FLASHPOINT IN UKRAINE

FLASHPOINT IN UKRAINE

HOW THE US DRIVE FOR HEGEMONY RISKS WORLD WAR III

EDITED BY

STEPHEN LENDMAN

CLARITY PRESS, INC.

© 2014 Clarity Press, Inc.
ISBN: 978-0-9860731-4-4
EBOOK: 978-0-9860731-5-1

In-house editor: Diana G. Collier
Cover: R. Jordan P. Santos
Cover photo: AP Photo / Sergei Chuzavkov

THE COVER IMAGE: Ukrainian [neo-Nazi] nationalists carry torches during a rally in downtown Kiev, Ukraine, late Wednesday, Jan. 1, 2014. The rally was organized on the occasion of the birth anniversary of Stepan Bandera, founder of a rebel army that fought against the Soviet regime and who was assassinated in Germany in 1959. See dramatic related video here: <http://99getsmart.com/ukraine-crisis-today-democracy-caught-on-camera-this-will-never-be-shown-on-mainstream-media/>

Clarity Press, Inc.
Ste. 469, 3277 Roswell Rd. NE
Atlanta, GA. 30305 , USA
http://www.claritypress.com

TABLE OF CONTENTS

Introduction / 9
Stephen Lendman

Washington's Recklessness Endangers the World / 15
Paul Craig Roberts

Washington Has Set the World on a Path to War / 19
Paul Craig Roberts

The New Cold War's Ukraine Gambit / 26
Michael Hudson

Obama's Ukrainian Power Grab, Sanctions and the Boomerang Effect / 46
James Petras

Ukraine and Regime Change / 50
Michael Parenti

Ukraine: Another Step in Capitalism's Global Dominance Strategies and Power Inside the Transnational Global Corporate Class and US-NATO Global Empire / 54
Peter Phillips, Mickey Huff and Nolan Higdon

Orange Revolution 2.0 / 64
Stephen Lendman

Libya, Syria, Venezuela, Ukraine: Another War Based on Lies, Pretexts, and Profiteering? / 80
Cynthia McKinney

The Geo-Politics Behind EuroMaidan / 90
Mahdi Nazemroaya

Crisis in Ukraine: Russia Extends its Control over the Black Sea and Strategic Waterways / 109
Michel Chossudovsky

**The Geostrategic Significance of Ukraine
in NATO's Drive to the East / 114**
Rick Rozoff

Who Benefits from the Ukraine Economic Crisis? / 119
Jack Rasmus

Mother Russia: An Elusive Prize / 131
John Kozy

**Hangover in Ukraine: Treaty of Versailles Spirits
Packaged in Bretton Woods Bottles. The Morning After / 138**
Jeffrey Sommers

The Labyrinth of Geography in a Time of Terror / 152
Matthew T. Witt

Containing Russia / 163
Stephen Lendman

The Ukraine Crisis and the Propaganda System in Overdrive / 171
Edward S. Herman and David Peterson

The Norms of Justice, International Law, and the 'Duty to Protect' / 200
Robert Abele

The Odessa Massacre / 215
Stephen Lendman

Ukraine: From Coup to Police State / 219
Andrew Kolin

The Kiev Putsch: Rebel Workers Take Power in the East / 227
James Petras

Is Ukraine a Turning Point in History? / 234
Rodney Shakespeare

Washington Intends Russia's Demise / 241
Paul Craig Roberts

The Ukraine Crisis: Decoding its Deep Structural Meaning / 244
John McMurtry

Contributors / 262

Index / 265

To all Ukrainians.
May they achieve peace, equity and justice.
May they inspire others globally.
May freedom triumph worldwide.

INTRODUCTION

STEPHEN LENDMAN

Ukraine is by far the most significant post-WW II geopolitical crisis. Escalating it risks global conflict.

Obama bears full responsibility. Complicit EU partners share it. Perhaps they bit off more than they can chew. They've got a tiger by the tail.

Putin won't accept blame for their lawlessness. He won't roll over for Western interests. Nor will allied Russian officials. They'll defend their own responsibly. They have every right to do so. They're obligated to do it.

Toppling foreign leaders by assassinations, coups or wars is longstanding US policy. William Blum did some of the best research. His books include *Rogue State*. They're must reading. He documented dozens of successful and failed post-WW II US interventions. They include:

- toppling Iran's Mohammad Mosaddegh in 1953; it was the CIA's first successful coup after an initial failure;
- ousting Guatemala's Jacobo Arbenz in 1954;
- failing to kill China's Chou En-Lai in 1955;
- failing hundreds times to kill Fidel Castro;
- failing to kill France's Charles de Gaulle;
- plotting Qaddafi's assassination for decades;
- killing him in 2011;
- eliminating Saddam Hussein in 2003

They very likely killed Hugo Chavez in 2013. Obama wanted him dead. He was either poisoned or infected with cancer causing substances. Four major surgeries in 18 months couldn't save him. Nor could world-class medical care overall.

Washington stops at nothing to advance its imperium. Millions of corpses attest to its barbarity. Replacing independent governments with subservient pro-Western ones is longstanding US policy.

Flashpoint in Ukraine: How the US Drive for Hegemony Risks World War III

Washington-supported Kiev putschists staged the most brazen coup d'etat since Mussolini's 1922 march on Rome. Claiming otherwise doesn't wash. It can't hide reality. Mob rule runs things.

Joining the EU's failed experiment looms. Seventeen Eurozone countries represent its weakest link. Uniting dissimilar ones under one size fits all rules failed dismally. Economic stagnation, longterm decline, high unemployment, growing poverty, deprivation, and political dysfunction characterize a doomed system.

Monetary union was engineered fraudulently to look workable. In 1979, Europe's Exchange Rate Mechanism (ERM) was introduced as part of the European Monetary System (EMS). Its purpose was to propel the continent to one European currency unit (ECU). ERM never worked. ECU is failing. Abandoning monetary and fiscal sovereignty reflects financial and economic madness.

For member states, joining means foregoing the right to devalue currencies to make exports more competitive, maintain money sovereignty to monetize debt freely, and legislate fiscal policy to stimulate growth.

Banking giants partnered with the EU, ECB and IMF Troika. Power they exert decides everything. Paying bankers comes first. Central bank lackeys do their bidding. They're more dangerous than standing armies. They wage war by other means. Finance is a new form of warfare.

Force-fed austerity mandates lowered living standards, deep social spending cuts, sacked public workers, and state assets sold at fire sale prices. Societies are hollowed out for profit. It's at the expense of suffering millions. EU member states are hamstrung by these and similar policies. They're fast becoming dystopian backwaters.

Ukraine faces the same future as other members. EU terms mandate structural adjustment harshness. So do IMF financial demands. Ordinary people are exploited ruthlessly. It's done for profit. Ukrainian interests lie more East than West. Getting in bed with predators assures millions harmed horrifically.

Ukraine matters. It's strategically located. It's in Europe's geographic center. It borders seven countries. In alphabetical order, they include Belarus, Hungary, Moldova, Poland, Romania, Slovakia and Russia. After Western/Central Russia, it's Europe's largest country territorially.

It's resource rich. Zbigniew Brzezinski once said "without Ukraine, Russia ceases to be an empire, but with Ukraine suborned and then subordinated, Russia automatically becomes an empire." More recently he said if Russia reunites with Ukraine, it'll be a Eurasian powerhouse. If Ukraine allies with Western Europe, Moscow will be significantly weakened geopolitically.

Introduction / Stephen Lendman

The battle for Ukraine's soul didn't end with putschists usurping power. It just began. It continues. Its future is up for grabs. It's up to ordinary Ukrainians to determine it. They have every right to do so. They'll have themselves to blame if not.

Putschists are illegitimate. What kind of government usurps power? What kind ousted a democratically elected one? What kind established itself by force? What kind rules extrajudicially?

What kind of legitimacy do ultranationalist, xenophobic, neo-Nazi, anti-Semites have? What kind substitutes unrestrained coercion for rule of law principles? What kind rules by intimidation? What kind eliminates political opposition? What kind bans opposing views? What kind mandates its message alone getting out?

The same kind substitutes fascist dictatorship for democracy.

On February 22, 2014, Ukrainian freedom died. Fascist extremism replaced it. Coup plotters seized power. They did so extrajudicially. They began consolidating rule straightaway.

Hardline ultranationalists control parliament. Illegitimate officials were installed. Neo-Nazis control powerful ministries. They openly display swastikas, Iron Crosses, SS insignia and other fascist symbols.

Obama's new friends are thugs. They're societal misfits. They represent mob rule.

Challenging them responsibly matters. Their agenda is reckless and dangerous. It makes peace activists cringe.

Potential civil war looms. Regional war could follow. At risk is spreading it globally. Preventing it matters most. We're all Ukrainians now. Humanity hangs in the balance. *Flashpoint in Ukraine* explains the major challenges ahead. Hegemons stop at nothing for unchallenged power. Global wars start this way. It bears repeating. Preventing WW III matters most. This book goes all-out to explain.

Horrific Ukrainian Human Rights Abuses

Kiev putschists reveal fascism's dark side. Today's Ukraine is its re-emergent epicenter. The May 2, 2014 Odessa massacre shows how far they'll go. Read my article, "The Odessa Massacre", herein.

Coup-appointed putschists plan horrors yet to unfold. They're waging war on their own people. They want all opposition elements crushed. They want fascist rule institutionalized. They want democracy prevented at all costs.

A Russian "White Book"[1] contains documented hard evidence. It reveals unconscionable Kiev human rights violations. It covers them from late November 2013 through March 2014. It does so in six chapters. They include:

(1) Violations of human rights.

(2) Interference by the European Union and United States.

(3) Weapons and violent methods used by protesters.

(4) Restrictions on basic freedoms and crackdown on dissidents.

(5) Discrimination based on ethnic background.

(6) Religious persecution.

According to Moscow's press service, content is "based on reports in the Russian and Western media, as well as statements by representatives of the current Kiev authorities and their supporters, eyewitness testimon(ies), observations and on-site interviews collected by Russian nongovernmental organizations."

Evidence indicts illegitimate putschists. It includes ultranationalist extremists, Nazism's reemergence, brazen pressure and threats, severe repression, physical violence, and suppressing press freedom.

Kiev fascists banned Russian TV channels. They include Vesti, Russia-24, Channel One international. RTS 'Pleneta,' and NTV World.They shut down independent Ukrainian media as well. They want their message alone getting out.

They harass, beat, and terrorize independent journalists. They brutalize anti-fascist activists. They're waging war on Eastern Ukrainian freedom fighters. They blame Russia and victims for their horrific crimes. These continue unabated. They promise worse ahead. They enjoy full Washington support. No-holds-barred brutality is official policy. Ukraine is unsafe to live in.

It's reminiscent of 1930s Nazi Germany. Maybe (1935-enacted) Nuremberg laws will follow. Nazis then targeted communists, social democrats, trade unionists, independent journalists, gypsies, homosexuals, Jews, and other opposition elements.They declared them enemies of the state. They targeted them for elimination. Death camps followed.

Anti-Semitism was rife. Jewish enterprises, shopkeepers, doctors, lawyers, academics, and ordinary people were vulnerable. Jews were humiliated in public. They were publicly assaulted. They were beaten. Their heads were shaved. Orthodox ones had their beards shorn.

Racist legislation followed. Infamous Nuremberg Laws forced landlords to break leases with Jews. Distinctions were removed between harming them physically and using legal ways to destroy their businesses, livelihoods, futures and lives.

After the March 1938 Austrian Anschluss, deadlier persecution followed. Nazi policy enforced Aryanizations, confiscations, arrests, physical violence, and cold-blooded murder. Hitler and Goebbels bore direct responsibility for Kristallnacht violence. It raged on November 9 and 10, 1938. It augured much worse to come. Jewish homes were looted nationwide. Scores of synagogues were attacked, burned and destroyed. So were thousands of large and small Jewish enterprises. Nearly 700 Jews perished. Around 30,000 went to concentration camps.

Apartheid more than ever became official policy. Jews and Aryians were separate and unequal. Separate laws governed them. Jews were fair game. Murder, beatings, other physical abuse, harassment, rapes, other sexual assaults, organized pogroms, confiscations, lootings, and other lawless acts followed.

Ahead of WW II's eruption, Aryians were accustomed to anti-Semitic violence and other forms of abuse. So-called "good Germans" were silent. They did nothing to interfere. It was part of normal daily life. Genocide horrors followed.

Ukrainians fear the worst with good reason. Nazism has reemerged. History has a disturbing way of repeating. Its core elements are unchanged. They include the worst of severe repression. Nazis tolerate no opposition. They persecute religious, ethnic and other societal groups. They target them for elimination altogether.

Neo-Nazi Right Sector leader Dmytro Yarosh openly boasts about "...killing Jews and Russians till [he] dies." Thousands like him foster similar ideologically extremist views.

It bears repeating. Ukraine is unsafe to live in. Thousands of Jews have already left. Others prepare to do so if necessary. Ukrainian Jews are threatened. Anti-Semitism is rife. Radical ultranationalism is virulent.

Odessa Jews are scared. They're preparing for mass evacuation. They're ready if violence too great to control erupts. So far they haven't been targeted.

They're vulnerable. According to Rabbi Refael Kruskal:

> When there is shooting in the streets, the first plan is to take (children) out of the center of the city.
> If it gets worse, then we'll take them out of the city.
> We have plans to take them both out of the city and even

to a different country if necessary, plans which we prefer not to talk about which we have in place.

He fears more clashes. "[N]ext weekend is going to be very violent," he said earlier.

Friday, May 9, is Victory Day. It marks Nazi Germany's capitulation to Soviet Russia. It was late May 8 evening Berlin time. It was May 9 Moscow time.

Fascist provocations were planned. Migdal International Center of Jewish Community Programs head Kira Verkhovskaya said: "If the situation gets worse, we are preparing to move."

Rabbi Avraham Wold represents Chabad community Hassidic Jews. He said they're taking extra security precautions.They posted armed guards. They prepared for possible evacuation. They allied with International Fellowship of Christians and Jews. They have 70 buses fueled. They're ready to go if needed.

Odessa's population approaches one million. Nearly one-third are Jews. They're justifiably scared. Earlier Nazis murdered millions of Ukrainians in cold blood. About 900,000 Jews perished. Some were burned alive. Odessans remember. They know how fascists operate. Anti-Semitism is rife. neo-Nazi Right Sector thugs threaten them. So do likeminded extremists.

They may have to flee for their lives. Perhaps on short notice. They fear the worst if not.

Ukraine's Jewish community is one of Europe's most vibrant. It includes dozens of active organizations and institutions. History has a disturbing way of repeating. Modern-day fascism may turn out no less horrifically than before. Ukrainians have just cause for concern. They'll get no Western help. They're on their own. Expect growing numbers to leave.

It bears repeating. *Flashpoint in Ukraine* is essential reading. It explains what everyone needs to know.

ENDNOTES

1 <http://www.mid.ru/bdomp/ns-dgpch.nsf/03c344d01162d351442579510044415b/38fa8597760acc2144257ccf002beeb8/$FILE/White%20Book.pdf>

WASHINGTON'S RECKLESSNESS ENDANGERS THE WORLD

PAUL CRAIG ROBERTS

The Washington-sponsored coup in Kiev is a reckless act. Such irresponsibility on the part of the US government should alarm the entire world.

Since the collapse of the Soviet Union, the US government has been raising the strategic threat that Washington poses to Russia. The US government violated its agreement not to take NATO into Eastern Europe. The US government withdrew from the ABM treaty.

The US government arranged with Poland to place US anti-ballistic missile bases on Russia's border. The US changed its war doctrine to permit pre-emptive nuclear attack. The US government financed "color revolutions" in Georgia and Ukraine, former constituent parts of both Russia and the Soviet Union.

The US government ignored Russia and attacked and dismembered Serbia. The US government trained and equipped the Georgian military and encouraged Georgia to attack the Russian peacekeeping force in South Ossetia. And now Washington has overthrown the democratically elected government of Ukraine and installed a puppet government.

Washington's Kiev coup is a direct strategic threat to Russia. Ukraine was long part of Russia and the Soviet Union. Indeed, southern and eastern parts of Ukraine are former territories of Russia that Soviet governments added to Ukraine for various reasons.

Crimea, overwhelmingly Russian, was stuck into Ukraine in 1954 by Khrushchev. Khrushchev did not include Sevastopol, the site of Russia's

Flashpoint in Ukraine: How the US Drive for Hegemony Risks World War III

Black Sea fleet, when he transferred Crimea to Ukraine. Sevastopol was transferred to Ukraine by US pressure when the Soviet Union broke apart and Ukraine emerged as an independent country.

In exchange, Russia was given a lease on the naval base until 2042. The lease permits 25,000 troops and specified numbers of military aircraft, tanks, and artillery in Crimea. The 16,000 Russian troops that the White House and presstitute media intentionally misreported as an invasion force were already present in Crimea under terms of the lease agreement.

Washington either overlooked or worked with the Russophobic ultra-nationalist groups in western Ukraine who sport Nazi emblems and speak of killing Russians and Jews.

Washington used its funded NGOs ($5 billion according to Assistant Secretary of State Victoria Nuland at the National Press Club in December 2013) to begin street protests when the elected Ukrainian government turned down the offer to join the European Union.

Initially, the protesters demanded that the Ukrainian government reverse its decision and join the EU. However, the ultra-nationalists, not the Ukrainian government, introduced violence into the protests and changed the demands from joining the EU to overthrowing the elected government.

Washington's stooges in the parliament seized power, disbanded the police, and issued arrest warrants for the President of Ukraine. The ultra-nationalist thugs stepped into the picture, intimidating the parliament, public prosecutors, and TV editors.

Videos are available online of the neo-Nazi thugs slapping around a public prosecutor and a TV editor and challenging parliamentarians by waving an Ak-47 in their face. Soon the intimidated American stooges were passing the ultra-nationalist agenda. The official use of the Russian language was banned. Proposals were introduced to arrest Ukrainians who held dual Russian/Ukrainian citizenship. War memorials to the Red Army that liberated Ukraine from Nazi Germany and to the Russian general whose tactics defeated Napoleon's Grand Army were destroyed.

The Russian populations of southern and eastern Ukraine were alarmed at the threats directed at them. These populations took to the streets demanding separation from the Russophobic thugs that the Washington-sponsored coup had raised to power in Kiev.

The Crimean government quickly voted Crimea's independence from Ukraine and announced a referendum in which citizens would determine whether to remain an independent country or return to Russia from whence Crimea came. The voter turnout was over 80%, and the vote to return to Russia was 97%. All international observers pronounced the vote fair, above board and totally free of coercion.

President Obama, his Secretary of State John Kerry, and the presstitute media that serves them lied through their teeth. These shameful liars said that Russia had invaded and annexed Crimea. Washington was so startled that events were not following its script that Kerry, having demonized Putin for "invading Crimea," now demanded that Putin invade Crimea and prevent the referendum vote, or else.

The "or else" was the empty threat of an incompetent and overstretched imperialist.

Crimea is now again part of Russia.

Having threatened sanctions, Washington and its EU puppets had to produce. But sanctions against Russia would have damaged Europe, so the "sanctions" were applied to 11 individuals: the deposed Ukrainian president and an aide, two Crimean politicians, and 7 Russians. The sanctions are for six months and have no effect unless those individuals sanctioned have foreign bank accounts, which none of the Russians do.

The presstitute media, of course, still speaks of the sanctions as if the wrath of God has fallen on Russia. Legally, as written, the sanctions only apply to the Obama and EU regimes as it was Washington and the EU that overthrew the elected Ukrainian democratic government. The government that Washington has put together is neither elected nor democratic.

The Crimean part of the story is over. But two dangerous parts remain. Putin, a real leader unlike the fakes that reign in the West, has said that he has not invaded, but he reserves the right should the Russian populations in eastern Ukraine be put down with force. So what did the idiots in Washington do?

Washington had its Kiev stooges appoint Ukrainian multi-billionaire Jewish oligarchs to rule over the Russian cities in eastern Ukraine. These oligarchs have their own private militias, and they have arrested the Russian leader in eastern Ukraine and sent him to Kiev. If Washington's stooges apply violence to the protesting Russian population, Putin would be forced to reclaim the Russian territory of eastern Ukraine.

The other dangerous part is western Ukraine, which defections could reduce to a rump state. If the ultra-nationalists prevail over the Washington-appointed stooges, the EU will not want Ukraine as a member. The EU is in the process of stamping out nationalism. That is the whole point of the euro.

How is a country a country when it no longer has its own currency? A neo-Nazi western Ukraine is not likely to have much support in Europe, making it easy for Putin to reabsorb Ukraine back into Russia where it was for as long as the US has existed.

If somehow Washington's stooges prevail and take Ukraine into the EU and NATO, the question becomes whether Russia will accept the situation and target the US bases in Ukraine with the Iskander missiles, or whether prior to the formalities of Ukraine securing Washington's protection as a NATO member, Russia will end the fiasco and terminate the rump state's short-lived independence.

It is entirely Russia's call. There is nothing Washington and its EU puppet states can do about it except launch nuclear war and terminate life on earth over Ukraine, or a rump state thereof, that has nothing whatsoever to do with US or EU interests.

Of course, Washington's militarists are reckless, and they are capable of any mistake as their foray into Ukraine proves.

WASHINGTON HAS SET THE WORLD ON A PATH TO WAR

PAUL CRAIG ROBERTS

Why is Washington so opposed to Crimean self-determination? The answer is that one of the main purposes of Washington's coup in Kiev was to have the new puppet government evict Russia from its Black Sea naval base in Crimea. Washington cannot use the government Washington has installed in Ukraine for that purpose if Crimea is no longer part of Ukraine.

What Washington has made completely obvious is that "self-determination" is a weapon it uses in behalf of its agenda. If self-determination advances Washington's agenda, Washington is for it. If self-determination does not advance Washington's agenda, Washington is against it.

The Washington-initiated UN Security Council resolution, vetoed by Russia, falsely declares that the referendum in Crimea, a referendum demanded by the people, "can have no validity, and cannot form the basis for any alteration of the status of Crimea; and calls upon all States, international organizations and specialized agencies not to recognize any alteration of the status of Crimea on the basis of this referendum and to refrain from any action or dealing that might be interpreted as recognizing any such altered status."

Washington could not make it any clearer that it totally opposes self-determination by Crimeans.

Washington claims, falsely, that the referendum cannot be valid unless the entire population of Ukraine votes and agrees with the decision by Crimeans. Note that when Washington stole Kosovo from Serbia, Washington did not let Serbians vote.

But let's overlook Washington's rank hypocrisy and self-serving double-standards. Let's apply Washington's argument that in order to be valid any change in Crimea's status requires a vote on the part of the population of the country that it departs. If this is the case, then Crimea has never been a part of Ukraine.

Under Washington's interpretation of international law, Ukraine is still a part of Russia.

When Khrushchev transferred Crimea (but not Sevastopol, the Black Sea base) to Ukraine, Russians did not get to vote.

Therefore, according to Washington's own logic, it is invalid to recognize Crimea as part of Ukraine. That also goes for other parts of Russia that Lenin transferred to Ukraine. Under the logic of Washington's UN resolution, large parts of Ukraine are not legitimately part of Ukraine. They have remained parts of Russia, because Russians were not allowed to vote on their transfer to Ukraine. Thus, there is no issue about "Russia annexing Crimea," because, according to Washington's logic, Crimea is still a part of Russia.

Do you need any more proof that the Ukrainian crisis is made up out of thin air by schemers in Washington who created the entire crisis for one purpose—to weaken Russia militarily.

No one was surprised that *The New York Times* published on March 14 the warmongering rant, written by neoconservatives for John McCain, which described Washington's aggression in Ukraine as Russia's aggression.

The US government overthrows an elected democratic Ukrainian government and then accuses Russia of "invading and annexing Crimea" in order to divert attention from Washington's overthrow of Ukrainian democracy. There is no elected government in Kiev. The stooges acting as a government in Kiev were put in office by Washington. Who else chose them?

What surprised some was Rand Paul joining the hysteria. Rand Paul wrote his propagandistic rant against Russia for *Time*. Rand Paul claims, falsely, that Putin has invaded Crimea and that it is an affront to "the international community."

First of all, the decision of Crimea to leave Ukraine is a decision of the Crimean population and the elected government, not a decision by Russia. But, for the sake of argument, let's take Rand Paul's lie as the truth:

Is "Vladimir Putin's [so-called] invasion of Ukraine a gross violation of that nation's sovereignty and an affront to the international community" like Washington's invasions of Iraq and Afghanistan, and Washington-sponsored invasions of Libya and Syria, and Washington's ongoing slaughter of Pakistanis and Yemenis with drones, and Washington's violation of Iran's sovereignty with illegal sanctions, and Washington's violation of Ukrainian sovereignty by overthrowing the elected government and imposing Washington's stooges?

If Putin is behaving as Rand Paul ignorantly asserts, Putin is just following the precedents established by Clinton in Serbia, by Bush in Afghanistan and Iraq, and by Obama in Afghanistan, Libya, Syria, and Ukraine. Washington's argument is reduced to: "We, the exceptional and indispensable nation can behave this way, but no other country can."

As some Americans have misplaced hopes in Rand Paul, it is just as well that he revealed in *Time* that he is just another fool prostituting himself for the neoconservative warmongers and the military/security complex. If Rand Paul is the hope for America, then clearly there is no hope.

As I have been pointing out, the propaganda and lies issuing from Washington, its European puppets, *The New York Times*, *Time*, and the entirety of the Western media are repeating the path to war that led to World War I. It is happening right before our eyes.

How much war does Washington want? Former US President Jimmy Carter said: "America does not at the moment have a functioning democracy."

I doubt that the Ukraine crisis precipitated by Washington's overthrow of the democratic government is over. Washington has won the propaganda war everywhere outside of Russia and Ukraine itself. Within Ukraine people are aware that the coup has made them worse off. The Crimea has already separated from the US puppet government in Kiev and rejoined Russia. Other parts of Russian Ukraine could follow.

In Kiev itself where the unelected, imposed-by-Washington dictatorial government resides, extreme right-wing Ukrainian nationalists, whose roots go back to fighting for National Socialist Germany, are at work intimidating public prosecutors, media editors, and the US imposed "government" itself. There is an abundance of videos available on the Internet, some made by the extreme nationalists themselves, that clearly reveal the intimidation of the imposed and unelected government installed by Washington..

In Kiev US bribes contend with naked neo-nazi force. Which will prevail?

The murder of ultra-nationalist Right Sector militant leader Myzychko by police of the acting Interior Minister of the American stooge government in Ukraine on March 25 has resulted in another Right Sector leader, Dmitry Yarosh, demanding the resignation of Arsen Avakov, the acting Interior Minister and the arrest of the police who killed Muzychko.

Yarosh declared: "We cannot watch silently as the Interior Ministry works to undermine the revolution." Right Sector organizer Roman Koval in Rovno, Ukraine, warned: "We will take revenge on Avakov for the death of our brother."

How this will play out is uncertain at this time. The violence provided by the Right Sector and other ultra-nationalist groups was essential to the success of the Washington-backed coup in overthrowing the elected democratic government.

But the Right Sector has emerged as both an embarrassment and a threat to the unelected coup government and to its Washington sponsors who are selling the Washington-installed puppet government as a progressive exercise in democracy. This sell is difficult when ultra-nationalist thugs are beating up the imposed government.

Could civil war break out in Kiev between the Right Sector and the government installed by Washington? We know that the Right Sector was sufficiently organized and disciplined to take over the protests. We don't know how well organized the Washington puppet government is or what force this group has at its disposal. We don't know whether Washington has provided mercenaries to protect the government it has installed. It is not clear at this time where the power balance lies between the Right Sector and the US stooge government.

The American, UK, Canadian, Australian, New Zealand, EU propaganda machine has blamed Putin for all the trouble. But so far the Russian government has not had to do anything except comply with the self-determination of the people in the Russian areas of Ukraine. Much of Ukraine, as it exists or existed today, consists of Russian territories added to Ukraine by Soviet rulers.

When Ukraine became independent with Russia's agreement when the Soviet Union collapsed, had the Russian territories first been put back into Russia from whence they came, Washington's coup would not have resulted in the same level of crisis.

Instead, under Washington's pressure, the Russian territory was retained by Ukraine, and in compensation Russia was given a 50-year lease on Sevastopol, Russia's Black Sea naval base.

The purpose of the Washington financed and orchestrated coup in Kiev was to put Ukraine, with its artificial boundaries, into the EU and NATO and to evict Russia from its warm water port and ring Russia with US missile bases. Washington and its European puppets described this as "bringing democracy to Ukraine."

Ukraine already had democracy, a young one trying to put down roots, and Washington destroyed it.

As Russian President Putin observed, overthrowing a brand new democracy destroys democracy. Washington's coup established for Ukraine the precedent that force and propaganda rule, not democracy.

But Washington cares not for democracy, only for Washington's agenda. And Russia, China, and Iran are in the way. The neoconservatives, who have controlled US foreign policy since the Clinton regime, concluded that the Soviet collapse meant that History has chosen America as the model socio-economic system for the world. They declared the US to be "exceptional" and "indispensable" and above international law.

Washington had a free pass to invade, murder, destroy, and dominate. The neoconservative claims of "American exceptionalism" sound like Hitler's claims for the German nation. When the White House sock puppet expressed in a speech the claim of American exceptionalism, Putin replied: "God made us all equal."

Washington's opinion is that the exceptional and indispensable nation—the US—is above not only all other nations but also above law. What Washington does is legal. What anyone else does in opposition is illegal.

Washington's intervention in Ukraine has unleashed dark forces. Yulia Tymoshenko, the criminal Ukrainian oligarch, who braids her hair or hair piece over her head like a crown, was released from prison by Washington's stooges and has not stopped putting her foot, or both feet, in her mouth.

Her intercepted and leaked telephone conversation declared that "It"s about time we grab our guns and go kill those damn Russians together with their leader". She declared that not even scorched earth should be left where Russia stands.

Tymoshenko was sentenced to prison by Ukrainians, not by Russians. Contrast her extreme language and Russophobia with the calm measured tones of Putin, who reaffirms Russia's interest to continue good relations with Ukraine.

On March 23 Tymoshenko was interviewed by the German newspaper, *Bild*, a mouthpiece for Washington. The crazed Tymoshenko declared that Putin was even more dangerous than Hitler.

This year 2014 is the 100th anniversary of World War 1. As my Oxford professor, Michael Polanyi, said, this was the war that destroyed Europe. He meant culturally and morally as well as physically. As John Maynard Keynes made clear in his prediction, the propagandistic way in which World War 1 was blamed on Germany and the "peace" that was imposed on Germany set up World War II.

We are witnesses today to the same kind of propagandistic lies with regard to Russia that caused World War 1. In *The Genesis of the World War*, Harry Elmer Barnes quotes the French chief editor of a French account of the organization of propaganda in France during World War I. The French built a massive building called La Maison de la Presse. In this building images of people were created with hands cut off, tongues torn out, eyes gouged out, and skulls crushed with brains laid bare.

These images were then photographed and "sent as unassailable evidence of German atrocities to all parts of the globe, where they did not fail to produce the desired effect." Also provided were "fictitious photographs of bombarded French and Belgian churches, violated graves and monuments and scenes of ruins and desolation. The staging and painting of these scenes were done by the best scene-painters of the Paris Grand Opera."

This vicious propaganda against Germany meant that Germany could be blamed for the war and that all of President Woodrow Wilson's guarantees to Germany of no reparations and no territorial loss if Germany agreed to an armistice could be violated. The propaganda success guaranteed that the peace settlement would be so one-sided as to set up the Second World War.

Russia has observed Washington's strategic moves against Russian national interests and Russian sovereignty for two decades. What does Putin think when he hears the vicious anti-Russian propaganda based 100% in lies?

This is what Putin thinks: The Americans promised Gorbachev that they would not take NATO into Eastern Europe, but the Americans did. The Americans withdrew from the ABM Treaty, which prohibited escalating the arms race with anti-ballistic missile systems. The Americans arranged with Poland to deploy anti-ballistic missile bases on Poland's border with Russia. The Americans tell us the fantastic lie that the purpose of American missile bases in Poland is to protect Europe from non-existent Iranian ICBMs.

The Americans change their war doctrine to elevate nuclear weapons from a retaliatory deterrent to a pre-emptive first strike force. The Americans pretend that this change in war doctrine is directed at terrorists, but we know it is directed at Russia. The Americans have financed "color revolutions" in Georgia and Ukraine and hope to do so in the Russian Federation itself.

The Americans support the terrorists in Chechnya. The Americans trained and equipped the Georgian military and gave it the green light to attack our peacekeepers in South Ossetia. The Americans have financed the overthrow of the elected government in Ukraine and blame me for the anxiety this caused among Crimeans who on their own volition fled Ukraine and returned to Russia from whence they came.

Even Gorbachev said that Khrushchev should never have put Crimea into Ukraine. Solzhenitsyn said that Lenin should not have put Russian provinces into eastern and southern Ukraine. Now I have these Russian provinces agitating to return to Russia, and the Americans are blaming me for the consequences of their own reckless and irresponsible actions.

The Americans say I want to rebuild the Soviet Empire. Yet, the Americans witnessed me depart from Georgia when I had this former Russian province in my hands, thanks to the short-lived war instigated by the Americans.

There is no end to the American lies. I have done everything possible to respond to provocations in a low-key reasonable manner, offering to work things out diplomatically, as has my Foreign Minister Lavrov. But the Americans continue to provoke and to hide their provocations behind lies.

The Americans brazenly bring to me a strategic threat in Ukraine. They intend to put Ukraine in NATO, the purpose of which expired with the Soviet collapse. They intend to put more missile bases on Russia's borders, and they intended to evict Russia from its Black Sea naval base, its warm water port. Americans have no intention of working anything out.

They intend to subjugate Russia. Washington wants Russia powerless, surrounded with ABM bases that degrade our strategic deterrent to uselessness. These Americans will not work with me. They will not listen to me or to Russia's Foreign Minister. They only hear their own call for American hegemony over the world. My only alternative is to prepare for war.

The government of China, having read Washington's plans for war against China and being fully away of Washington's pivot to Asia, in which the "indispensable nation" announced its "safe-guarding of peace" by surrounding China with naval and air bases, understands that it has the same Washington enemy as does Russia.

What the entire world faces, every country, every individual regardless of their political orientation, is a Washington-engineered confrontation with Russia and China. This confrontation is enabled by Washington's bought-and-paid-for European and UK puppet states.

Without the cover provided by Europe, Washington's acts of aggression would result in war crimes charges against the government in Washington. The world would not be able to enforce these charges without war, but Washington would be isolated.

The European, Canadian, Australian, New Zealand, and UK governments have betrayed not only their own peoples but also the peoples of the entire world by lending the support of Western Civilization to Washington's lawlessness.

The propaganda that the West represents the hope of the world is a great lie.

THE NEW COLD WAR'S UKRAINE GAMBIT

MICHAEL HUDSON[1]

Finance in today's world has become war by non-military means. Its object is the same as that of military conquest: appropriation of land and basic infrastructure, and the rents that can be extracted as tribute. In today's world this is taken mainly in the form of debt service and privatization. That is how neoliberalism works, subduing economies by indebting their governments and using unpayably high debts as a lever to pry away the public domain at distress prices. It is what today's New Cold War is all about. Backed by the IMF and European Central Bank (ECB) as knee-breakers in what has become in effect a financial extension of NATO, the aim is for U.S. and allied investors to appropriate the plums that kleptocrats have taken from the public domain of Russia, Ukraine and other post-Soviet economies in these countries, as well as whatever assets remain.

In a recent interview in *The New York Review of Books*, George Soros outlines what he thinks should be done for the Ukraine. It should "encourage its companies to improve their management by finding European partners."[2] This means that kleptocrats should sell major ownership shares in their companies to Westerners. This would give the West a stake in protecting them, pressuring their government to tax labor rather than the wealthy, and helping them cash out and keep their takings in London and New York to finance Western economies, not that of Ukraine.

The West's ideological conquest of the Post-Soviet economies

That is not how replacing Soviet communism with a free market was supposed to work out—at least, not for the Soviet side. Mikhail Gorbachev and his supporters hoped that ending the Cold War would enable Russia to dismantle the arms race whose costly military overhead prevented the Soviet Union from devoting resources to produce consumer goods and adequate housing. In addition to the peace dividend, the aim was to establish a price feedback system that would raise industrial productivity and living standards.

The West's ideological victory—or more to the point, the neoliberal anti-labor, anti-government and pro-Wall Street game plan—was sealed at the Houston summit in July 1990. Russian Prime Minister Gorbachev and other Soviet leaders endorsed the World Bank/USAID plan for shock therapy, privatization, deindustrialization and a wipeout of domestic personal savings (characterized as an "overhang") to start by impoverishing the population at large and vesting an overclass with the most unequal distribution of wealth in the Northern Hemisphere. U.S. Cold War advisors urged Russia and other post-Soviet states to give hitherto public assets and property to individuals, preferably to plant managers and political insiders. The cover story was that it did not really matter who got them, because private ownership in itself would lead the new owners to re-organize production along the most profitable lines. Pinochet's Chile was held out as a shining success story, and a right-wing Pinochetista movement started in Russia.

The Communist Party *nomenklatura*, Komsomol leaders such as Mikhail Khodorkovsky and Red Directors were excited by these neoliberal promises to turn over natural resources, real estate, infrastructure and factories to themselves. The sanctimonious pretense was that property has its own logic of self-interest, which serves the social good because wealth will trickle down to uplift the population at large. In practice the neoliberal "free market" turned out to be a euphemism for looting. Subsidized by U.S. support and imposed by Yeltsin's presidential fiat (unconstitutionally, over the objections of the Duma), ownership of hitherto public investment and natural resources were given to managers who made their fortunes by selling their takings to Western investors.

Already before 1990 billions of dollars in roubles already were being siphoned off via Latvia (Grigory Loutchansky and Nordex played a major role), while co-op leaders KGB and army leaders already were creating proto-predatory financial structures. U.S. bankers, officials and academics went to Russia and other former Soviet republics to explain that the most practical path was to create joint-stock companies and sell shares to Western buyers to bid up the price. Western banks helped kleptocrats keep the proceeds from these sales abroad so that they didn't have to reinvest it at home (or pay taxes). The tax burden was placed on labor and consumers, not on the windfall gains and natural resource rents, land rent or monopoly rent being siphoned off.

Instead of bringing about Western European or American-style industrial capitalism with their heavily subsidized technology and protected agriculture, the effect has been to de-industrialize Russia and other post-

Soviet economies, except for East Germany and Poland. In effect, the former Soviet Union was colonized in the world's largest resource grab since Europe's conquest of the New World five centuries ago.

As in the other former Soviet republics, Ukraine embraced the neoliberal plan to make kleptocracy the final stage of Stalinism. As Mikhail Khodorkovsky described: "Decent people get out of the system, leaving 'idiots and lowlife'—great material for building up the machinery of state. And yet that is indeed our state."[3] Along these lines one Russian journalist excoriates Ukraine's sequence of oligarch-politicians as gangsters:

> Kuchma gave orders to kill the journalist Gongadze. Yanukovich, still the country's only legally elected president, did a couple of stretches in the clink even in Soviet times—for snatching fur-hats in public toilets.
> Former Ukraine Premier Lazarenko is now doing time in the U.S.A. for money laundering, fraud, and extortion. His business colleague Yulia Timoshenko, whose complicity in those crimes was proved beyond all reasonable doubt by U.S. investigators, fearing the same fate, sought immunity by moving into politics.
>
> Timoshenko is the person whom ordinary people of Ukraine have called *vorovka*, feminine for thief, to her face. Indeed, the source of the billions this "engineer-economist" (her position in Soviet times) amassed in the '90s is perfectly obvious: pocketing the money for gas that came from Russia to Ukraine and Europe. Getting payment for the gas [sold by] Timoshenko's corporation was always a wrangle, and at times impossible. She salted away her booty in European banks, often carrying bags of cash across the border, for which she was repeatedly arrested but wriggled out of jail sentences by suborning judges and such. Again, all this is on record.[4]

These leaders have left Ukraine looking like a Northern Hemisphere Nigeria. Real wages plunged by more than 75 percent from their 1991 level wages already by 1998 and have stagnated ever since.[5] This "cheap labor" makes Ukraine appealing to European investors, who now are making their own move to obtain what Ukraine's oligarchs have grabitized. The West has made it clear that it will help these individuals convert their takings into cash and move it safely into Western banks, luxury properties and other *nouveau riches* assets.

The coup seeks to break up Ukraine, Libya- or Iraq-style

From a military vantage point, the New Cold War aims to prevent revenue from these privatized assets from being used to rebuild, re-industrialize, and hence potentially to re-militarize the Russian and Near Abroad economies. This is why U.S. strategists have moved to pry Ukraine out of the Russian orbit. The dream is to achieve the Cold War's *coup de grace* along the lines outlined by Zbigniew Brzezinski in his 1997 *Grand Chessboard*: "Without Ukraine, Russia ceases to be a Eurasian empire." The aim is to break as much of Ukraine as possible out of the Russian orbit and to draw it into the West, and into NATO itself.

This has been the plan ever since President Clinton broke the disarmament agreement made by George H.W. Bush with Gorbachev and extend NATO to the former Warsaw Pact members, starting with the Baltics. The logical extension of this tactic is to promote separatist movements in Russia itself, much as U.S. strategists are seeking to stir the pot of ethnic resentment in China, and as they have done in Libya, Iraq and Syria.

They found their most recent opening when Ukrainians mounted a mass demonstration against the rampant political and economic corruption built in from the outset of independence. The hoped-for aid from Europe turned out to be only to subsidize the kleptocracy, not to promote meaningful democracy. President Yanukovich reacted to Eurozone demands for yet more austerity by choosing Russia's far better offer. Meanwhile, "Occupy Maidan" was filling up with middle-age demonstrators, women, students, Russian-speakers, nationalists and others whose common aim was to end the thieving. They wanted reforms, and were protesting against the oligarchs, not only Yanukovich but also Timoshenko and the others.

But the Obama Administration seems to be channeling Dick Cheney these days. Its Assistant Secretary of State for European and Eurasian Affairs was the neocon Victoria Nuland, who wanted Arseniy Yatsenyuk to be in charge, an economist willing to turn the Ukrainian economy away from the Russian orbit toward the Eurozone. To accelerate matters instead of waiting for the scheduled autumn elections, a preemptive coup. U.S.-backed separatists mounted a coup, bringing in right-wing neo-Nazi groups and foreign snipers to escalate a violent confrontation on February 20.

Public relations spinning made it difficult to understand who was behind the snipers firing on demonstrators and police. An public campaign by the coup leaders and U.S. spokesmen accused Yanukovich's police of doing the firing. But a TV investigative team sent from Germany's ARD confirmed what had been trickling into the news contradicting the American version of events. The April 10 report found that contrary to the claims of the coup leaders in Kiev, the demonstrators were hit from behind by snipers shooting from the roof of "their own headquarters, the Hotel Ukraina."[6] One doctor found that all the bullets taken from bodies he examined were identical, suggesting a single group of snipers. The German team quoted family members about how the coup's new Attorney General, Oleg Machnitzki, has stonewalled them with regard to the details of the death or injury of their relatives. He is a member of the right-wing Swoboda party, appointed to investigate snipers who seem to have come from his own group.

The ARD program quotes a senior member of the new government's Investigative Committee saying that "The results of my investigations which I have found, simply do not match up with what the prosecutor says" in blaming Yanukovich. The program concluded: "the fact that a representative of the nationalist Svoboda Party as Attorney General quite obviously hindered the elucidation of the Kiev massacre, creates a bad image of the new transitional government—and thus also of all those western governments that support the new rulers in Kiev."

In a travesty of reality, White House spokesmen portrayed the U.S.-orchestrated violence as representing a spontaneous nationalistic anti-Russian spirit of the Maidan demonstrators, as if they were supporting pro-EU and hence anti-Russian passions. But what evidently happened is that the coup leaders sought to jump in front of the anti-corruption parade by creating chaos and then restore "order" by removing politicians from the Eastern Russian-speaking region.

Yanukovich reached an agreement with the protest leaders to step down and appoint an interim government, but his palatial home was sacked and he fled for safety to Russia. The coup leaders (calling themselves the "transitional government") fanned regional tensions by banning the use of Russian on television and other public places, and even began to cut off water to Crimea, while replacing local Eastern Ukraine officials with "Right Sector" apparatchiks in an attempt to force the region's oligarchs and factory owners to turn away from their main markets in Russia and re-orient the economy toward Europe.

Matters have not worked out as planned. The U.S.-backed destabilization moves were so blatant that they prompted former President Jimmy Carter 'to warn that: "The rest of the world, almost unanimously, looks at America as the No. 1 warmonger. That we revert to armed conflict almost at the drop of a hat—and quite often it's not only desired by the leaders of our country, but it's also supported by the people of America."[7]

Commenting on the anarchy into which the U.S.-backed coup has plunged Ukraine, Singapore's Prime Minister Lee Hsien Loong summed up what so often has been the result of foreign uprisings backed by U.S. promises. "I think you should have thought of that before encouraging the demonstrators on the Maidan. I think some people didn't think through all the consequences. ... can you take responsibility for the consequences and when it comes to grief, will you be there? You can't be there, you've got so many other interests to protect."[8] Having encouraged the Ukrainian coup by holding out a quixotic dream of joining the EU and even NATO, the United States really has no means to follow through. It is in many ways a reply of the Hungarian 1956 uprising and that of the Czechs in 1968.

The effect is to make the United States look like what Mao Tse Tung called it: a Paper Tiger. Having waved a big stick, the United States and its NATO satellites are now leaving Ukraine broke. The aim of prying it out of the Russian orbit has left the country heavily in debt to Russia for arrears in payments for gas (now no longer subsidized) and in danger of losing Russia as its major market for industrial exports. To cap matters, Western separatists are talking of blowing up the pipelines carrying Russian gas to Germany and other European consumers, to reduce Russia's trade balance and thus presumably deter its ability to spend on the military.

To support President Obama's assurances that the US-backed side was not conducting the terrorism, the U.S. news media have blacked out the German investigation and similar testimony. Obama's claims and those of Samantha Power at the United Nations may go down in history as his analogue to George W. Bush's fictitious "weapons of mass destruction" in Iraq.

As Warren Buffett has quipped, finance and debt pyramiding are weapons of mass destruction. They go hand in hand with mass deception. Opposition to the U.S.-backed coup and its attempt to impose Eurozone austerity on Ukraine is not necessarily pro-Russian, but simply opposed to plans to tear the country away from its major export market and fuel. Of all the post-Soviet states, Ukraine's economy is most closely interlocked with that of Russia, even with its military production. Disrupting these linkages can only be mass unemployment and austerity. The aim of a Ukrainian anti-Russian turn thus is not to help Ukraine, but to use that unfortunate country as a pawn in the New Cold War.

America's Ukraine adventure as a New Cold War gambit

Why would an American president take so great a risk with his reputation, if not to make a major geopolitical move for a showdown with Russia? The $5 billion of U.S. support (to which Victoria alluded in her notorious phone remarks explaining U.S. support for the coup) has been spent to fuel a movement dreaming of joining the EU. But the drive to turn Russia's naval base at Sevastopol and into a NATO Black Sea port was stymied by the coup leaders' over-reaching drive to ban the Russian language in public venues. A majority of Crimeans sought protection by being absorbed into Russia, which Putin hardly could have refused.

Failing to pry away the entire Ukraine, Plan B is to break it into parts, much as U.S. strategists are fomenting Uighur and Tibetan separatism in China. Dismemberment usually is achieved most easily in today's world under the *force majeur* of IMF "stabilization" such as tore Yugoslavia apart (an early venture of Jeffrey Sachs). The aim is to break away as much of Ukraine as possible from the Russian orbit, and to do so in ways designed to hurt Russia the most. This entails refusal to pay for gas arrears, and stopping Ukrainian military exports to Russia. IMF and EU-sponsored austerity would lead to deeper dependency on Western Europe for credit that a bankrupt Ukraine, driven into even deeper unemployment, could not pay. The IMF-EU then would insist that its government must pay Western creditors by proceeds from privatization sell-offs. The problem with this is that most Ukrainian debt is owed to Russia—not only for gas but also for other Russian claims including a reimbursement of Russian prepayment for its Crimean naval base.

The Ukrainian coup also aims to impose on Russia the kind of military burden that originally led its leaders to undertake their rapprochement with the West. The idea is to drain its budget militarily by heating up the New Cold War along its borders, leaving less to invest in real economic growth. And if sabre rattling over the Ukraine can taunt Russia into over-reacting, this will revive fears of the Russian bear in the Baltics and other neighboring states, fanning their ethnic anti-Russian tensions. This will help keep their elections from being fought over neoliberal austerity and the pro-oligarchy, anti-labor tax policies put in place since 1991.

Like most national security advisors, Brzezinski depicted Russian resistance to U.S. geopolitical strategy as a threat to re-establish the kind of powerful imperial state that has become economically impossible in today's world, except for the United States alone. The U.S. aim is to become unilateral global military tsar (or mother-in-law, or whatever metaphor you might want to use), using the IMF, ECB and EU bureaucracy, NATO, the covert operations of America's National Endowment for Democracy (NED) and Freedom House to block foreign resistance to smash-and-grab austerity policy and privatization selloffs.

This perpetual U.S. national security nightmare suspects any industrial power of being potentially military in character. Hence, any nation with a potential to pursue an economic alternative to austerity is a potential enemy.[9] To military game-players, China and Russia appear as the two great current and present dangers, given their industrialization, control of their own resources and most of all, financial autonomy from the dollar.

Putin made it clear that Russia would be satisfied to see Ukraine as a federalized buffer state, with regional autonomy for each of its ethnic regions. But U.S. strategists fear that this would enable the eastern region, whose export industry is tied to Russian markets, to resist the Eurozone austerity that would force Ukraine to borrow, default, and then pay back by selling off its public domain, banks, farmland, basic infrastructure and industry to Western investors.

The U.S. problem is how to convince Ukraine and other post-Soviet economies to submit to an IMF-EU financial order imposing chronic austerity. The trick is to make Russia look like the major danger, not Western financial austerity and the kleptocracy it supports. When countries waver from following this policy, the fallback game is to make them fear the alternative—a combination of Russian menace and IMF-NATO punishment for not submitting.

In setting the stage for this New Cold War global policy, former U.S. Ambassador to Russia Michael McFaul demonizes Putin. Until his election, "Russia was gradually joining the international order,"[10] by which McFaul means that it was on its way to becoming a U.S. economic colony, with its stock market leading global indexes and making fortunes for Wall Street investors. McFaul goes on to accuse Putin of "nationalistic resurgence," by which he means protecting Russia against U.S. smash-and-grab attempts to gain control of its raw materials when he stopped Khodorkovsky's sale of Yukos Oil to Exxon and its partners.

McFaul admitted in another interview: "The reset's been over for a long time. ... When President Medvedev was there, we got a lot of things done that made Americans safer and more prosperous ...The American national interest, that's what the reset was about. The reset was never about better relations with Russia. Outcomes were what mattered."[11] Putin was demonized once Russia stopped saying "Yes."

McFaul must be aware of Putin's own explanation for ending the U.S. dream: Contrary to George H.W. Bush's assurances, President Clinton expanded NATO into the former Warsaw Pact members of the old Soviet Union. What ended the "reset" was Obama's violation of his promise to enforce a no-fly zone in Libya, only to have NATO bomb Libya apart. As Putin explained in a speech before the Duma:

> This disregard to rule of law was evident in Yugoslavia in 1999, when NATO bombed the country without a UN Security Council mandate …. There was Afghanistan, Iraq and the perversion of the UNSC resolution on Libya, when instead of imposing a no-fly zone NATO bombed the country into submission. ...

"They were cheating us once more, took decisions behind our back, presented us with a fait accompli," he said, adding that the pattern is identical to that which accompanied NATO's expansion to the east, the deployment of an anti-ballistic missile system, visa restrictions and numerous other issues.

"They are constantly trying to corner us in retaliation for our having an independent position, for defending it, for calling things by their names and not being hypocritical," Putin accused. "Everything has its limits, and in Ukraine our western partners crossed the red line."[12]

Foreign Minister Lavrov explained that contrary to international law and U.S. promises,

> western states, despite their repeated assurances to the contrary, have carried out successive waves of Nato enlargement, moved the alliance's military infrastructure eastward and begun to implement antimissile defence plans. ... Attempts by those who staged the secession of Kosovo from Serbia and of Mayotte from the Comoros to question the free will of Crimeans cannot be viewed as anything but a flagrant display of double standards. No less troubling is the pretense of not noticing that the main danger for the future of Ukraine is the spread of chaos by extremists and neo-Nazis.[13]

Putin pointed out that "our partners in Europe recognize the legitimacy of the current Kiev authorities, but are doing nothing in order to support Ukraine; not a single dollar, not a single euro."[14] It was Russia that was continuing "to give it economic support and subsidize Ukraine's economy with hundreds of millions and billions of dollars for now. This situation, of course, can't continue eternally." In fact, Gazprom cancelled two major gas discounts for Ukraine, normalizing the price from $268 to $485 per thousand cubic meters starting as of April 1.

The gas dimension and Ukraine's debts to Russia

The usual Western financial strategy for taking an economy's assets is to subject it to austerity and then foreclose and privatize. The problem is that most Ukrainian debt is owed to Russia. Ukraine has not been paying for its gas this year. Prime Minister Medvedev pointed out that, as President, he "signed the Kharkov Agreement with President Yanukovych. Under the terms of this agreement, we extended our use of the naval base [in Sevastopol] for a long period—25 years," paying $11 billion in advance. So on balance, Ukraine owes Russia $16 billion over and above the gas debt.

There is a principle in international law, in accordance with which an agreement remains in force only so long as the circumstances that gave rise to it prevail—*clausula rebus sic stantibus* … I think it is perfectly fair to raise the question of having Ukraine's budget compensate these funds. This could be done through the courts, in accordance with the revoked agreement's terms. Of course, these are tough measures, but at the same time, the agreement no longer has effect, but the money we paid is real, and our Ukrainian partners must understand that nobody hands over money just like that, for nothing.

> At the same time, I remind you that Ukraine's debt, public and corporate, to Russia is quite large as it is. This includes the $3-billion loan that we gave them recently in accordance with our agreement to buy Eurobonds, and the nearly $2 billion that Ukraine owes in accumulated debt to Gazprom. All in all then, Ukraine's total debt comes to a very large sum.
> VLADIMIR PUTIN: 11 billion plus 5 billion?[15]

Most pressing, of course, is Ukraine's gas bill. Without paying, it may see the gas turned off. And if Ukraine simply siphons off gas being transmitted to Europe, a gas turn-off would threaten about 15 percent of Europe's gas supply.[16] Yet this seems to be what US-NATO strategy is trying to bring about. If Russia stops sending gas to Europe through Ukraine and does not get paid, the ruble could weaken, spurring capital flight to the West and leaving Russia with less foreign exchange available to rebuild its industrial economy.

Interim Prime Minister Yatsenyuk claimed that the new price for gas was an act of "aggression" and refused to pay anything at all. But he saw no such aggression in the IMF's demand to remove gas subsidies for Ukrainians. The rise in price evidently is to be blamed on Russia withdrawing its discount, not on revoking the domestic gas subsidy. The government's insolvency likewise will be blamed on Russian demands for payment of the debts falling due. To counter this double standard of blame, President Putin pointed out that "the lowest prices were in effect at the beginning of this year and Ukrainian partners stopped paying even at those prices. … April 7 marked a yet another date for payments under the gas contract for March

2014 and they didn't pay us a single dollar or ruble of the $540 million they were supposed to pay."[17]

When Ukraine failed to pay the $2.2 billion payment due on April 7 for the March gas, Gazprom's CEO Alexei Miller pointed out that under the terms of its contract this ended the special discount Ukraine had been receiving. It had been "given on the condition that Ukraine would pay all its gas debts and pay 100% for the current deliveries, and it was clearly indicated that if this did not happen, the discount would be annulled in the second quarter of 2014."[18] Prime Minister Medvedev reiterated that no future shipments would be made without prepayment,[19] and President Putin wrote to European leaders:

> Instead of consultations, we hear appeals to lower contractual prices on Russian natural gas—prices which are allegedly of a "political" nature. One gets the impression that the European partners want to unilaterally blame Russia for the consequences of Ukraine's economic crisis.
>
> Right from day one of Ukraine's existence as an independent state, Russia has supported the stability of the Ukrainian economy by supplying it with natural gas at cut-rate prices. In January 2009, with the participation of the then-premier Yulia Tymoshenko, a purchase-and-sale contract on supplying natural gas for the period of 2009-2019 was signed. Ukraine, right up till August 2013, made regular payments for the natural gas in accordance with that formula.
>
> However, the fact that after signing that contract, Russia granted Ukraine a whole string of unprecedented privileges and discounts on the price of natural gas, is quite another matter. This applies to the discount stemming from the 2010 Kharkiv Agreement, which was provided as advance payment for the future lease payments for the presence of the (Russian) Black Sea Fleet after 2017. This also refers to discounts on the prices for natural gas purchased by Ukraine's chemical companies. This also concerns the discount granted in December 2013 for the duration of three months due to the critical state of Ukraine's economy. Beginning with 2009, the total sum of these discounts stands at 17 billion US dollars. To this, we should add another 18.4 billion US dollars incurred by the Ukrainian side as a minimal take-or-pay fine. In other words, only the volume of natural gas will be

delivered to Ukraine as was paid for one month in advance of delivery.

Undoubtedly, this is an extreme measure. We fully realize that this increases the risk of siphoning off natural gas passing through Ukraine's territory and heading to European consumers.[20]

Putin might also have mentioned that when Russia lent Ukraine $3 billion in 2013 to support its currency by buying Eurobonds, it included a clause in the contract "that stipulates that the total volume of Ukrainian state-guaranteed debt cannot exceed 60% of its annual GDP. If that threshold is breached, Russia can legally demand repayments on an accelerated schedule," forcing Ukraine to default.[21] This prospect seems likely in view of the Maiden coup's intention to break Ukraine away from the Russian orbit, disrupting its major export market.

Ukraine's fragile economic structure and balance of payments

Reflecting the geographic specialization of labor established in Soviet times, Ukraine is still a major exporter of military equipment to Russia. But Kiev's first deputy prime minister, Vitaliy Yarema, threatened to halt all arms supplies to Russia, stating that "Manufacturing products for Russia that will later be aimed against us would be complete insanity." One report calculates that the range of exports includes "the engines that power most Russian combat helicopters; about half of the air-to-air missiles deployed on Russian fighter planes; and a range of engines used by Russian aircraft and naval vessels. The state-owned Antonov works in Kiev makes a famous range of transport aircraft, including the modern AN-70. The Russian Air Force was to receive 60 of the sleek new short-takeoff-and-landing aircraft, which now it may have to do without."[22]

Ukraine's oligarchs also sell steel and other industrial products to Russia. In the US-NATO plan, these factories would be sold to European investors to produce for Western markets. But Eurozone economies are shrinking as a result of their post-2008 austerity imposed to squeeze out debt service for foreign creditors. So the anti-Russian stoppage of export sales threatens to plunge the hryvnia's exchange rate even further than the 35% decline against the dollar in the first three months of 2014, making it already the world's worst performing currency this year. As Mark Adomanis at *Forbes* summed up the economic costs of the coup's anti-Russian stance: "Russia has always had the ability to wreck economic havoc on Ukraine, and this should have made the West a lot more cautious about the Eastern Partnership and the general effort to incorporate Ukraine into European institutions. In retrospect the entire effort to sign the association agreement appears to have been a rather reckless gamble which no one knew the stakes of." To avoid a drastic collapse that would plunge the economy into deep depression, the West would have to provide much "more generous (and politically risky) packages of financial assistance." Instead, all the IMF, Eurozone and United States have done is to egg Ukraine down the road toward financial catastrophe.[23]

Blaming Russia for Ukraine's coming austerity and new privatization sell-offs

The problem confronting US-NATO strategists is how to persuade Ukrainian voters to support the neoliberal austerity model of deep unemployment that will force labor to emigrate westward in a wave of "Ukrainian plumbers." Fanning the flames of resentment from the years of Soviet domination is a tactic that has worked well in the Baltics. Latvia has just joined the Eurozone (following Estonia's lead) and resentment of the World War II and postwar Russian dominance is so strong that the Russian language is limited to 40% of instruction in secondary schools and effectively banned from public universities (with some small exceptions such as Russian literature). The Maidan coup leaders are playing a similar anti-Russian card to focus the coming election on past sufferings instead of on how the coming IMF-dictated austerity will further impoverish Ukraine's economy.

A decade ago Russian President Boris Yeltsin went to Latvia and tried to divert this attitude by saying Russians themselves also were exploited by Stalinist bureaucracy. It didn't have much effect. The trauma of Soviet domination was so strong that Russian-speakers are treated as second-class citizens (many of the older ones without even being granted citizenship). The effect in Ukraine can be imagined by thinking what would happen if Canada were to ban the use of French language in public documents, universities and the mass media. Such a move certainly would prompt Montreal and Quebec to secede. Likewise if New York banned the use of Spanish and encouraged groups expressing a desire to start killing ethnic Hispanics.

For neoliberal US-IMF-NATO strategists, the advantage of fanning ethnic rivalries is to keep focusing Baltic elections on anti-Soviet memories instead of the disaster of neoliberal austerity programs. Playing off ethnic groups against each other has helped lock the Baltics into a pro-EU, pro-austerity program. Ukraine's coup leaders have been even harsher in closing TV stations that broadcast in Russian, arrested and beaten up leaders opposed to the Maidan coup, and deemed opposition to IMF-EU austerity criminal and "separatist." All this has led to Ukraine's Russian-speaking eastern provinces to turn to Russia for protection. Foreign Minister Sergei Lavrov claims that the United States is accusing Russia of doing what it itself is guilty of. The Western coup leaders are responsible for breaking up the nation, not Russia. "I will leave these claims on the conscience of our American partners. One shouldn't lay one's own fault at somebody else's door."[24] As one report has summarized the coup leaders' behavior:

> Over the last week and a half the Ukrainian government has tried to arrest every protest leader it can find and charge him with being a separatist. Conviction carries a jail sentence of 5 to 8 years.
>
> The banks here, most notably Privat Bank which is owned by the oligarch Kolomoyskyi, are limiting and freezing the accounts of people throughout the south-east region. For the last month, persons working in the coal and manufacturing industries have been told that if they joined the protests, or even spoke about them on the job, they would be fired. And, for the last two weeks, 30% of the workers' pay has been deducted to support the new National Guard, which is composed mostly of Pravy Sector fighters who have been threatening the population of the region.
>
> Yulia Tymoshenko was quoted last week as saying, "It doesn't matter who wins the presidential election, we all win. We all hate Russia!" By "Russia," she also means the people of south-east Ukraine who won't accept being ruled by an ultra-nationalist government.[25]

The aim seems to be to goad Russia to act intemperately and with brutality, perhaps even to make a serious military move against which NATO can deliver a devastating response from the ships it has moved into the Black Sea. A Russian incursion would support NATO's claim that Europe needs its protection, and also help keep Ukrainian and Baltic voters more fearful of Russia than of the IMF and ECB. The irony is that NATO was supposed to protect Europe from the threat of military conflict with Russia. Its adventurism at the hands of U.S. neocons now threatens to put Europe at risk, while devastating Ukraine's economy.

What blocks Russia from offering an economic alternative

The Eurozone is turning into an economic dead zone, but neither Russia nor major European parties are proposing to change the regressive rent-extracting tax and financial system that is imposing austerity and enables kleptocrats to bleed the post-Soviet economies, and toward which the West itself is moving.

As noted above, one problem blocking both Russian and Eurozone opponents of financial austerity from presenting such an alternative is the U.S. ethnic divide and conquer strategy of playing to distract populations from debating the real economic issues at hand. Another deterrence is the Thatcherite claim that There Is No Alternative.

Of course there is an alternative. But without going back to the events of 1991-94 and rejecting the path that Russia took under Yeltsin at the hands of the notorious Harvard Institute for International Development (HIID), the US Agency of International Development (AID) and World Bank planners, all that President Putin can do is use personal persuasion. His attempt to stop the bleeding has led the U.S. press to depict him as a tsar, not as a liberator from World Bank-Harvard neoliberalism. When he sought to rebuild Russia, he was accused of becoming an autocrat blocking "free markets," the American euphemism for the kleptocracy that has crippled Russia's ability to steer its development in the way that the United States and Western Europe industrial economies have done.

Given the political alliances in which Ukrainian politics are controlled by an oligarchy, what can Vladimir Putin offer the country? What is needed is a full-blown alternative to neoliberal tax and financial policy. Yanukovich rejected the IMF-EU "aid" with its destructive "conditionalities" of fiscal austerity and financial deflation, but all that Russia can offer Ukraine are subsidies for its politically gerrymandered oligarchy. In Russia, Putin used "jawboning" to urge the oligarchs and them to invest their takings at home to rebuild Russian industry. But without formulating an alternative to the financial and tax system, and indeed an alternative economic model, Russia can't offer a better economic system to its Near Abroad.

The cure for a rent-seeking oligarchy is to tax away rent seeking and de-privatize public monopolies. What Ukraine's kleptocrats have taken (and what foreign investors seek to extract) can be recovered by promoting classical progressive policies taxing land and natural resources, regulating monopolies and providing public infrastructure investment, including a public option for banking and other basic services. That is what drove the U.S. and Western European industrial takeoffs, after all.

It involved a long political conflict with the post-feudal landlord class and financiers, and a similar fight must be waged today. By the time World War I broke out a century ago, social democracy was winning the battle and socialism appeared on the horizon. But today that battle is not even being fought and the economic tools to guide reform—the concept of economic rent as unearned income, and the ability of central banks to create credit in the same way that commercial banks do—have all but disappeared from public discussion.

Russia shies from offering a solution along these lines, because that is labeled "socialist." Without enacting at least the classical criteria of a free market—a land tax, a natural resource and windfall gains tax on "unexplained enrichment, it is hardly in a position to promote these policies in the Ukraine or Baltics.

Neither Russia nor other post-Soviet republics in 1990 understood what finance capitalism and rent seeking are all about— except for the grabitizers advised by Western interests, of course. When it came to helping rebuild the Soviet economies after they sought Western support in integrating after 1990, the World Bank and U.S. neoliberals promoted a neofeudal political and fiscal counter-revolution against Progressive Era reforms. The Cold War thus was ended by a lethal rapprochement between Western financial interests and local political insiders and gangs.

It was the antithesis of political and economic democracy. Yet this is what still binds today's post-Soviet oligarchy to the West, supported by Wall Street, the City of London and German business, hoping to take the privatization windfall in partnership with the kleptocrats. Since 1991 Russia has suffered an average reported $25 billion in capital flight annually, amounting to more than half a trillion dollars over the past two decades. This is revenue that might have been used to modernize its economy and raise living standards. It was deterred by the failure to recognize that the precepts of neoliberalism are the opposite of what made the United States and Western Europe prosperous industrial economies.

At the very least, Ukraine and other post-Soviet economies need modern versions of Teddy Roosevelt, FDR and preferably a Eugene Debs. Economically, they need a Thorstein Veblen, John Maynard Keynes and Hyman Minsky. Such voices existed in Russia in 1991, including Dmitri Lvov at the Russian Academy of Sciences. Many non-neoliberal foreign economists urged alternatives to the World Bank-Harvard promoters of kleptocracy. But instead of creating a system of public checks and balances, the Soviet Union refrained from taxing the economic rents it was privatizing. The result was a travesty of free markets. Instead of the ideas of Adam Smith, John Stuart Mill and other classical economists urging markets free *from* unearned income, economic rent and predatory pricing, the West pretended that the antidote to Soviet bureaucracy would be neofeudal economies free *for* enclosures of the public domain, rent seeking and predatory pricing.

Flashpoint in Ukraine: How the US Drive for Hegemony Risks World War III

Do Russia, Ukraine and other post-Soviet economies have an alternative to neoliberal austerity?

In 1991 the United States and Western Europe did the opposite of helping the Soviet Union create a mixed economy, subsidize industry with a progressive tax system and keep natural resource rent, land rent and financial gains in the public domain rather than being privatized. What the West wanted was to extract these rents for its own investors. Russia was turned into an exporter of oil and gas, metals and other raw materials, while weakening its industrial ability to withstand US-NATO military encirclement.

What is needed today to restore natural resource wealth and post-Soviet land and infrastructure from oligarchs sending their takings abroad is a tax code of land and resource rents for starters. What has been relinquished can be recovered to finance public investment to rebuild their economies. This was the essence of the successful Western model, which saw industrial capitalism evolve toward socialism. It is the antithesis of neoliberalism.

Given the hesitancy of wealthy individuals to give up what they have taken, governments probably need to leave them with the wealth they have taken abroad. But new bleeding can be stopped by a rent tax to recapture the pre-1990 economic patrimony that has been relinquished to the oligarchs and, via them, to foreign investors. The economic rent that Wall Street envisions being paid out as dividends will be taxed away, legally under international law, by a tax code distinguishing economic rent from profits on *new* manmade capital investment and production.

Neoliberals will denounce this policy as if it signals a return to Soviet Stalinism, as if this ever were Marxist. To neoliberals, kleptocracy and neofeudalism are simply the final stage of socialism. But their present system is more an ideological coup d'état, imposed on the former Soviet Union in a moment when disillusion with bureaucratic collectivism was at its peak.

Reading the *Communist Manifesto* should dispel any thought that Russians had much familiarity with Marxist economics, or for that matter with the classical political economy out of which Marxism emerged. Marx and Engels described the positive achievement of capitalism as bringing bourgeois Europe out of feudal landlordism and inherited wealth. The ghost of Marx might have spoken to Gorbachev, advising him to pave the ground for industrial capitalism by enacting at least the reforms that Europe's 1848 Revolution advocated: taxing economic rent, followed by instituting consumer protection laws, establishing labor unions, and public banking to take the power of fiat credit creation away from foreign creditors.

The political problem for neoliberalism is how to deter voters from acting in their self-interest along these lines. In Latvia and Ireland voters have submitted to the anti-labor, anti-government policies of global finance. Neoliberals have come to see that they can win at the polls by imposing even *more* austerity. We are dealing with something like the Stockholm syndrome, most typically when kidnapped victims look to their kidnappers for protection. Poverty begets fear, prompting the weak to vote out of servility to the rich—or against each other in ethnic rivalries. The wider the polarization, the more the poor victims rely on their exploiters, hoping to survive by becoming abject clients in a predatory patronage system.

This means that the further economic inequality widens and the more a population is ground down into poverty and debt, the more the weak identify their interests with those of their oppressors. They believe that their best hope is that somehow the rich will reciprocate by accepting them in a patronage system. The effect is to demoralize populations and make them so fearful that they feel even *more* dependent on their oppressors, whom they hope will see how obediently they are behaving and will treat them better.

The past century has seen a counter-revolution against the Enlightenment, classical economics and its culmination in socialist hopes to steer industrial capitalism to evolve into democratic socialism. What is occurring today is a self-destructive financial dynamic of impoverishment, dependency and breakdown in many ways like what happened when Rome's creditor oligarchy plunged the Empire into the Dark Age two thousand years ago. The post-feudal real estate and financial oligarchies, the landed aristocracies of Europe and the great banking families and American trust builders have made a comeback, and the New Cold War is intended to lock in their victory. Ukraine is simply the latest battlefield, and battlefields end up devastated.

ENDNOTES

1. Michael Hudson is Distinguished Research Professor of Economics at UMKC, and former Professor of Economics and Director of Economic Research at the Latvia Graduate School of Law. His most recent articles on the post-Soviet economies are "Stockholm Syndrome in the Baltics: Latvia's neoliberal war against labor and industry," in Jeffrey Sommers and Charles Woolfson, eds., *The Contradictions of Austerity: The Socio-Economic Costs of the Neoliberal Baltic Model* (Routledge 2014), pp. 44-63, and "How Neoliberal Tax and Financial Policy Impoverishes Russia – Needlessly," *Mir Peremen* (The World of Transformations), 2012 (3):49-64 (in Russian). МИР ПЕРЕМЕН 3/2012 (ISSN 2073-3038) Неолиберальная налоговая и финансовая политика приводит к обнищанию России, 49-64.
2. "The Future of Europe: From Iran to Ukraine: An Interview with George Soros," The New York Review of Books, April 24, 2014, p. 69.
3. Mikhail Khodorkovsky, My Fellow Prisoners (2014), reviewed by John Lloyd, Financial Times, April 12, 2014.
4. Sergei Roy, "Ukraine: Triumph, Tragedy, or Farce?" *Johnson's Russia List*, April 5, 2014.
5. Manlio Dinucci, "Ukraine, IMF "Shock Treatment" and Economic Warfare," *Global Research*, March 21, 2014, citing IMF statistics at <http://www.imf.org/external/

Flashpoint in Ukraine: How the US Drive for Hegemony Risks World War III

6   pubs/ft /scr/2003/cr03174.pdf.>

6   "Fatal shootings in Kiev: Who is responsible for the carnage from Maidan," ARD German television, April 10, 2014http://www.wdr.de/tv/monitor//sendungen/2014/0410/maidan.php5, translated on *Johnson's Russia List*, April 14, 2014, #1. The German investigators confirmed from journalists with the protestors that "the hotel on the morning of February 20 was firmly in the hands of the opposition."

7   David Daley, "'America as the No. 1 warmonger': President Jimmy Carter talks to Salon about race, cable news, 'slut-shaming' and more," *Salon*, April 10, 2014.

8   Gideon Rachman, "Lunch with the FT: Lee Hsien Loong," *Financial Times*, April 12, 2014.

9   The classic statement is by Deputy Secretary of Defense Paul Wolfowitz: "Our first objective is to prevent the re-emergence of a new rival, either on the territory of the former Soviet Union or elsewhere, that poses a threat on the order of that posed formerly by the Soviet Union. This is a dominant consideration underlying the new regional defense strategy and requires that we endeavor to prevent any hostile power from dominating a region whose resources would, under consolidated control, be sufficient to generate global power." <http://en.wikipedia.org/wiki/Wolfowitz_Doctrine>, quoting from a Department of Defense planning document, "Prevent the Re-Emergence of a New Rival," February 1992, in P. E. Taylor, "U.S. Strategy Plan Calls for Insuring No Rivals Develop. A One-Superpower World," *The New York Times*, March 8, 1992.

10   Michael A. McFaul, "Confronting Putin's Russia," *New York Times* op-ed, March 24, 2014.

11   Patt Morrison, "Michael McFaul — an eye on Russia," *Los Angeles Times*, March 26, 2014.

12   "Putin: Crimea similar to Kosovo, West is rewriting its own rule book," <http://www.russiatoday.com>, March 18, 2014, from *Johnson's Russia List*, March 18, 2014 #4. See also "Address by President of the Russian Federation," Kremlin.ru, March 18, 2014. Complete text in Russian at http://kremlin.ru/news/20603.

13   Sergei Lavrov, "It's not Russia that is destabilising Ukraine," *The Guardian* (UK), April 8, 2014.

14   "Russia Continues Economic Aid to Ukraine Despite Illegitimate Govt.—Putin," RIA Novosti, *Johnson's Russia List*, April 9, 2014, #1.

15   "Meeting with permanent members of the Security Council," Kremlin.ru, March 21, 2014 (from Johnson's Russia List).

16   Daria Marchak and Jake Rudnitsky, "Ukraine Rejects Gas Price as Putin Waits on Prepayment," Bloomberg, April 10, 2014 (*Johnson's Russia List*, April 10, 2014, #42). Putin said Europe cannot refuse the delivery of Russian gas without harming its own economic interests. "European countries take around 34%-35% of their gas balances from Russia. Can they stop purchasing Russian gas? In my view, it's impossible," Putin said. ("Putin's Q&A Session 2014," *Johnson's Russia List*, April 17, 2013, #7.)

17   "Putin says situation with Ukraine's non-payments for gas absolutely unacceptable," NOVO-OGAREVO, April 11. /ITAR-TASS/ (*Johnson's Russia List*, April 11, 2014 #4).

18   Shaun Walker, "Fears of gas war as Ukraine refuses to pay increased prices set by Russian firm," theguardian.com, 6 April 2014.

19   Jack Farchy, Roman Olearchyk and Andrew Jack, "Kiev faces Russian gas threat," *Financial Times*, April 10, 2014.

20   President Vladimir Putin's letter to leaders of European countries. Full text, ITAR-TASS, April 10, 2014 (*Johnson's Russia List*). At his April 17 annual question-and-answer session, Putin moderated his stance and "said Moscow is ready to withstand the situation on Ukraine's payment for Russian gas for another month, but then will switch to upfront payments for gas, amid Ukraine's inability to pay its debts. 'We are ready to tolerate a bit more, we'll put up with it another month. If over the next month there are no payments, then we will transfer over to the so-called prepayment plan in accordance with the contract,' Putin said. *Johnson's Russia List*, April 17, 2013, #7: "Putin's Q&A Session 2014: Crimea, Ukraine, Gas, Foreign Policy and Mass Surveillance."

21. Mark Adomanis, "Ukraine's Economy Is Nearing Collapse," Forbes.com, April 15, 2014.
22. Fred Weir, "Can Russia's military fly without Ukraine's parts?" *Christian Science Monitor,* April 10, 2014.
23. Adomanis, op. cit.
24. Sergei Lavrov, "It's not Russia that is destabilising Ukraine," *The Guardian* (UK), April 8, 2014.
25. George Eliason, "A Changing Narrative in Ukraine," <http://www.opednews.com>, April 9, 2014.

OBAMA'S UKRAINIAN POWER GRAB, SANCTIONS AND THE BOOMERANG EFFECT

JAMES PETRAS

Introduction

In the biggest power grab since George Bush seized Eastern Europe and converted it into a NATO bastion confronting Russia, the Obama regime, together with the EU, financed and organized a violent putsch in the Ukraine which established a puppet regime in Kiev.

In response the citizens of the autonomous Crimean region, fearing the onslaught of cultural and political repression, organized self-defense militias and pressured the administration of Russian President Vladimir Putin to help protect them from armed incursions by the NATO-backed coup regime in Kiev. Russia responded to the Crimean appeal with promises of military assistance—effectively halting further Western absorption of the entire region.

Immediately following the proxy putsch the entire US-EU propaganda machine spun into high gear. The nature of the Western power grab of the Ukraine was ignored. Russia's defensive action in Crimea became the focus of media and Western government attacks. Unconditional support for the for the violent seizure of the Ukraine by the US and EU-backed coup was broadcast by the West's entire stable of journalistic hacks and accompanied by screeds calling for measures to destabilize the Russian Federation itself through a full-scale economic and diplomatic war.

The US and EU convoked meetings and press conferences calling for trade and investment sanctions. Threats emerged from the White House and Brussels calling for a "freeze of Russian assets" in Western banks, if Moscow did not hand over the Crimea to the coup regime in Kiev. Russian capitulation became the price of mending East-West ties.

The Obama regime and a host of US Congress people, media pundits and policy advisers called for, or engaged in, imposing sanctions on strategic sectors of the Russian economy, including its financial assets in the West.

Opinions in Europe divided over this issue: England, France and the rabidly anti-Russian regimes of Central Europe (especially Poland and the Czech Republic) pushed for harsh sanctions, while Germany, Italy and the Netherlands were more measured in their response.[1]

The Washington-based advocates for imposing sanctions against Russia view this as an opportunity to: (1) punish Russia for acceding to the Crimean autonomous government's call for defense against the Kiev putsch by activating Russian troops stationed in the region; (2) weaken Russia's economy and isolate it politically from its major Western trading and investment partners; (3) legitimatize the violent seizure of power by neoliberal and neo-Nazi clients of the US; and (4) promote destabilization within the borders of the Russian Federation.

At a minimum, economic sanctions have become an aggressive tool for energizing the corrupt pro-Western elites and oligarchs in Russia to influence the Putin government to accept the de-facto regime in Kiev and deliver the autonomous Crimean nation into their hands. "Sanctions" are seen by the White House advisers as: (1) projecting US power, (2) securing the Ukraine as a strategic new base for NATO, (3) ethnically cleansing this diverse and complicated region of its Russian-speaking minority and (4) opening the Ukraine for the wholesale plunder of its economic and natural resources by Western multinational corporations.

The Obama regime cites the "success" of the financial and economic sanctions against Iran as a "model" for what can be achieved with Russia: A weakened economy, diminution of its trade, destabilizing its currency, and provoking consumer scarcities and mass unrest.[2] US Secretary of State John Kerry is pushing for more extreme forms of economic reprisals: trade and investment sanctions, which obviously could lead to a break in diplomatic relations.[3]

Impact of Sanctions on Russia, the US and EU

Energy and financial sanctions on Russia, assuming that they can be imposed, would have a severe impact on Russian energy companies, its oligarchs and bankers. Trade and investment agreements would have to be abrogated. As a result Europe, which relies on Russian oil and gas imports for 30% of its energy needs, would slip back into an economic recession.[4]

The US is in no position to replace these energy shortfalls. In other words, trade and investment sanctions against the Russian Federation would have a "boomerang effect", especially against Germany, the economic 'locomotor' of the European Union.

Financial sanctions would hurt the corrupt Russian oligarchs who have stashed away tens of billions of Euros and Pounds in European real estate, business investments, sport teams and financial institutions. Sanctions and a real freeze on the overseas assets of the Russian billionaires would curtail all those profitable transactions for major Western financial institutions, such as Goldman Sachs, JP Morgan-Chase and other "giants of Wall Street" as well as in the "City of London."

In "punishing" Putin, the EU would also be "spitting on itself."Sanctions might weaken Russia but they would also precipitate an economic crisis in the EU and end its fragile recovery.

Russia's Response to Sanctions

Essentially the Putin Administration can take one of two polar responses to the US-EU sanctions: It can capitulate and withdraw from Crimea, sign an agreement on its military base (knowing full well that NATO will not comply), and accept its own international status as a quasi-vassal state incapable of defending its allies and borders; or the Putin Administration can prepare a reciprocal set of counter-sanctions, confiscate Western investments, freeze financial assets, renege on debt payments and re-nationalize major industries.

The Russian state would be strengthened at the expense of the neoliberal and pro-Western oligarchical sectors of Russia's policy elite. Russia could terminate its transport and base agreements with the US, cut off the Pentagon's Central Asian supply routes to Afghanistan.

President Putin could end sanctions with Iran, weakening Washington's negotiating position. Finally, Russia could actively support dissident anti-imperialist movements in the Middle East, Africa and Latin America while strengthening its support for the Syrian government as it defends itself from US-supported violent jihadists.

In other words, US-EU sanctions while attempting to undermine Russia could actually radicalize Moscow's domestic and foreign policy and marginalize the currently pro-Western oligarchs who had influenced the heretofore conciliatory policies of the Putin and Medvedev administrations.

The EU and Obama might consolidate their hold over the Ukraine but they have plenty to lose on a global scale. Moreover, the Ukraine will likely turn into a highly unstable vassal state for the NATO planners. EU, US and IMF loans for the bankrupt regime are conditional on (1) 40% cutbacks on energy and gas subsidies, (2) 50% cuts in public sector pension payments, (3) major increases in consumer prices and (4) the privatization (plunder) of public firms.

The result will be large-scale job loss and a huge jump in unemployment. Neoliberal austerity programs will further erode the living standards of most wage and salaried workers and likely antagonize the neo-Nazi 'popular base' provoking new rounds of violent mass protests.

The West would move forward with ‹agreements' with their Ukraine clients 'at the top' but face bitter conflicts ‹below.' The prospect of Brussels and the IMF dictating devastating economic policies as part of an austerity program on the masses of Ukrainian citizens will make a mockery of the puffed-up nationalist slogans of the far Right putschists. Economic collapse, political chaos and a new round of social upheaval will erode the political gains assumed in the power grab of February 2014.

Conclusion

The unfolding of the US-EU-Russian conflict over the Ukraine has far-reaching consequences, which will define the global configuration of power and foster new ideological alignments

Western sanctions will directly hit Russian capitalists and strengthen a "collectivist turn." The Western power grab of the ‹soft underbelly of Russia' could provoke greater Russian support for insurgent movements challenging Western hegemony. Sanctions could hasten greater Sino-Russian trade and investment ties, as well as military cooperation agreement.

Much depends on Obama and the EU's calculation of another weak and pusillanimous response from the Russian government. They are confident that the Russian Federation will once again, as in the past, ‹bluster and object' to Western expansionist moves but will ultimately capitulate.

If these calculations are wrong, if the West goes through with financial and energy sanctions and President Putin makes a robust riposte, we are heading into the eye of a new political storm in which a polarized world will witness new class, national and regional conflicts.

ENDNOTES

1	*Financial Times*, 3/5/14, p. 2.
2	*Ibid.*
3	*Ibid, p. 1.*
4	*Ibid, p. 2.*

UKRAINE AND REGIME CHANGE

MICHAEL PARENTI

In early 2014 more than 83 percent of the qualified voters of Crimea, on their own volition, participated in a referendum to rejoin Russia. And of that number, nearly 97 percent voted to separate themselves from Ukraine and once again become a part of Russia, in what was a massively one-sided victory. Returning to Russia meant better wages and better pensions, and somewhat better living conditions. The eagerness to reconnect was not anchored totally in ethnic emotionality; Crimean voters also hoped for a better standard of living.

It should be remembered that Crimea would never have pursued such an action, and Russia would never have been receptive to such a course, were it not that Ukraine was in the grip of disruptive forces that were driving toward regime change.

Regime change is a form of action designed to make it impossible for the existing government to govern. We have seen this well-orchestrated chaos and endless disruption in various countries. Militantly organized groups are financed and equipped by outside western interests. NGOs (nongovernmental organizations) surface in substantial numbers and produce rebellious publications and events designed to unsettle the besieged government---in Ukraine's case, a government that was democratically elected not long before. The NGOs handle billions of dollars worth of supplies used to mobilize and sustain the protests. Even though they are supposed to be independent ("nongovernmental") some NGOs get all their funds from the U.S. government. As Assistant Secretary of State, Victoria Nuland, proudly exclaimed, the United States had poured some $5 billion into the struggle for regime change.

Ultra-nationalists and mercenaries soon took hold of the protesting crowds and set the direction and pace of action, secure in the knowledge that they had the powerful reach of the western nations at their backs. This included NATO's military might and the western (corporate and public) mainstream media with a global reach that pretty much shut out any contrary viewpoint. The most retrogressive elements among these operatives in Kiev launched slanderous attacks against Jews, Blacks, Chinese, Muscovites, and—of course—Communists.

In Ukraine, crypto-fascist groups like Svoboda, the Right Sector, and others secured ample funds to keep thousands of people fed and comfortable enough on the streets of Kiev for weeks at a time, complete with well-made marching flags, symbols, and signs in various languages (including English). Svoboda henchmen were being financed by someone. They wore insignia that bore a striking resemblance to the swastika. Svoboda's top leaders openly denounced "Russian scum," and the "Muscovite Jewish mafia." Disguised men in unmarked combat fatigues attacked unarmed police and security guards. They moved among the gathered crowd and at times, according to independent sources, delivered sniper shots into the crowd---which could then be readily blamed on the nearly asphyxiated government. Meanwhile the western media reported everything the way the White House wanted, for instance, unfailingly referring to the perpetrators as "protestors."

This manufactured uprising in Kiev is something we have seen in numerous other countries: from Venezuela to Thailand during this very same time frame. The scenario is much the same, and the goal of these western-financed attacks has been to make the world safe for the 1%, the global super rich. Ukraine citizens who think they are fighting for democracy will eventually discover that they are really serving the western plutocracy. They will be left with a new government filled with old intentions. Ukrainians will end up with nothing to show for their efforts except a still more depressed and more corrupt economy, an enormous IMF debt, a worsening of social services, and an empty "democracy," led by corrupt neo-Nazis and ultra-nationalists.

Russia has stepped in on behalf of Russian Crimea. And Russia does not seem quite ready to leave Eastern Ukraine to the mercy of the regime changers. So Russia is now maligned by the western plutocrats who seek ways to put Moscow in isolated retreat. Putin is denounced and demonized at every turn. What exactly have been the demonic moves Putin has committed? Specifics are seriously wanting. What we have witnessed is a longstanding ploy of U.S. global aggrandizing. When confronted by a country or a political movement that decides to work out its own problems, a country that does not open its land, labor, natural resources, and capital to the U.S. empire's voracious embrace, U.S. leaders play the heroic rescuers. The leaders of such countries and movements are demonized: Castro, Mossadegh, Allende, Aristide, Noriega, Milosevic, Qaddafi, Hugo Chavez, and others too numerous to mention.

Flashpoint in Ukraine: How the US Drive for Hegemony Risks World War III

Leaders who serve U.S. interests by killing off and otherwise repressing the democratic reformers in their countries, are hailed as friends and heroes as, for instance, was Saddam Hussein hailed by Washington until he started asking for a larger oil quota. Those leaders who step out of line, as did Saddam, by committing economic nationalism, refusing to throw open the land, labor, capital, and resources of their countries to the western investors, are demonized and targeted, depicted as purveyors of mass destruction and whatever other terrorist menace. Once a leader is properly demonized, the U.S. empire builders exercise their presumed license to bomb his people.

So with Ukraine. In Kiev, all through January and February of 2014, the ominously dressed and masked squads that threw fire bombs and sniped from windows and roofs were uncritically and ever respectfully described as "protestors" and "demonstrators" by the western mainstream media. The American Confederacy flags and KKK symbols they hung in the parliament building, after they took it over by force, were pictured on the Internet by freelancers but never mentioned or shown in the corporate news. The "protestors" waged a forceful and successful takeover of the democratically elected government---a government that was promising new elections in a few months. This regime-change campaign earned nary a critical utterance from the U.S. mainstream media. But in March 2014, Russian-speaking citizens in eastern Ukraine who engaged in demonstrations and municipal building takeovers were immediately labeled "terrorists" and "militant agitators" bent on making trouble for the Kiev "authorities."

And what of the wicked Putin? How really wicked is he? Has anyone in the U.S. media ever read Putin's speeches? If so, they are keeping it a secret. Putin's utterances are so much more clear and sane than the twisty pretenses put out by Obama. Take for instance Obama's Brussels speech of March 2014, at the Palais des Beaux-Arts in which he dared to claim, with a straight face, that the United States has saved and democratized Iraq! In Iraq, the president and his cohorts did not grab control, he reassured his EU audience: "We left Iraq to its people in a fully sovereign state." No, we left Iraq with a million casualties, hundreds of thousands in destitution, a shattered infrastructure, a breakdown of public safety, and a demoralized population choking on wretched sectarian violence.

In this same speech, Obama asserted that Washington selflessly felt obliged to help Ukraine. He noted that issues in Ukraine did not infringe upon U.S. interests. Still the United States had a commitment to international law and to the humanitarian rights of all nations, even poor little ones, or maybe especially poor little ones. "We cannot turn our backs on smaller nations" (but Russia is obliged to turn its back on Crimea). Obama was unswerving in his claim that the United States was dedicated to fighting "the bully." And in this instance, the bully was Russia, led by bully-boy Putin. Russia must learn, Obama went on, that it cannot "run roughshod over its neighbors" and it would accomplish nothing "through brute force" (advice not proffered to the Kiev regime changers themselves). Furthermore, Obama reminded us, we Americans "need to defend democracy" (except when we impose regime change on an elected democratic government as in Ukraine). Moscow's "invasion of Ukraine" was a violation of international law and is deserving of all the sanctions imposed upon Russia---and more to come. Meanwhile, the changed regime that now represented Ukraine was to be bolstered with a $17.1 billion loan from the International Monetary Fund and an increased U.S. military presence in neighboring Poland. Immediate disbursement by the IMF of $3.2 billion will allow Ukraine to avoid a potential debt default. In other words, it will protect the rich creditors, not the Ukrainian taxpayers. It will enable Ukraine to pay its maturing debts by going still deeper into debt

As the weeks went on, Obama was now making it clear that all decent nations had to stand up to Moscow and challenge the way that Russia was behaving. Some day we might have a U.S. president who does not use diplomacy to play the irate schoolmaster, who does not patronize or scold one or another country with complaints about their behavior. The presumption is that U.S. leaders have no questionable motives, no hidden agendas of any kind. Self examination is not in order.

But others have examined things. Putin himself, on 29 April 2014, remarked that Washington was behind Ukrainian events all along, though keeping low. "I think what is happening now shows us who really was mastering the process from the beginning."

The U.S. empire's ultimate intent is to encircle and reduce Russia to a frightened and discombobulated satellite. But that is much easier said than done. At this time, as I write, Moscow reportedly no longer accepts telephone calls from the White House. Meanwhile protests against the NATO-supported Ukrainian regime are on the rise. Anti-Kiev activists are seizing administrative buildings and calling for a referendum on federalization. Ukraine's acting President, Aleksandr Turchinov, put the Ukrainian army on full alert due to the "threat of a Russian invasion." Turchinov admitted that the government in Kiev could not control the situation in eastern Ukraine. It did not even seem able to control the situation in Kiev itself.

Obama may have a few tricks and trumps left to play. But he is fishing in troubled waters and might invite more danger and tribulation than he---or we---can handle. As Putin put it: "The situation is serious" and we need "to find serious approaches to the solution."

UKRAINE: ANOTHER STEP IN CAPITALISM'S GLOBAL DOMINANCE

STRATEGIES AND POWER INSIDE THE TRANSNATIONAL CORPORATE CLASS AND US-NATO GLOBAL EMPIRE

PETER PHILLIPS
MICKEY HUFF
NOLAN HIGDON

The US-NATO Military Empire operates in service to transnational corporate capital's global domination agenda. In an unrelenting quest for capital growth, the empire seeks full neoliberal economic control of the world's resources and the full subjugation of human labor. To say any less ignores how 500 years of capitalism has resulted in world wars, enslavement and death of millions, and a state of permanent aggression from established powers against any resistance by the peoples. The current crisis in the Ukraine is another step in the unrelenting consolidation and control of transnational capital. The recent events in the Ukraine can only be understood by appreciating similar patterns of regime change in recent history that include events in Libya, Syria, Iraq, Afghanistan, Venezuela, Yugoslavia, Sudan, Indonesia, Vietnam, Panama, and numerous other nations, all in the context of 500 years of capital consolidation by rotating imperial powers.

Concentration of Capital and the Formation of a Transnational Corporate Class[1]

Capitalist power elites have long existed around the world. The globalization of trade and capital brings the world's elites into increasingly interconnected relationships—to the point that sociologists have begun to theorize the development of a transnational capitalist class (TCC). In one of the path breaking works in this field, *The Transnational Capitalist Class* (2000), Leslie Sklair argued that globalization elevated transnational corporations to more influential international roles, with the result that nation-states became less significant than global trade agreements developed through the World Trade Organization (WTO) and other international institutions.[2]

William Robinson followed in 2004 with his book, *A Theory of Global Capitalism: Production, Class, and State in a Transnational World.*[3] Robinson claimed that 500 years of capitalism had led to a epochal global shift in which all human activity is transformed into capital. In this view, the world had become a single market, which privatized social relationships. He saw the Transnational Corporate Class (TCC)[4] as increasingly sharing similar lifestyles, patterns of higher education, and consumption. The global circulation of capital is at the core of an international bourgeoisie, who operate in oligopolist clusters around the world. These clusters of elites form strategic transnational alliances through mergers and acquisitions with the goal of increased concentration of wealth and capital. The process creates a polyarchy of hegemonic elites. The concentration of wealth and power at this level tends to over-accumulate, leading to speculative investments, economic crisis, and global/regional wars.

The TCC makes efforts to correct and protect its interests through global organizations like the World Bank, the International Monetary Fund, the G20, World Social Forum, Trilateral Commission, Bilderberg Group, Bank for International Settlements, and other transnational organizations. These transnational institutions, including major corporate media outlets in service to the TCC, rely on US-NATO military hegemony for the enforcement of global agreements and the support of governments favorable to the TCC agenda of expanding and concentrating global capital. Governments unsupportive to transnational capitalist interests are pressured to comply or are undermined in a quest for regime change. Inside the governments of the US and NATO allies are various intelligence agencies who operate from within what scholar Peter Dale Scott calls a deep state that remains outside the public realm.[5] Within this system, nation-states become little more than population containment zones, and the real power lies with the decision makers who control global capital and encourage the implementation of overt and covert actions to maintain and expand their domination.[6]

Flashpoint in Ukraine: How the US Drive for Hegemony Risks World War III

Patterns of Regime Change: Deep State Power Politics and the Undermining of Non-cooperating Governments

The US-NATO deep state intelligence apparatuses engage in systematic undermining of regimes targeted for change to governments more acceptable to international capital. Practices of how the US-NATO Empire conducts deep state efforts for regime change in various countries are becoming more sociologically observable. If we review the histories and the US-NATO deep state activities evident in what has happened in the past two decades in Afghanistan, Iraq, Iran, Venezuela, Yugoslavia, El Salvador, Libya, Syria and Ukraine we can begin to see similar practices that demonstrate the unrelenting surge of TCC power inside the US-NATO military empire. While in some of these cases regime change has not yet been successful, each case has been ideologically justified by a war on terror or "humanitarian intervention." The following are historically evident patterns of deep state activities involved in regime change.

1. Long term external funding of opposition parties, special projects on "democracy building," covert operations, assassinations, counter intelligence activities, bribing of officials, and infiltration of regime bureaucracies are all part of covert and overt manipulations meant to undermine target governments for regime change. U.S. Agency for International Development (USAID) and National Endowment for Democracy (NED) often work in cooperation with domestic and foreign intelligence agencies, private corporations, non-governmental organizations and US ambassadors/CIA in country. These efforts include the organization of opposition leaders ready for assumption of governmental authority at the correct time. All the above is associated with a continuing public relations effort by private PR firms in service to TCC US-NATO Empire and a cooperative corporate media inside a managed news system.

2. Funds are provided to opposition groups to organize public events, mass rallies, marches, and demonstrations against the regime. Creation of incidents and events reflecting human rights violations are widely denounced in the global media. Covert consultation and funding of violent opposition efforts can often occur at this junction.

3. Efforts are undertaken to create violent incidents whereby innocent victims are injured and killed. Support of covert false flag operations such as the use of sarin gas in Syria, and sniper shootings in Libya, Ukraine, and Venezuela are blamed on the targeted regime. TCC media puts the blame for deaths on the police or the military of the evil regime.

4. TCC media and the US-NATO Empire then issue global demands calling for a humanitarian intervention combined with economic and trade sanctions, and cutting off the regime's access to international banking and credit. This phase includes United Nations resolutions, proposed military activities by NATO and the US, IMF and World Bank sanctions and indictments of specific regime individuals by International Criminal Court (ICC).

5. Finally, either the regime collapses or a violent military coup takes place removing non-cooperating officials, and opposition forces take command of the government, or the US-NATO Empire forces initiate military actions such a no-fly zones, bombings, and/or invasions and occupations. In the cases of Libya and Ukraine, the gold deposits of the regime are transferred to US-NATO control.

While these patterns of intervention are mostly readily observable from the histories of the past two decades, various elements of these patterns have a long-term history inside the expansion of US-NATO and allies' desire for concentration of capital of the past century.

Such practices required a continuing ideological justification. In US history, manifest destiny, democracy building, fighting the communist global conspiracy, war on terror, have each in turn been ideological justifications for capital expansion and economic control of various regions and people. Certainly for the US the ideological ideas of manifest destiny allowed the subjugation of an entire continent of native peoples and the annexation of Mexican territories. Bringing democracy to the people was an ideological justification for US invasions and occupations of Hawaii, Cuba, Puerto Rico and the Philippines a century ago, and many nations since. The ideological construct of fighting the global communist conspiracy after World War II justified the US and capitalist allies' engagements in Korea, South East Asia, and various other nations including Guatemala, Iraq, and Iran.

The ideological justification of fighting communism served well as a justification for capital expansion until 1991. The big ideological divide and ultimate power struggle after World War II between Communism and Capitalism ended with the collapse of the USSR. However, the five-century agenda of global capital domination never ended and has continued to the present under the guise of a war on terror and "humanitarian interventions" in service to empire. However, the ideological justification for US-NATO Empire intervention in Ukraine does not really fit in the context of the so-called "war on terror" or "humanitarian interventions." The US-NATO capitalist challenge to Russia is clearly more evident in the case of Ukraine. So it appears that starting in 2013, we are seeing the ideological rhetoric of Cold War nuclear warfare re-emerging. The reemergence of a TCC propaganda war along Cold War lines further reflects these developments.

TCC Media's Imperial Frames: Cold War 2.0 as Propaganda Redux

The world's corporate media is owned and controlled by the TCC, which pays no attention to academic concepts like "transnational capitalist class." Thus, a recent LexisNexis search of news coverage, recently completed, using the term "transnational capitalist class," returned only three news stories in the past decade, two from foreign media, and the third a letter to the editor by Leslie Sklair. The concept of a transnational capitalist class is absent from corporate news coverage, and often, state run media outlets are also heavily influenced by the TCC.

The corporate media in the US-NATO Empire covers foreign unrest issues in various countries as if they are silos. Countries in war or crisis are treated as isolated cases where nation-state decision makers and various opposition groups and parties create tensions that may result in civil unrest and regime changes (these can be legitimate pro-democracy movements, though these can also be used by outside parties to unwitting ends). During these periods of internal chaos, human rights violations often occur whereby the corporate media identify the supposed perpetrators of violence as evil Hitler-like regimes deserving of the ongoing unrest and in need of being sanctioned by the international community. If human rights violations are serious enough, "humanitarian intervention" (an Orwellian term for military invasion and/or occupation) is demanded by so-called democratic peace loving people around the world. Further, TCC media often manufacture much of the political support in democratic societies for such interventions.[7]

In October 2013, the largest economic contributor to the Republican Party, Sheldon Adelson, called for the nuclear bombing of Iran.[8] In December 2013, California Republican Congressman Duncan Hunter followed suit, supporting nuclear weapons against Iran.[9] Similarly, former Vice Presidential candidate and reality television show star Sarah Palin, speaking to Obama about Russia, averred that "The only thing that stops a bad guy with a nuke is a good guy with a nuke."[10] These types of irrational remarks justifying the US as the only nuclear power in the world are returning in the context of a new (or continuing) Cold War. Duncan Hunter claimed, "Pakistan does not share the same values we have" and thus should not have nuclear weapons.[11] As if that degree of nationalist hubris wasn't enough, a recent study noting the ignorance of the American public found that the further off an American's guess was about the location of Ukraine on a map, the more likely they were to support US intervention in Ukraine.[12]

When the Berlin Wall came crashing down in 1991, it prompted political scientist Francis Fukuyama to declare "the end of history."[13] However, it appears to be merely a pause in the progression of Cold War tendencies both abroad and on the home front. The 21st century government spying by the US and Russia offered corporate media an opportunity to dissect worldwide government spying. Instead, the corporate media railed against Russian spying and justified similar US spying. In 2012, the corporate media justified international and domestic spying by the US, by attacking the revelations of whistleblower Edward Snowden and *The Guardian's* Glenn Greenwald.[14] However, that same corporate media lambasted the Russian Government for spying. In 2014, Russia hosted the winter Olympics in Sochi. The conservative news and opinion website *The Daily Caller* reported that in Sochi, Russia was "using spy cameras installed in hotel bathrooms and showers."[15] Owen Matthews of *NewsWeek* claimed that "The 2014 Sochi Olympics have become a giant testing ground for some of the most intensive, extensive and intrusive electronic surveillance operations ever mounted."[16] NBC made up a story later proved false if not impossible which claimed that visitors would be hacked the moment they landed in Russia.[17] The media blitz against Russian spying during the Olympics was especially hypocritical considering that both the *Wall Street Journal* and The United States Computer Emergency Response Team (US-CERT), a division of the Department of Homeland Security, admitted that the US spied on people attending the 2002 Olympics in Salt Lake City, Utah.[18]

      The Cold War mindset historically kept the US corporate media from discussing the worldwide problem of media ownership as they pounced on the bias in Russian media. The Russian Government funds the news network Russia Today (RT).[19] Abby Martin, host of RT's *Breaking The Set,* was hailed by the US corporate media shortly after Russia's 2014 invasion of Ukraine for saying "I can't stress enough how strongly I am against any state intervention in a sovereign nation's affairs. What Russia did was wrong."[20] RT reporter Liz Wahl quit RT on the air to protest the invasion.[21] FOX, CNN, and NBC lauded the anchors for challenging Russia.[22] However, the praise was short lived once Martin criticized US media for not responding to the Iraq invasion the way she responded to Ukraine. Martin noted that the US media in "The lead-up to the Iraq war, [US media was] parroting exactly what the establishment said."[23] Martin's claim is widely supported by massive amounts of evidence and academic studies that the corporate media in the US have been loath to acknowledge.

      There has been a worldwide crackdown on journalists, but a discussion of it was ignored as the corporate press' Cold War bias covered Russia's curtailing of free speech.[24] The US media criticized Russia in January of 2014 after David Satter—a distinguished former correspondent with the *Financial Times*—became the first US journalist to be expelled from Moscow since the Cold War. The female Russian punk rock group Pussy Riot, which has about 11 members, was arrested and attacked in Russia for their protests, which railed against the close ties of Russia with the church.[26] CNN, FOX, and MSNBC sympathetically reported on the attacks against Pussy Riot at the 2014 Winter Olympics in Sochi.[27] Corporate coverage ignored how the US has committed equally egregious atrocities on free speech and journalism. For example, despite whistleblowers being legally protected under the Whistleblower Protection Act of 1989, the Obama Administration has indicted more of them under the Espionage Act than all previous Presidents combined.[28]

The corporate media's Cold War bias curtailed reporting on worldwide imperialist aggression. The corporate media, without noting any hypocrisy, disseminated criticism of Russia's imperialist aggression by US officials responsible for imperialist aggression of their own. In March 2014, the writer of President George W. Bush's Iraq invasion speeches, David Frum, tweeted "If Russia acts the outlaw nation, can it be expected to be treated as anything but an outlaw?"[29] John Kerry claimed "[Y]ou just don't invade another country on phony pretext in order to assert your interests." However, when Kerry was a Senator from Massachusetts he voted to support the Iraq invasion in 2003.[30] When asked about the similarity to Russian invasion of Crimea and the US invasion of Iraq, President Barrack Obama said at least "America sought to work within the international system."[31]

The obviousness of this hypocrisy has been noted by many independent journalists, most notably Robert Parry, but this view even made it to CNN online via *The Guardian's* Simon Tisdall (with an editor's note clearly saying the views were those of the author, not that of CNN).

History Matters: Past as Prologue

The 2013-2014 news coverage of the Ukraine, and Syria vis-á-vis Russia and the US-NATO Empire illuminates the continued existence of the Cold War bias in corporate media and a reemergence of a strong anti-Russia framework. TCC media see nothing more than evil leaders in the Ukraine and Syria who are committing human rights violations and the president of Russia is encouraging these evil doers as a co-partner in the crimes.

Regarding the Ukraine, the TCC media are setting a Cold War framework of international tension and brinkmanship similar to situations early in the Cold War in Berlin, Vietnam and Cuba. The US-NATO allies are accelerating the crisis with tension-filled statements, and military threats. The brinksmanship now appearing in the Ukraine must be understood as inevitable in the context of the 500 year history of capital expansion and the unrelenting deep state manipulations by US-NATO Empire intelligence agencies in service to and in cooperation with TCC. Key multinational corporations standing to benefit from new resource access and or war spending will often be included in the planning and implementation of covert operations. Understanding a theory of deep state power and observing recent similar patterns of crisis creation is now more readily observable.

If we review the histories and the deep state patterns evident in what has happened since the collapse the USSR in Iraq, Afghanistan, Yugoslavia, Venezuela, Egypt, El Salvador, Libya, Syria and Ukraine we can begin to see core mechanisms reflecting the unrelenting surge of TCC power inside the US-NATO military empire.

The "war on terror" is simply not sustainable as a long-term justification for global power concentration. The Ukraine underscores this idea in that a larger framework similar to the US v. USSR is reemerging to justify intervention there. An understanding of the need for a new Cold War media framework can help a lot in terms of recognizing the continuing efforts by the deep state US-NATO Empire's efforts to bring total neoliberal capital control over the entire world. Also the patterns of deep state politics will become increasingly easier to observe as capital concentrates globally. The TCC is becoming more transparent as the 99% recognizes the power and need to continued growth and consolidation by the 1/1000 of the 1 % that comprise the TCC.

By watching and calling out the lies and distortions of the TCC US-NATO Empire, we can encourage leaders elsewhere to recognize the patterns of power, and take the necessary steps to peaceably resist these ongoing imperial strategies of global dominance while working to strengthen democratic people's movements, both at home, and abroad.

ENDNOTES

1. The framework for the analysis in this article using the TCC was first laid out and published in Mickey Huff, Andy Roth, and Project Censored, *Censored 2014: Fearless Speech in Fateful Times* (New York: Seven Stories Press, 2013).
2. Leslie Sklair, *The Transnational Capitalist Class* (Oxford, UK: Blackwell, 2001).
3. William I. Robinson, *A Theory of Global Capitalism: Production, Class, and State in a Transnational World* (Baltimore: John Hopkins University Press, 2004).
4. For purposes of this study we use the term transnational corporate class and transnational capitalist class (TCC) interchangeably.
5. For a discussion of deep state techniques and strategies see, Peter Dale Scott, *American War Machine, Deep Politics, the CIA Global Drug Connection and the Road to Afghanistan*, Rowman & Littlefield Publishers, 2010.
6. Robinson, *A Theory of Global Captialism*, 155–156.
7. Noam Chomsky, Edward Herman, *Manufacturing Consent: The Political Economy of Mass Media*, (New York: Pantheon Books, 1988).
8. Noah Rayman, "GOP Mega Donor Sheldon Adelson Wants To Nuke Iran," *Time*, Oct. 23, 2013, accessed 5/1/2014, <http://swampland.time.com/2013/10/23/sheldon-adelson-nuke-iran/>
9. Ben Armbruster, "Congressman Says U.S. Should Use Nuclear Weapons If It Attacks

Flashpoint in Ukraine: How the US Drive for Hegemony Risks World War III

10. Iran," *Think Progress,* December 4, 2013, accessed 5/1/2014, <http://thinkprogress.org/security/2013/12/04/3018431/duncan-hunter-iran-nukes/>
10. Heather, "Palin: 'Mr. President, The Only Thing That Stops A Bad Guy With A Nuke Is A Good Guy With A Nuke'," *Crooks and Liars,* March 9, 2014, accessed 5/1/2014,<http://crooksandliars.com/2014/03/palin-mr-president-only-thing-stops-bad>
11. *Real Time With Bill Maher.* HBO. April 11, 2014.
12. Kyle Dropp, Joshua D. Kertzer and Thomas Zeitzoff, "The less Americans know about Ukraine's location, the more they want U.S. to intervene," *Washington Post,* April 7, 2014, accessed 5/1/2014, <http://www.washingtonpost.com/blogs/monkey-cage/wp/2014/04/07/the-less-americans-know-about-ukraines-location-the-more-they-want-u-s-to-intervene/>
13. Francis Fukuyama. *The End of History and the Last Man.* (Free Press, 1992).
14. Nolan Higdon, "The Millennial Media Revolution Part IV: The Response Tells You If It's Working," *Project Censored,* March 2, 2014, accessed 5/1/2014, <http://www.projectcensored.org/millennial-media-revolution-part-iv-response-tells-working/>
15. Josh Voorhees, "Russian Official Lets It Slip That There Are Cameras In the Olympic Hotel Bathrooms," *Slate,* February 6, 2014, accessed 5/1/2014, http://www.slate.com/blogs/the_slatest/2014/02/06/russia_olympic_shower_cams_hosts_dismiss_hotel_complaints_by_citing_video.html Sarah Hofmann, "RED STARE: Russians spy on media with cameras installed in Sochi showers," *Daily Caller,* February 6, 2014, accessed 5/1/2014, <http://dailycaller.com/2014/02/06/red-stare-russians-spy-on-media-with-cameras-installed-in-sochi-showers/#ixzz2x65sj6LT>
16. Owen Mathews, "Russia Tests Total Surveillance at the Sochi Olympics," February 12, 2014, accessed 5/1/2014, <http://mag.newsweek.com/2014/02/14/russia-tests-total-surveillance-sochi-olympics.html>
17. "Hacked Within Minutes," *NBC Nightly News,* February 6, 2014, accessed 5/1/2014, http://www.nbcnews.com/video/nightly-news/54273832/#54273832 Phillip Nickinson, "NBC News and the bullshit 'ZOMG Sochi Olympics Android hack' story," *Android Central,* February 6, 2014, accessed 5/1/2014, <http://www.androidcentral.com/nbc-news-and-bullshit-zomg-sochi-olympics-android-hack-story>
18. Desert News Staff, "Report: NSA was spying on Salt Lake City during Olympics," *Desert News,* August 21, 2013, accessed 5/1/2014, < http://www.deseretnews.com/article/865585064/Report-NSA-was-spying-on-Salt-Lake-City-during-Olympics.html?pg=all https://www.us-cert.gov/ncas/tips/ST14-001>
19. "Is RT state-run?," *Russia Today,* June 16, 2011, accessed 5/1/2014, <http://rt.com/usa/rt-government-broadcasting-radio>
20. John Aravosis "Russia censors RT news host's blistering critique of Ukraine invasion," *America Blog,* March 4, 2014, accessed 5/1/2014, <http://americablog.com/2014/03/russian-state-media-host-blasts-russian-invasion-ukraine-video.html>
21. Josh Feldman, "RT Anchor Resigns On-Air: I Can't Be Part of Network 'That Whitewashes the Actions of Putin' *Mediaite,* March 5, 2014, accessed 5/1/2014, < http://www.mediaite.com/tv/rt-anchor-resigns-on-air-i-can%E2%80%99t-be-part-of-network-that-whitewashes-the-actions-of-putin/>
22. "Russia Today Anchor Who Quit on Air Says It Was Not a Political Stunt," *Your World with Neil Cavuto,* March 6, 2014, accessed 5/1/2014, http://foxnewsinsider.com/2014/03/06/russia-today-anchor-who-quit-air-says-it-was-not-political-stunt Henry Austin, "Russia TV Anchor Refuses Crimea Job After Slamming Invasion," *NBC,* March 4, 2014, accessed 5/1/2014, <http://www.nbcnews.com/storyline/ukraine-crisis/russia-tv-anchor-refuses-crimea-job-after-slamming-invasion-n43746>"European Leaders Meet in Brussels; Explosive Interview with Pope Francis; RT Anchor Resigns On Air; Mom Drives Kids Into Ocean," *CNN, March 6, 2014, accessed 5/1/2014,* <http://edition.cnn.com/TRANSCRIPTS/1403/06/nday.02.html> Greg Botelho, "Anchor quits: I can't be part of network 'that whitewashes' Putin's actions," *CNN, March 6, 2014, accessed 5/1/2014,* <http://www.cnn.com/2014/03/05/world/europe/russia-news-

23. anchor-resigns/> Catherine Taibi, "Russia Today Anchor Speaks Out Against Invasion Of Ukraine: 'What Russia Did Is Wrong," *The Huffington Post*, March 4, 2014, accessed 5/1/2014, <http://www.huffingtonpost.com/2014/03/04/russia-today-anchor-abby-martin-putin-ukraine-rt_n_4895679.html>

23. Jack Mirkinson, "RT Anchor Abby Martin Rips American Media, Spars With Piers Morgan," *The Huffington Post,* March 6, 2014, accessed 5/1/2014, <http://www.huffingtonpost.com/2014/03/06/abby-martin-piers-morgan-russia-today_n_4910744.html>

24. Mickey Huff, Andy Lee Roth, and Project Censored. *Censored 2014*: *Fearless Speech in Fateful Times.* (New York, NY: Seven Stories Press, 2013.)

25. Luke Harding, "Russia expels US journalist David Satter without explanation," *The Guardian*, January 13, 2014, accessed 5/1/2014, <http://www.theguardian.com/world/2014/jan/13/russia-expels-american-journalist-david-satter>

26. Associated Press, "2 jailed members of Russian band Pussy Riot released under new amnesty law, *FOX News,* December 23, 2013, accessed 5/1/2014, http://www.foxnews.com/world/2013/12/23/jailed-member-russian-punk-band-pussy-riot-released-under-new-amnesty-law/ Charles Clover, "Pussy Riot dig claws into Putin," *Financial Times*, March 16, 2012 accessed 5/1/2014, <http://www.ft.com/cms/s/0/8efa1f1e-6f82-11e1-b3f9-00144feab49a.html#axzz30UMZ2mRN> Carole Cadwalladr, "*The Guardian*, July 28, 2012, accessed 5/1/2014, <http://www.theguardian.com/world/2012/jul/29/pussy-riot-protest-vladimir-putin-russia>

27. "Members of Pussy Riot attacked, whipped, unmasked in Sochi," *FOX Sports,* February 19, 2014, accessed 5/1/2014, <http://msn.foxsports.com/olympics/story/pussy-riot-band-members-attacked-cossack-militia-sochi-whipped-ski-masks-taken-off-021914> Richard Engel, Albina Kovalyova and Erin McClam, "Pussy Riot Detained for Hours in Sochi, Leave Station Singing," *NBC*, February 18, 2014, accessed 5/1/2014, <http://www.nbcnews.com/storyline/sochi-olympics/pussy-riot-detained-hours-sochi-leave-station-singing-n32531> Jethro Mullen, "Pussy Riot members attacked in Russian city while eating at McDonald's," *CNN*, March 7, 2014, accessed 5/1/2014, <http://www.cnn.com/2014/03/07/world/europe/russia-pussy-riot-attack/>

28. Associated Press, "Architect on Obama's War on Whistleblowers: 'It's Good to Hang An Admiral Once in a While as an Example'," *Tech Dirt,* July 22, 2013, accessed 5/1/2014, <http://www.techdirt.com/articles/20130722/01430523882/architect-obamas-war-whistleblowers-its-good-to-hang-admiral-once-while-as-example.shtml>; Huff, Roth, *Censored 2014.* "Information on Whistleblower Protection Act and Whistleblower Protection Enhancement Act," *Security and Exchange Commission*, accessed 5/1/2014, <https://www.sec.gov/eeoinfo/whistleblowers.htm>

29. David Frum, "If Russia acts the outlaw nation, can it be expected to be treated as anything but an outlaw?," *Twitter,* March 3, 2014, accessed 5/1/2014, <https://twitter.com/davidfrum/status/440521158308659200> Rania Khalek, "Hypocrisy of US Elites Over Russia's Invasion of Ukraine Is Out Of Control," *Dispatches From The Underclass,* March 5, 2014, accessed 5/1/2014, <http://raniakhalek.com/2014/03/05/hypocrisy-of-us-elites-over-russias-invasion-of-ukraine-is-out-of-control/>

30. U.S. Senate Roll Call Votes 107th Congress - 2nd Session, "On the Joint Resolution (H.J.Res. 114)," October 11, 2002, accessed 5/1/2014,<http://www.senate.gov/legislative/LIS/roll_call_lists/roll_call_vote_cfm.cfm?congress=107&session=2&vote=00237>. Jim VandeHei, "In Hindsight, Kerry Says He'd Still Vote for War," *Washington Post*, August 10, 2014, accessed 5/1/2014, <http://www.washingtonpost.com/wp-dyn/articles/A52839-2004Aug9.html>

31. Ryan Grim, "Obama Defends Iraq Invasion: At Least America 'Sought' To Get UN Backing," March 26, 2014, accessed 5/1/2014, <http://www.huffingtonpost.com/2014/03/26/obama-iraq_n_5036771.html>

ORANGE REVOLUTION 2.0

STEPHEN LENDMAN

Ukrainian protests bore clear earmarks. Ordinary Ukrainians were manipulated. Extremist street thugs were involved. They were recruited to cause trouble. They were paid to do it. Washington's dirty hands bore full responsibility. They still do.

Color revolutions are a US specialty. At issue is eliminating independent sovereign states. It's co-opting former Soviet Republics and Warsaw Pact countries. It's turning them West. It's incorporating them into NATO to further US dominance, using EU membership as bait. It's doing so despite no tangible benefits. Promises made to be broken substitute. Marginalizing, weakening, and isolating Russia are prioritized.

So-called spontaneous uprisings were manufactured. Ukrainians should know better. They went through this before. Memories are short-lived. Washington manipulated Ukraine's 2004 Orange Revolution. Ordinary people ended up losers. Promises made were fake. Exploitation followed. Once deceived should have been enough.

Good sense isn't a man on the street attribute. PT Barnum said "(t)here's a sucker born every minute." Con men, corporate predators, and rogue states with hegemonic ambitions take full advantage. Ukrainians were had once. They were set up again. They weren't mindful enough to understand. Awakenings usually come too late to matter. Shutting stable doors after horses bolt won't get them back. What's ahead looks grim.

Washington developed manipulating tactics long ago. It did so through years of trial and error. They're down to a science. They often work. Rand Corporation strategists were involved. In the 1990s, they developed the concept of "swarming." It relates to communication patterns and movements of bees and other insects. They're applied to military conflicts and street protests. Key US organizations are involved. More on swarming below.

The usual suspects include the National Endowment of Democracy (NED), the International Republican Institute (IRI), the National Democratic Institute (NDI), Freedom House, the Soros Foundation, and other corporate groups. They serve US imperial and corporate interests. They exploit ordinary people doing so. Various activities are ongoing in different countries. Different strategies are featured. Sustained mass protests often turn violent. They're one step removed from open conflict.

So-called color revolutions mask dark intentions. Ordinary people are easy marks. They're manipulated like pawns.

Ukrainians protested against their own self-interest. Succeeding assured harming their welfare. They were too out of touch to know.

Daily images weren't encouraging. Opposition MPs allied with Western interests. They demanded President Viktor Yanukovych resign. So did street protesters.

Washington's dark side is longstanding. It's notorious. It's too ugly to conceal. Assistant Secretary of State for European and European Affairs Victoria Nuland was caught red-handed. More on this below. She's hardcore neocon. She's a career foreign service officer. She's worked with Democrat and Republican administrations.

Early in her career, she covered Russian internal politics at Washington's Moscow embassy. She served on Washington's Soviet Desk. She worked in the State Department's Bureau of East Asian and Pacific Affairs. She served in Guangzhou, China. She was Deputy to the Ambassador-at-Large for the Newly Independent States of the former Soviet Union. She directed a task force on Russia, its neighbors and an expanding NATO. She was Clinton's Deputy Secretary of State Strobe Talbott's chief of staff. She was Deputy Permanent Representative to NATO. She was Dick Cheney's Principal Deputy National Security Advisor. She was Permanent US Representative to NATO. She was a National War College faculty member. She was Obama's Special Envoy for Conventional Armed Forces in Europe. On September 18, 2013, she was appointed Assistant Secretary of State for European and European Affairs.

Her husband is Project for the New American Century (PNAC) co-founder Robert Kagan. He's a neocon foreign policy theorist/hardliner. He advised John McCain's 2008 presidential campaign. He served on Hillary Clinton's Foreign Affairs Policy Board. The Foreign Policy Initiative (FPI) is PNAC's current incarnation. He's a board of directors member. He represents the worst of America's dark side.

So does Nuland. She supports regime change. She backed fascist governance replacing Ukrainian democracy. She was involved in manipulating street thug violence. She was part of a US-instigated insurrection. She wanted legitimate Ukrainian governance toppled. She wanted pro-Western stooge governance replacing it. She lied saying: «We stand with the people of Ukraine...»She demanded Ukrainian President Viktor Yanokovych engage «with Europe and the IMF.»

She was caught red-handed urging regime change on tape. Her conversation with hardline US Ukraine ambassador Geoffrey Pyatt was recorded. It circulated on You Tube.[1] Perhaps it remains there now. It's more evidence of America's dark side. It bears repeating. It's too ugly to hide. The leaked video is damning. It's four minutes long. It's titled "Maidan puppets." It refers to Kiev's Independence Square.

The *Kiev Post* (KP)[2] broke the story. On February 6, it headlined " 'F..k the EU,' frustrated Nuland says to Pyatt, in alleged leaked phone call." On February 4, the Nuland/Pyatt conversation was posted on You Tube. It's unclear by whom. Both US officials expressed frustration over EU "inaction and indecision," said KP. Nuland was heard saying "f..k the EU."

Pyatt called opposition figure Vitali Klitschko the "top dog." He heads the Ukrainian Democratic Alliance for Reform party (UDAR). Pyatt and Nuland agreed he's "too inexperienced to hold a top government post." He agreed not to run for president. In late March, he announced his Kiev mayoral candidacy.

A US Kiev embassy spokeswoman had no comment about Nuland's damning conversation. State Department spokeswoman Jennifer Psaki downplayed what happened."I'm not going to confirm or outline details," she said. "I understand there are a lot of reports out there and there's a recording out there, but I'm not going to confirm private diplomatic conversations." When pressed about You Tube authenticity, she said she "didn't say it was inauthentic. I think we can leave it at that." She was pressed again about the conversation revealing US intentions opposite of public comments about Ukrainians deciding their own future.

She lied, saying they aren't "inconsistent in the least bit." Her convoluted explanation didn't wash. She claimed Washington is working with Ukraine's government, opposition elements, as well as "business and civil society leaders to support their efforts..." Obama planned regime change. He wanted Ukraine's democratically elected government toppled. Not according to Psaki. She lied claiming it's "up to the Ukrainian people themselves to decide their future. (It's) up to them to determine their path forward, and that's a consistent message that we're conveying publicly and privately."

Psaki was hard-pressed explaining why Nuland felt the need to apologize. Doing so shows You Tube dialogue was authentic. Psaki called the incident a "new low in Russian tradecraft in terms of publicizing and posting this." "I don't have any other independent details about the origin of the You Tube video," she added.

Deep-seated internal Ukrainian problems persist. Poverty, unemployment and widespread corruption need addressing. Ukrainians are justifiably angry. Allying with troubled EU economies won't help. Their best interests lie more East than West. Moscow offers Ukraine tangible benefits. So do China, Iran and other non-Western states. Washington and EU partners assure harder than ever hard times.

It's hard making ordinary Ukrainians understand. Even Western oriented ones. They have an illusion of EU-aligned future prosperity. Hard lessons often are learned too late to matter. Brussels offers sticks, not carrots. They mandate structural adjustment harshness. So do IMF financial demands. They include mass layoffs, deregulation, deep social spending cuts, wage freezes or cuts, unrestricted free market access for Western corporations, business friendly tax cuts, marginalizing trade unionism, and harsh crackdowns on nonbelievers.

Professor Stephen Cohen is a longtime Russian expert. CNN interviewed him. He was blunt, saying:

> We are witnessing as we talk the making possibly of the worst history of our lifetime. We are watching the descending of a new Cold War divide between West and East. Only this time, it is not in far away Berlin. It's right on Russia's borders through the historical civilization in Ukraine. It's a crisis of historic magnitude. If you ask how we got in it (and how) we get out, it is time to stop asking why Putin - why Putin is doing this or that, but ask about the American policy, and the European Union policy that led to this moment.[3]

Western officials and media scoundrels wrongfully blame Putin for policy made in Washington. Complicit Western partners concurred. They created a horrendous mess. Civilizations may clash. Global war could erupt. Encircling the Russian Federation with NATO bases risks it. Ukraine shares a 1,400 kilometer border with Russia.

Imagine nearby US nuclear-armed long-range missiles aimed at its heartland. Imagine what Putin won't tolerate. Or any other responsible leader. The so-called EU agreement Yanukovych rejected had a clause he couldn't accept. Doing so meant "abid[ing] by NATO military policy," said Cohen. It reflects an "ongoing march towards post-Soviet Russia," he added. Putin had no choice. He had to act. He did so defensively. He did responsibly."(I)f you put him in a corner, you are going to see worse," said Cohen.

Washington's Cold War never ended. At issue is eliminating a major rival. Imagine risking war to do it. Imagine what no responsible leader would dare.

Throughout months of conflict, Russia went all-out to avoid confrontation. It remains committed to diplomatic resolution. Foreign Minister Sergei Lavrov is a consummate diplomat. He "urge[d] the West to show a responsible approach and set aside geopolitical interests and (respect) the interests of the Ukrainian people." He knows what he's up against. He knows Washington's real intentions. He knows targeting Ukraine is prelude to what's planned for Russia.

Throughout months of protests, Russian President Vladimir Putin attributed them to attempts to undermine Ukraine's government. "As far as the events in Ukraine are concerned," he said earlier, "to me they don't look like a revolution, but rather like 'pogrom.' However strange this might seem, in my view it has little to do with Ukrainian-EU relations."

Putin called protests pre-arranged. He said opposition elements intended them ahead of February 2015 presidential elections. They jumped the gun, he added. Ukrainian presidents serve for five years. Yanukovych was elected in 2010. He hoped for another term.

Putin called Kiev protests a "false start due to certain circumstances." Video footage showed "how well organized and trained militant groups operate," he added. People were manipulated. "They say that the Ukrainian people are being deprived of their dream. But if you look at the contents of the (EU) deal - then you'll see that the dream" is more illusion than reality. EU terms are "very harsh," Putin stressed. They involve sticks, not carrots. "I want to stress," he added, "that regardless of the choice of the Ukrainian people, we will respect it."

Dark US and other Western sources accused him of pressuring Yanukovych to back down. Russian Federation Council international affairs committee head Mikhail Margelov[4] blamed Brussels for Ukraine's refusing an alliance deal. "Brussels mistook Ukraine for some microstate, for which joining the European Union mean[t] making history," he said. "And it is mostly Brussels rather than some pressure from Russia that is to blame for Kiev's decision not to sign the agreement in Vilnius."Ukraine is a "coveted prize," he added. Brussels thinks inviting a former Soviet republic is too high an honor to refuse. No matter that membership minuses far exceed pluses. Ukraine benefits most by turning East. Brussels offers little incentive to do otherwise.

Unacceptable meddling in other nations' affairs is longstanding US policy. Doing so includes spreading malicious misinformation. Western Ukrainians favor an EU alliance. Why they'll have to explain.

Eastern ones are opposed. They favor a customs union with Russia, Belarus and Kazakhstan. Two-thirds of Ukrainians oppose joining NATO. They do so for good reason They're against global militarism. They don't want Ukraine involved in NATO wars. The Atlantic Alliance serves America's imperial ambitions. Most Ukrainians oppose compromising good relations with Russia.

In 1997, RAND Corporation researchers John Arquilla and David Ronfeld developed regime change street tactics. They titled their concept "Swarming & the Future of Conflict."[5] It involves waging war by other means. It exploits the information revolution. It takes full advantage of "network-based organizations linked via email and mobile phones to enhance the potential of swarming."

In 1993, Arquilla and Ronfeldt prepared an earlier document titled "Cyberwar Is Coming!"[6] They said "warfare is no longer primarily a function of who puts the most capital, labor and technology on the battlefield, but of who has the best information" and uses it advantageously. State-of-the art IT techniques use "advanced computerized information and communications technologies and related innovations in organization and management theory," they explained. Information technologies "communicate, consult, coordinate, and operate together across greater distances."

Cyberwar today is what blitzkrieg was to 20th century warfare. In 1993, Arquilla and Ronfeldt focused on military conflicts. In 1996, they studied net and cyberwar. They did so by examining "irregular modes of conflict, including terror, crime, and militant social activism." In 1997, they developed the concept of swarming. They suggested it might "emerge as a definitive doctrine that will encompass and enliven both cyberwar and netwar." They envisioned "how to prepare for information-age conflict." They called swarming a way to strike from all directions.

Effectiveness depends on various elements able to interconnect using revolutionary communication technology. What works on battlefields proved effective on city streets. US-instigated color revolutions achieved regime change in Serbia (2000/2001), Georgia (2003), Ukraine (2004), and Kyrgyzstan (2005).

Other efforts fell short. Color revolutions reflect America's modern day new world order strategy. They followed Soviet Russia's dissolution. Proxy and direct hot wars rage at the same time. US strategy is multi-faceted. Subversion, mass surveillance, and destabilization play major parts. Successful swarming tactics accomplish coups d'état by other means.

Anti-Iranian Green Revolution efforts failed. Street protests and clashes followed June 2009 elections. CIA elements instigated black operations. They did so to destabilize Tehran's government. Regime change plans haven't changed. What happens going forward bears close watching.

Flashpoint in Ukraine: How the US Drive for Hegemony Risks World War III

Ukraine remains in the eye of the storm. Protests began on November 21. They continued for three months. Neo-Nazi putschists usurped power. They staged the most brazen coup since Mussolini's 1922 march on Rome. They did so with Western support. What happened followed GHW Bush's broken promise. In 1989, he told then Soviet leader Mikhail Gorbachev NATO wouldn't expand east. It wouldn't do it to Russia's borders provided Moscow let its former republics become independent and abandoned its Warsaw Pact.

Former Russian republics Estonia, Latvia, and Lithuania are NATO members. Other Eastern European ones include Albania, Bulgaria, Croatia, the Czech Republic, Hungary, Poland, Romania and Slovenia. Washington wants all remaining Eastern European nations co-opted. Especially Ukraine. It wants them part of NATO.

NATO's a US imperial tool. It's been this way from inception. Washington provides most funding. It's over 70%. Claiming a NATO "political and military alliance for peace and security" doesn't wash. It never did. It's polar opposite truth. NATO's mission is offense, not defense.

It includes 28 member states, 22 Euro-Atlantic Partnership Council (EAPC) ones, seven Mediterranean Dialogue countries, and four Istanbul Cooperation Initiative (ICI) states. They comprise nearly one-third of world nations. NATO plans exponential expansion. It wants new members and partners on all continents. It wants them virtually everywhere. It's a global killing machine. It wants all adversaries and potential ones eliminated. It wants unchallenged world dominance.

Washington controls NATO. Its bases encroach on Russian and Chinese borders. They do so menacingly. So-called missile defense systems intended for offense target them. Neither country threatens America.

Imagine if Russia or China positioned nuclear armed missiles on America's northern and/or southern borders.

Imagine if their warships patrolled off its east and/or west coasts. Imagine if they entered Gulf of Mexico waters.

Imagine if their strategy called for ravaging and destroying one country after another. Imagine if they wanted all pro-Western governments toppled.

Imagine if they wanted subservient puppet regimes replacing them. Imagine if they prioritized permanent wars to achieve objectives.

Imagine a potential WW III scenario. Imagine possible armageddon.

Obama risks what no responsible leader would dare. His new friends include xenophobic, ultranationalist, anti-Semitic, hate-mongering militant fascists. Ukrainian independence was stolen. It's gone with them in charge. Dystopian harshness took over.

Growing numbers of Eastern Ukrainians reject Kiev putschists. It remains to be seen whether Western ones join them. The full impact of fascist repression combined with extreme neoliberal harshness hasn't hit home. All bets are off when it does. National rebellion may follow. Perhaps civil war. At risk is spilling it cross-border. Today is the most perilous time in world history. A potential East/West confrontation looms.

Obama and Putin are geopolitical opposites. Their ideologies clash. They're world's apart. Putin supports peace and stability. Obama wages permanent wars. He does so one after another.

Putin affirms the UN Charter and other rule of law principles. Obama ignores them. He claims a divine right to pursue unchallenged hegemony. He does it belligerently.

Putin believes nation-state sovereignty is inviolable. Obama wants pro-Western puppet governments replacing independent ones. His Ukrainian policy alone threatens humanity. He's recklessly out-of-control. He's surrounded by neocon advisors. His rage to dominate risks WW III. Stopping him matters most. Daily developments should scare everyone.

This writer's open letter to Obama said the following:

> Congratulations, Mr. President. You're the latest in a long line of lawless leaders. You achieved rogue status without really trying.
>
> Contempt for rule of law principles, duplicity and moral cowardice define your administration. Pretense otherwise doesn't wash.
>
> Instead of improving lives for ordinary Americans, you created worse than ever conditions.
>
> You more than ever made America a gangster state. Millions worldwide call it a pariah one. They do so for good reason.
>
> You stole public wealth. You handed Wall Street crooks trillions of dollars. You gave war profiteers trillions more.
>
> You impoverished millions. You left 100 million working-age Americans unemployed or underemployed.
>
> You ignore human need. Homelessness and hunger aren't your concerns.
>
> You're systematically destroying middle class society. You're heading America on a fast track toward third world status. A second one toward full-blown tyranny.
>
> You promised hope and change. You campaigned for peace. You promised all US forces out of Afghanistan in your first year in office.

You assured Palestinian sovereignty free from occupation harshness. You said decades of what Israel imposed would end.

You promised Guantanamo closure once and for all. You pledged within one year of taking office.

Bush administration war criminals will be held accountable, you said. Torture will end by decree.

So will indefinite detentions. Lawless military commissions trials won't be tolerated.

Labor rights will be supported. So will public education. And you can keep your doctor, you said.

You guaranteed universal healthcare with a public option. It'll be more affordable than before, you claimed.

You'll end unconstitutional executive authority. You'll help Americans facing foreclosure keep their homes.

You promised real immigration reform within one year of taking office. You'll "revisit the Patriot Act."

You'll "overturn unconstitutional executive decisions during the past eight years."

You'll be a uniter, not a divider. You'll serve all Americans equitably, justly, fairly and honorably.

"It's time to turn a page," you said. "We'll restore our values." The "days of compromising them are over."

We'll "secure a more resilient homeland." We'll "adhere to the Geneva Conventions."

Freedom is too precious to lose. You've gone all-out to destroy it on your watch. You've done so at home and abroad.

You said openness and transparency in government will be highlight your administration. You'll increase whistleblower protections.

Big Brother will be banished. "[N]o more illegal wiretapping of American citizens," you pledged.

No more "spy[ing] on citizens who are not suspected of a crime." No more privacy invasions.

No more human and civil rights violations. No more ignoring inconvenient laws.

No more extrajudicial operations. No more favoring monied interests over popular ones. No more wars for power and profit.

No more less than treating everyone equitably and justly. No more defending the indefensible.

Arundhati Roy once called Tony Blair a "psychopath." She described Bush the same way. She said you're no different from them. And then some, this writer adds.

You did more to make America unfit to live in than any of your predecessors. You've waged political, economic and hot wars on humanity.

You threaten its survival. Your policies risk WW III. You're unapologetic. Your rampaging continues.

Your waging multiple direct and proxy wars. You target all independent countries. You do so for regime change.

You're waging war on Syria. You launched it. You killed tens of thousands. You bear full responsibility. You want a subservient pro-Western stooge replacing Assad.

You ravaged and destroyed Libya for the same reason. You turned it into a charnel house. You're doing the same thing to many countries. Countless millions suffer horrifically on your watch.

Ukraine is your latest victim. Congratulations. You claimed another imperial trophy. As long as you can keep it.

It's at the expense of millions of Ukrainians deserving better. You want them marginalized, exploited, and impoverished. You want them denied fundamental freedoms.

You want Ukraine run by fascist extremists. You bought victory on the cheap. Keeping it is something else entirely.

Reports estimate you spent over $5 billion transforming Ukraine from a democracy to a pro-Western fascist police state.

It's pocket change compared to multi-trillions waging war on Afghanistan, Iraq, Libya, Syria, and other countries below the radar.

You elevated anti-Semitic, hate-mongering, xenophobic, ultranationalist neo-Nazis to power.

You expressed support for their extremism. You called them "the voice of the people." You blamed Ukraine's legitimate government for their street crimes.

You endorsed their power grab. You did so disgracefully. You planned it. You initiated it. You funded it.

You want total control over Ukrainian policy. You want ordinary Ukrainians having no say. You went all-out to prevent it. You stole their future. Eastern Ukrainians resist you valiantly. They're struggling to get it back.

Russia is geopolitically opposite. It's proud and assertive. Putin challenges Washington responsibly. He's not about to roll over. He won't accept US dominance. He won't sacrifice Russian sovereignty. Geopolitical issues especially concern him. He wants Moscow's influence increased. He wants rule of law principles respected. He wants peace and stability. He abhors violent confrontations. He opposes interfering in the internal affairs of other nations. International law prohibits it.

The UN Charter provisions recognize sovereign state rights, equality among all nations, non-interference in their internal affairs, and responsibility to settle disputes peacefully without threats or use of force. Article 2(7) states:

> Nothing contained in the present Charter shall authorize the United Nations to intervene in matters which are essentially within the domestic jurisdiction of any state or shall require the Members to submit such matters to settlement under the present Charter; but this principle shall not prejudice the application of enforcement measures under Chapter VII.

They exclude «the use of armed force....» Under Article 51, it's permitted only in self-defense against externally generated aggression.

UN Charter provisions explain under what conditions intervention, violence and/or coercion (by one state against another) are justified. Article 2(3) and Article 33(1) require peaceful settlement of international disputes. Article 2(4) prohibits force or its threatened use, including no-fly zone acts of war. Articles 2(3), 2(4), and 33 prohibit unilateral or other external threat or use of force not specifically allowed under Article 51 or otherwise authorized by the Security Council in accordance with UN Charter provisions.

Three General Assembly resolutions prohibit non-consensual belligerent intervention. They include:

- the 1965 Declaration on the Inadmissibility of Intervention in the Domestic Affairs of States and the Protection of Their Independence and Sovereignty;[7]
- the 1970 Declaration on Principles of International Law Concerning Friendly Relations and Cooperation among States in Accordance with the Charter of the United Nations; and

- the 1974 Definition of Aggression.

No nation, or combination thereof, may intervene in the internal affairs of others without lawful Security Council authorization.

Washington uses political, economic, and military force. Its financial wars cause more harm than hot ones. It targets one independent country after another. It wants pro-Western puppet states replacing them. It violates international law doing so.

Article 8 of the 1933 Montevideo Convention of Rights and Duties says "No state has the right to intervene in the internal or external affairs of another." Under Article 10, differences between states "should be settled by recognized pacific methods." Article 11 calls sovereign state territory "inviolable..."

Non-intervention is mandated in:

- the Organization of American States;
- the Organization of African Unity; and
- League of Arab States.

It was affirmed at conferences in:

- Montevideo;
- Buenos Aires;
- Chapultepec; and
- Bogota, as well as in decisions of the:
- Bandung Asian-African Conference;
- First Conference of Heads of State or Government of Non-Aligned Countries in Belgrade;
- Programme for Peace and International Cooperation adopted at the end of the Second Conference of Heads of State or Government of Non-Aligned Countries in Cairo; and
- declaration on subversion adopted at Accra by the Heads of State and Government of the African States.

The 1648 Treaty of Westphalia established the principle of state sovereignty. It considered states immune from foreign interference or intervention. State sovereignty is inviolable.

During the 18th and 19th centuries, philosophers like Immanuel Kant said states, as well as individuals, should be subject to international law. Political, economic or military force by one nation against another is prohibited. Kant's "Preliminary Articles" provided ways to prevent conflicts.

Flashpoint in Ukraine: How the US Drive for Hegemony Risks World War III

They included:

> (1) Prohibiting secret peace treaties that tacitly include the possibility of future war.
> (2) Abolishing standing armies.
> (3) Prohibiting national debts from provoking external conflicts.
> (4) Affirming that no state shall forcefully confront others.

Three other articles included ways to establish peace:

> (1) Every state constitution should be republican.
> (2) The law of nations shall be founded on a federation of free states.
> (3) The law of world citizenship shall respect "Universal Hospitality" conditions.

Kant defined it to mean unrestricted global free movement.

League of Nations initiatives failed to prevent conflicts. So did Kellogg-Briand. In August 1928, America, Germany France, Britain, Italy, Japan, and nine other nations became signatories. They promised wars would no longer resolve "disputes or conflicts of whatever nature or of whatever origin they may be, which may arise among them." Violating parties would "be denied the benefits furnished by this treaty."

The 1950 Nuremberg Principles defined crimes against peace. It did so to prevent them from repeating. The UN Charter failed "to save succeeding generations from the scourge of war" and other forms of conflict. How can it when America's hegemonic ambitions take precedence. Intervention is longstanding US policy.

Putin and Obama clash on fundamental principles. At issue is lawless aggression. It's interfering in the internal affairs of other countries. It's imposing Washington rules.

In February 2007, Putin addressed the 43rd annual Munich Conference on Security Policy. He called US foreign policy "very dangerous (in its) uncontained hyper-use of force—military force—in international relations, force that is plunging the world into an abyss of permanent conflicts." HE said US imperialism "overstep(s) national borders in every way."

"(U)nilateral illegal actions have not resolved any single problem. They have become a hotbed of further conflicts."

"We are seeing increasing disregard for the fundamental principles of international law."

"No one feels safe! Because no one can feel that international law is like a stone wall that will protect them."

"Of course, such a policy stimulates an arms race. The dominance of force inevitably encourages a number of countries to acquire weapons of mass destruction."

Putin opposes Washington's "unipolar world" agenda. He called it one "in which there is one master, one sovereign."

"And at the end of the day, this is pernicious not only for all those within this system, but also for the sovereign itself because it destroys itself from within."

"We are constantly being taught about democracy. But for some reason those who teach us do not want to learn themselves."

America deplores democracy. It tolerates none at home and abroad. It opposes what it claims to support.

In February 2012, *Moskovskiye Novosti*[8] (*The Moscow News*) published the text of Putin's foreign policy comments on "Russia and the changing world". Putin said: Moscow faces "key foreign challenges..." Decisions made affect "our economy, our culture, and our budgetary and investment planning." Given America's belligerence, they impact Russia's survival. Moscow pursues "an independent foreign policy." It will continue doing so. Global security depends on cooperation, not confrontation. Washington stresses other priorities.

Putin affirmed the "inalienable right to security for all states, the inadmissability of the excessive use of force, and the unconditional observance of the basic principles of international law." Failure to abide by these principles assures destabilized international relations.

Washington and NATO conduct "contradict the logic of modern development..." Expansion assures confrontation. Global security and stability are undermined."Regrettably," America and other Western nations remain dismissive of Russia's concerns.

Aggressive wars masquerade as liberating ones. They undermine state sovereignty. Doing so creates "a moral and legal void..."

The Security Council and other UN bodies long ago breached their mandates. Nations usurp their obligations with impunity. Force is lawlessly used against sovereign states. Destabilization policies target them. America and NATO undermine global peace. They do it consistently. They do it repeatedly. They do it lawlessly. States are victimized by "humanitarian" intervention and "missile-and-bomb democracy..."

Washington and key NATO partners "developed a peculiar interpretation of security that is different from ours."

America is "obsessed" with using force to "becom([e] absolutely invulnerable." The more it tries, the greater the destabilizing consequences. Absolute invulnerability for one nation assures none "for all others" outside its aggressive alliance.

Middle East and other uprisings replaced one "dominant force with another even more aggressive." It's hostile to popular needs.

Destroying nations to save them is cover for global dominance. Russia stands fundamentally opposed. "No one should be allowed to employ the Libyan scenario in Syria." Or against any other nation.

Washington prioritizes doing so. Conflict resolution is spurned. Warmongering interventionism substitutes.

Putin's doctrine endorses cooperation, not confrontation. Diplomacy works, he says. Protecting civilians requires ending violence, not escalating it. People yearn for democracy. They deserve it, he said. America wants unchallenged dominance and dictatorship. On vital geopolitical issues, Russia and America remain fundamentally at odds.

"...US attempts to engage in 'political engineering'" undermine relations, said Putin. Washington's missile shield targets Russia aggressively. It "upsets the military-political balance established over decades."

"Russia intends to continue promoting its security and protecting its national interest by actively and constructively engaging in global politics and in efforts to solve global and regional problems."

"We are ready for mutually beneficial cooperation and open dialogue with all our foreign partners."

"We aim to understand and take into account the interests of our partners, and we ask that our own interests be respected."

Washington pursues hegemonic dominance. Doing so risks global war. Syria is in the eye of the storm. Ukraine remains there post-coup. Washington-manipulated violence targets Venezuela. Iran's turn awaits. Other independent countries are threatened. War on humanity threatens its annihilation. America heads toward full-blown tyranny. Resistance is a universal right. It's an obligation.

Ordinary people can change things. We're all in this together. We have a choice. Resist or perish. There's no in between.

ENDNOTES

1. <http://www.youtube.com/watch?v=MSxaa-67yGM&feature=youtu.be>
2. <https://www.kyivpost.com/content/politics/fuck-the-eu-frustrated-nuland-says-to-pyatt-in-alleged-leaked-phone-call-336373.html>
3. <http://transcripts.cnn.com/TRANSCRIPTS/1403/01/cnr.09.html>
4. http://voiceofrussia.com/news/2013_12_04/Brussels-to-blame-for-Ukraines-refusal-to-sign-association-deal-Russian-official-2089/
4. <http://www.youtube.com/watch?v=MSxaa-67yGM&feature=youtu.be>
5. <http://www.rand.org/content/dam/rand/pubs/documented_briefings/2005/

RAND_DB311.pdf>
6 <http://www.rand.org/pubs/reprints/RP223.html>
7 <http://jurist.law.pitt.edu/2131.htm>
8 <http://www.globalresearch.ca/foreign-policy-russia-and-the-changing-world/31174>

LIBYA, SYRIA, VENEZUELA, UKRAINE:

ANOTHER WAR BASED ON LIES, PRETEXTS AND PROFITEERING?

CYNTHIA McKINNEY

It is one thing for the world to go up in flames by a series of miscalculations; it is quite another for those flames to be the intentional product of national policy and then to brazenly lie about it. The Obama Administration destabilizes the world, destroying whole countries, blames its actions on provocations from another country or a non-existent organizational threat to the U.S., and then proceeds to behave as if the prevarication is the truth. If the International Community, whoever that is, actually buys this heap of lies, then the world is in worse shape than I thought. We all watched in amazement as "colored revolutions" swept across North Africa. Yes, people want to be free; and I do, too. But free from whom and free to do what?

I remember sitting in a tent in Tripoli, Libya in February 2011 and listening to Muammar Qaddafi say that we—Afro-descendants who had been called to Tripoli from all over the African Continent and the Diaspora—will witness the great North African squeeze of the state in the middle. He said that the only way the U.S. could drop the independent Libyan Jamahiriya (which means nation of the masses of the people) domino into the ashes was to first take out Tunisia and Egypt. He said that the Presidents of both Tunisia (Ben Ali) and Egypt (Mubarak) would never allow U.S. or foreign boots on the ground for an outright invasion. When the agitation began and the neighboring dominoes began to fall, he knew that the target was Libya--and him personally.

Qaddafi told us that the West had long wanted its hands on Libya for strategic reasons. Indeed, Israel had claimed the Green Mountains in the eastern part of the country as a Jewish homeland and Libya had rebuffed U.S. efforts to locate a base for the Pentagon's Africa Command (AFRICOM) on the Continent. But even more than that, Libya did not agree to the unfolding Mediterranean Compact. Both the Euro-Mediterranean Partnership and the Mediterranean Union—an idea cooked up by disgraced former President of France, Nicolas Sarkozy—faltered on the lack of cooperation from Libya. Qaddafi informed us that his demand to Europe was that if the Europeans were all to join this Union, then all of Africa should join it, too. Turkey also balked at the prospect that the Mediterranean Union would become a substitute for Turkish membership in the European Union, which Sarkozy and other Europeans opposed. Consequently, the project made little headway.

However, these acts by Libya only sharpened the bullseye over its North African location on the map and Libya was accused of being an obstructionist to everything that the West wanted. As Libya's turn came, the demonization of "The Guide" or " Brother Leader" Muammar Qaddafi intensified on CNN, BBC, Al Jazeera, and other special interest media outlets supportive of Libya's incineration. The entire seven million inhabitants of Libya were reduced to a single individual who deserved what was coming. Anyone who has been demonized, as I have been, knows this drill. As a child of the southern U.S.A., I remember the mass media treatment that was applied to Dr. Martin Luther King, Jr. Sheldon Appleton wrote in "Assassinations,"[1] that such demonization allows the public to conclude that the targeted group or individual brought it on themselves. Appleton wrote that nearly one third of poll respondents, after the assassination of Dr. Martin Luther King, Jr., felt strongest that Dr. King had brought his assassination on himself. Negative media treatment has its purpose. It works best on those who believe the media without questioning its own special interest in covering a story in the way that it does. In fact, other research on the media found that the media can actually take sides while leading its audience to believe that it has not taken sides.[2] Moreover, in the United States, it is important to know that the media have been given a license to lie to the public in U.S. Courts.[3] These same media outlets are now trying to arouse hatred of the President of Russia, Vladimir Putin, as if he is my enemy and the enemy of my next door neighbor. The nearly 150 million people in Russia are now reduced to one man. Our hatred of that man will be justified and anything that the U.S. or U.S. proxies do to him or to his country will be his fault. That is, if the propaganda war works.

Perhaps the most important activity creating a serious chink in the armor of U.S. activities on the African Continent and toward nations of color in the Global South sounding the death knell for Libya's Jamahiriya was taking place on an entirely different continent: South America. At the very same time that Muammar Qaddafi and the Libyan Jamahiriya were pushing a strategic, ideologically correct, and principled Pan-African drive for a United States of Africa with its own standing army, development bank as an alternative to the World Bank, Continental bank as an alternative to the International Monetary Fund (IMF), and gold-backed currency, Hugo Chavez on the continent of South America was pushing the exact same types of institutions serving a united Latin America and Caribbean. Just as Libya was providing independent communication for the African Continent so that calls from Africa were not relayed through Europe and back to Africa—with Europe picking up a hefty fee, of course—Chavez had started Radio South, a radio network that broadcasts African and Western Hemisphere stories and news through a sharing arrangement. TeleSur, a television network, began beaming Spanish language news and items of interest from the Venezuelan perspective around the world; TeleSur English (being established now in Ecuador) would broaden the TeleSur reach to English-speaking areas.

Libya was using its oil money to invigorate the entire African economy and its leadership to foster more independence from European domination; Hugo Chavez was doing the same thing in the so-called New World. Hugo Chavez had institutionalized this vision of South-South cooperation within the region with the founding of the Bolivarian Alliance for the Peoples of Our America (ALBA), an organization with a different set of values, offering an alternative to neoliberalism and free trade agreements that allow the legal pillage of countries of the South by their former European metropoles and the United States. Hugo Chavez inaugurated the Africa South America Summit (ASA). A Bank of the South (Banco del Sur) was initiated at the conclusion of one of the ASA summits and the use of an alternative currency (the Sucre) has begun in the Latin American region. Why would an independent Ukraine want to get into debt peonage with the international cartel of bankers of London and New York represented at the IMF when alternatives exist that tout national dignity, independence, and alternative values?

The Third ASA Summit was to be held in 2011 in Libya. Instead, Libya became host to North Atlantic Treaty Organization (NATO) member countries' boots on the ground, very well paid mercenaries, and U.S. and NATO dropping incendiary bombs from drones and bomber airplanes, including depleted uranium ones, including earth rattling bunker busters. And one of the many stories of the death of Muammar Qaddafi had him hiding in a tunnel on the side of the road where he was serendipitously found, then sodomized, and then killed by gleeful, celebrating Libyans. Gone was the Libyan Jamahiriya government that paid for all hospital and health care expenses of sick Libyans anywhere in the world; gone was the Jamahiriya government that paid the total tuition for Libyan students and all the living expenses of their families everywhere in the world they were studying. Gone were the credit card jubilees where Libyan credit card debts were paid off, and gone was the government of a country that had no debt to anyone in the world.

Hillary Clinton, then Secretary of State, gloated in classic war criminal fashion: "We came, We saw, He died."[4] This should serve as her ethical disqualification enough from future elective or appointed public office in the United States and enough for a judicial indictment and sentence from The Hague; instead some Americans are lining up to salute Hillary as future Commander-in-Chief and the next President of the United States of America. That tells me all I need to know about the condition of moral collapse that plagues the political class inside the United States today.

Thus, it is by directed U.S. policy that Libya leads the way where I hope Syria, Venezuela, and now Ukraine do not go. Some aspects of the initiating irritant are the same; other aspects are quite different. For example, Libya is the only country that to date suffered outright "kinetic activity"—as "Son of Africa" and U.S. President Barack Obama would euphemize war. However, the roadmap used to get Libya where it is today—its complete dissolution as a governable entity—is exactly the same template used so successfully in Syria, Ukraine, and that is now playing out in Venezuela. Libya's allies, mainly the governments of China and Russia, should be ashamed of themselves for allowing Libya to go down in flames as it has. This has been as detrimental to the African Continent as was the U.S.-approved murder of Patrice Lumumba, the first democratically elected Prime Minister of Congo.[5]

An annual peaceful protest in eastern Libya served as the camouflage for a violent takeover of Libya's military barracks and police station—complete with the theft of military and police weapons by a sleeping cell, later found to be led by individuals who were on the payroll of the U.S. National Endowment for Democracy and other U.S. organizations. International NGOs fell into line rhetorically, like Amnesty International, and the Libyan leaders who were loyal to the Jamahiriya were all killed, tortured, imprisoned, forced to renounce their loyalty to the Jamahiriya, or forced to flee the country that they loved. Today, Libya is run by armed hooligans who have been set loose on an innocent population, albeit today a Green resistance thrives in the desert areas of Libya's south.[6]

Thank goodness, Syria was saved from this fate by Chairman of the U.S. Joint Chiefs of Staff, General Martin Dempsey, who opposed President Obama's planned bombing of that country.[7] General Dempsey diverted the unilateral bombing action of the President to a debate in Congress, instead, where the authorization for bombing Syria was withheld. But the situation in Syria had started out in the exact same way as in Libya: a peaceful protest march that all of a sudden became a site of carnage that is blamed on the government. Remember, this was the exact same template used in Venezuela in 2002 when Chavez was kidnapped in the unsuccessful U.S.-backed coup attempt. The Irish videographers that just happened to be in Caracas at that time, recorded the violence perpetrated by the Chavez opposition, that had been blamed on the Chavez government. This opened the media up for closer scrutiny. In Ukraine, the presence of snipers who were killing individuals on both sides of the political divide was documented by European investigator, Estonian Foreign Minister Urmas Paet who spoke with EU Foreign Ministry representative Catherine Ashton. In that conversation, Foreign Minister Paet reveals that, upon having just returned from Ukraine, he found unsettling evidence that the snipers in Ukraine were killing people on both sides, which suggests that the snipers were not from the government.[8] Paet says, "The stronger and stronger understanding is that the sniping is from the new Ukraine governing coalition." Upon reporting the Foreign Minister's remarks, all the *Guardian* could do was lace its report with "claims" and "conspiracy theory."

I traveled to both Libya and to Syria during the unraveling of Libya and while Syria was under attack. In both Syria and Libya, most of those fighting the government were foreigners. A lot of those in Syria had been recruited and armed in Libya. In Libya, not only were the government soldiers and police outgunned, they also had a "no-shoot" order that had been given. The authorities that had initiated the no-shoot order turned out later to have been a part of the plot to overthrow the Jamahiriya government. Libya did not have a General Dempsey to come to its rescue or defense. Plus, Libya gave up its ability to fight back when it gave up its deterrent chemical weapons arsenal in order to make peace with the U.S. There is an inherent lesson in this for all other independent countries. Now that Libya and Syria no longer hold chemical weapons due to U.S. pressure, it is the turn of the U.S. to destroy its chemical, biological, and nuclear weapons.

What Syria has to its advantage is that allies Iran and Russia are not too far off on the horizon—and their militaries. Thus, the only "double veto" by Russia and China in the United Nations Security Council blocked military action against Syria. As a result, Syria dies a slow death, but it is a death nonetheless. Recovery will take generations. Just as the sowers of chaos in the West want. Chaos and a debilitated polity that fails to have even a minimal diplomatic imprint in the world is exactly what is envisioned for Libya and Syria's neighborhood of the world. This also includes Yemen and Somalia, now under consistent U.S. bombing. We are witnessing the "Iraqization" of Africa and West Asia. Orchestrated chaos destabilizes and tears up countries, and cliodynamics is the science that tells intelligence agencies how long it will take those targeted countries to overcome the civil strife and become a functioning state again.

Thanks to WikiLeaks and its release of millions of e-mails from the intelligence firm called Stratfor located in Texas, U.S.A., we learned of the existence of a relationship between the leader of OTPOR, a youth organization credited with creating enough chaos in Serbia to allow the U.S. an excuse to lead in the bombing of Serbia, resulting in the eventual resignation of President Milosevic. OTPOR means resistance in the Serb language. On November 27, 2006, WikiLeaks Cable #06HAVANA23546 discusses a "landmark" meeting of opposition youth who were shown a documentary of OTPOR as inspiration for similar action in Cuba—undoubtedly for the "Cuban Spring." As it turns out, the leader of OTPOR, Srdja Popovic, was also on the payroll of Stratfor, the intelligence outfit that calls itself a "shadow CIA." [9] Flash mobs, the internet, cell phones, and out-of-control young people were to be used to create trouble from Cuba to Bosnia to Belarus to Ukraine. In Ukraine, the replica youth organization is called "Pora," according to WikiLeaks Cable #05ALMATY2838, dated August 4, 2005. In fact, I remember Qaddafi telling us about how disgruntled youth, who had no real appreciation or the struggle for Libyan independence and the threat to that independence represented by the sweet talk of the United States, were the instrument that was being used to create chaos in Libya. He mentioned that these impressionable young adults were also given access to drugs. I remember one Libyan told me that they were bored, they didn't have to work, the state took care of them. They thought life in the U.S. was better. Consider the millions of young people including myself—in the U.S. who struggle under massive student loan debt or are in the military because they wanted to go to school: some of whom end up imprisoned when they refuse to commit war crimes for the President who sent them off to war.

As General Dempsey proved, the U.S. military is the only thing standing between the U.S. arsenal of weapons and its actual use anywhere on the planet. Libya did not have a vocal General Dempsey, norPutin, nor Xi. In 2011, Dmitry Medvedev was President of Russia and Hu Jintao was President in China. Neither exercised a veto at the United Nations in order to save Libya from its current fate. In the Congress, Dennis Kucinich put up a valiant fight to stop the bombardment of Libya, but failed in the end. Is there presently any incumbent in Congress who is willing to do whatever it takes to save lives and the future for these countries—and our own—and end this madness of U.S.-led war?

Today, young people are throwing stones and overturning cars and defacing buildings in Venezuela. An uncritical eye would think that the wave of pro-democracy fervor had reached Venezuela—but, wait—the Bolivarian Revolution *is* democracy in Venezuela for millions of people of color who were previously disenfranchised there. U.S. policy under President Obama thwarts the enfranchisement of Indigenous and Afro-Venezuelans, who are more visible in government positions now than ever before in the history of Venezuela—much to the dismay of the Venezuelan White minority opposition that identifies more with the U.S. and Europe than their own fellow country-men and -women. And so, today, Venezuela suffers the same kind of targeting that Libya and Syria experienced. And the interesting aspect of this development is that whether it is Libya, Syria, Venezuela, or Ukraine—or the United States when its turn comes—anti-democracy work now looks like pro-democracy agitation. Just as anti-racism work was spun to appear to be racist work, so too now anti-democracy work is spun today to appear to be democracy work. We must be very careful and watch these events with a critical eye. All that is needed is an innocent audience to take it all in on what I call the special interest media, and never ask a question.

    What is happening in Ukraine is the classic U.S. destabilization template for the Twenty-First Century. Indeed, the U.S. admits that it has already spent $5 billion for "democracy promotion" in Ukraine. This is illegal and the U.S. Congress should have voted to cut off the funding a long time ago. Especially after the admission of the expenditure of such a huge amount was made by Assistant Secretary of State for European Affairs Victoria Nuland, wife of Robert Kagan, cofounder of Project for a New American Century (PNAC). So, neocon fingerprints are all over this Ukraine operation. Could that be why there is no sign of courage coming from Congress any time soon? Those who could be counted on to condemn this policy and to agitate against it are no longer there: House of Representatives Members Dennis Kucinich, Ron Paul, and I are history there. The document from OTPOR shows how Venezuela will be destabilized; it reads like a textbook of what is happening in Ukraine today. Only, Ukraine has gone further with the abdication of the democratically-elected President and the installment of a U.S.-oriented puppet regime. A primary difference is that Venezuela stands naked before the world as its Bolivarian Revolution is being tested. Only the people of the U.S. and European countries can save the Venezuelan people from the pernicious—and illegal, by the way—policy of the U.S. Ukraine has the backing of a very nearby Russia and its 800,000-strong military. Its proximity to Russia is its lure for the West and its impulsion for Russia. The only remaining question is whether the U.S. can get its proxies in the region, like Poland, to launch the unthinkable war that the U.S. politicians seem all-too-ready to join, but only by providing the pretext. Thus, if a U.S. proxy does anything to destabilize the already-tense situation in Ukraine, it will not be by accident, but by ruthless calculation for war against the wishes of the U.S. public that is sick and tired of U.S. wars based on lies, pretexts, and war-profiteering. The people of the U.S. are increasingly becoming aware of just how much war really is a racket.

One big caveat that seems to be unfolding is this: General Martin Dempsey, who intervened to stop the hot and overt war against Syria, has not bothered to show up when war is threatened against Russia and maybe China over Ukraine. When he posted on his Twitter account from Poland that U.S. soldiers were joining Polish forces in a joint training exercise, Dempsey was immediately challenged by those opposed to war. Dempsey posted further, on his FaceBook page on April 23, 2014 that the U.S. was also sending "elements" to train with Lithuania, Latvia, and Estonia. His FaceBook posts ends with some bravado about being "stronger together."

My caveat is: the foreign policy establishment today is the same foreign policy establishment of the United States of my youth: Cold Warriors thought that the U.S. could assure its primacy by conquering the Eurasian landmass. That means Russia, China, and the land in-between. Ukraine is a part of that land in-between—contested geography since the Cold War. U.S. military leaders dreamed about going to war against Russia—back then, the Soviet Union. I even studied Security Studies at the Fletcher School of Law and Diplomacy. Many of the professors there had outside gigs with the U.S. military. What the U.S. government pumped to the public at large was also pumped in universities across the country. Condoleezza Rice is a student of this kind of thinking—trained by the best of the Cold Warriors and Zionists, including the father of Madeleine Albright, who was her undergraduate political science teacher. Dr. Rice became a specialist on a country that does not even exist any longer. But that doesn't stop Cold Warriors from dreaming of the ultimate war to buy more time for U.S. hegemony.

U.S. hegemony is the latest incarnation of European domination—sure to come to an end as China and India assume their place on the global stage. Perhaps some have staked more than just the fate of Ukraine on the outcome of these global trends and have decided that a world war is worth it. I doubt that anyone will publicly broach the impact of racial identity on current and future global trends—especially on this talk of war. However, global demographic trends might be an underlying variable worth considering. Indeed, here's how some have been seeing it:

> It was a balance where you knew you were the rich countries, the powerful countries and all the organs of running the world were designed to accommodate that fact ... The Western countries were able to stay ahead firstly because of manufacturing. Well that got taken out and manufacturing moved to Asia. The second thing that happened after that was that in service industries, it moved to the Western countries and now that's been taken out.

In terms of Asian dominance in the service areas. And thirdly was in technology, we were able to stay ahead, ... the technological advance has now shifted as well. So the challenge for our country is, what the hell is it that's going to be left for us, if Asia is eating our lunch and dinner in terms of the things that we used to be able to do. And it's not just the United States, it is truly that group of the so-called billion plus that were previously the dominant factor who had 80% of the world's GDP ... If it were me today, the number one thing that I would be thinking about ... is that the 80 -20 rule which I had comfortably in my hip pocket is going to be a 35 - 65 rule and that puts a challenge of dramatic proportions to anybody who is in a business school today.[10]

What better way to go out guns blazing if you feel that your very identity as master of the universe and your current system, controlled by central banks and a cadre of elites, is possibly at stake and will exist no more if peace becomes the viable option?

ENDNOTES

1 Sheldon Appleton, "Assassinations," *Public Opinion Quarterly* 64, no. 4 (Winter 2000): 495 – 522.
2 For research on British Broadcasting Corporation (BBC) coverage of Hugo Chavez, please see Lee Salter and Dave Weltman, "Class, nationalism and news: The BBC's reporting of Hugo Chavez and the Bolivarian revolution," *International Journal of Media and Cultural Politics* 7, no. 3 (2011): 253 – 273.
3 For more information on this Court decision, please see <http://www.projectcensored.org/11-the-media-can-legally-lie/> and the actual court decision here: http://www.2dca.org/opinions/Opinion_Pages/Opinion_Page_2003/February/February%2014,%202003/2D01-529.pdf
4 For the video of then-Secretary of State Hillary Clinton laughing about the murder of Muammar Qaddafi in an interview and her defense of her words, please visit <https://www.youtube.com/watch?v=Fgcd1ghag5Y> and <https://www.youtube.com/watch?v=i1fJwS_SWD8> both accessed on April 30, 2014.
5 For U.S. admission of its authorization of and payment for the murder of Patrice Lumumba, please see *Foreign Relations of the United States, 1964 – 1968, Volume XXIII, Congo 1960 – 1968*, released 19 years late because the U.S. did not want to acknowledge its role in this heinous act, located at <http://history.state.gov/historcaldocuments/frus1964-68v23> accessed on April 30, 2014.
6 For more information on the illegal aggression against Libya, please see Cynthia McKinney (ed.) *The Illegal War on Libya* (Atlanta, Georgia: Clarity Press, 2012).
7 For more information on President Obama's decision to bomb Syria and then direct the decision to Congress, please see <http://www.whitehouse.gov/the-press-office/2013/09/07/weekly-address-calling-limited-military-action-syria> and <http://www.buzzfeed.com/evanmcsan/obama-i-have-decided-to-bomb-syria-but-i-want-congress-to-we> both accessed on April 30, 2014.
8 <http://www.theguardian.com/world/2014/mar/05/ukraine-bugged-call-catherine-

ashton-urmas-paet>

9   See the expose of the sordid history of cooperation between Syrdja Popovic, co-founder of Otpor! and its offshoot, CANVAS, with Stratfor and the U.S. government by Carl Gibson and Steve Horn, "Exposed: Globally Renowned Activist Collaborated with Intelligence Firm Stratford," Occupy.com, 12/2/2013, <http://www.occupy.com/article/exposed-globally-renowned-activist-collaborated-intelligence-firm-stratfor>

10   James D. Wolfensohn speech before the Stanford University Graduate School of Business, "Big Shift Coming," delivered January 11, 2010 located at <http://www.youtube.com/watch?v=6a0zhc1y_Ns&feature=youtu.be>, accessed on May 3, 2014.

THE GEO-POLITICS OF EUROMAIDAN

MAHDI NAZEMROAYA

The takeover of power in Kiev by the mainstream opposition is a coup that has been executed by force, which overlooks the opinions of at least half of the Ukrainian population. Yet, you would not know this from listening to such media outlets and networks as CNN or Fox News or reading the headlines being produced by *Reuters* and the state-owned British Broadcasting Corporation (BBC). The events in Kiev are misleadingly being billed and framed by these media sources and the so-called "Western" governments they support, either directly or indirectly, as the triumph of people power and democracy in Ukraine.

While the mainstream media in North America and the EU look the other way regarding who the ultra-nationalists in the coup government in Kiev really are, the facts speak for themselves. Both the EU and the US governments have rubbed their elbows with the ultra-nationalists. Oleh Tyahnybok, the leader of Svoboda (formerly the Social Nationalist Party of Ukraine), was even part of the opposition triumvirate that all the US and EU officials visiting Kiev met with while performing their political pilgrimages to Ukraine to encourage the protesters to continue with their demonstrations and riots demanding Euro-Atlantic integration.

Svoboda has popularly been described as a neo-Nazi grouping. The World Jewish Congress has demanded that Svoboda be banned. The ultra-nationalist party was even condemned by the EU's own European Parliament, which passed a motion on Dec. 13, 2012 categorically condemning Svoboda.

The text adopted by the European Parliament states:

> Parliament goes on to express concern about the rising nationalistic sentiment in Ukraine, expressed in support for the Svoboda Party, which, as a result, is one of the two new parties to enter the Verkhovna Rada. It recalls that racist,

anti-Semitic and xenophobic views go against the EU's fundamental values and principles and therefore appeals to pro-democratic parties in the Verkhovna Rada not to associate with, endorse or form coalitions with this party.

Several members of Svoboda have been given key cabinet and government posts. One of the two junior deputy prime ministers, or assistant deputy prime ministers, is Oleksandr Sych. The ministry of agriculture and food has been given for management to Ihor Shvaika. The environment and natural resources ministry has been assigned to Andry/Andriy Mokhnyk. The defense minister is Ihor Tenyukh, a former admiral in the Ukrainian Navy who obstructed Russian naval movements in Sevastopol during the Russo-Georgian War over South Ossetia and who was later dismissed by the Ukrainian government for insubordination. Oleh Makhnitsky, another member of Svoboda, has been assigned as the new prosecutor-general of Ukraine by the coup government.

Andry Parubiy, one of the founders of Svoboda, is now the post-coup secretary of the National Security and Defense Council of Ukraine (RNBO). He was the man controlling the so-called "Euromaidan security forces" that fought government forces in Kiev. His job as secretary is to represent the president and act on his behalf in coordinating and implementing the RNBO's decisions.

As a figure, Parubiy clearly illustrates how the mainstream opposition in Ukraine is integrated with the ultra-nationalists. Parubiy is an Orangist and was a leader in the Orange Revolution. He has changed parties several times. After founding Svoboda, he joined Viktor Yushchenko's Our Ukraine before joining Yulia Tymoshenko's Fatherland Party and being elected as one of the Fatherland Party's deputies, or members of parliament.

The ultra-nationalists are such an integral part of the mainstream opposition that the US-supported Orangist president of Ukraine, Viktor Yushchenko, posthumously awarded the infamous Nazi collaborator Stepan Bandera the title and decoration of the "Hero of Ukraine" in 2010. Foreign audiences, however, would not know that if they relied on reportage from the likes of the US state-run Radio Free Europe, which tried to protect Yushchenko because he wanted to reorient Ukraine toward the U.S. and EU. Parubiy also lobbied the European Parliament not to oppose Yushchenko's decision.

Other smaller ultra-nationalist parties were also given government posts, and several of the independent cabinet members are also aligned to these parties. Dmytro Yarosh from Right Sector (Pravyi Sektor) is the deputy secretary of the RNBO, and the Trizub Party was given the education ministry. Trizub had Sergey Kvit appointed to the post of education minister.

Flashpoint in Ukraine: How the US Drive for Hegemony Risks World War III

The ultra-nationalists have intransigently anti-Russian attitudes. Many of them also dislike a vast spectrum of other groups, including Jews, Armenians, Roma, Poles, Greeks, Germans, Turks, Tartars (Tatars), socialists, communists, and supporters of the Party of Regions. In this context, it should be no surprise that one of the first decisions that the post-coup regime in Kiev made was to remove the legal status of the Russian language as the regional language of half of Ukraine.

The Right Sector, itself, is a coalition of militant ultra-nationalists. These militants were instrumental in fighting government forces and taking over both government buildings in Kiev and regional governments in the western portion of Ukraine. Despite the protests of First Deputy Defense Minister Oleynik, Deputy Defense Minister Mozharovskiy and Deputy Defense Minister Babenk, Arseniy Yatsenyuk's post-coup government has even given the ultra-nationalist opposition militias official status within the Ukrainian military and security forces. Yatsenyuk and the Orangists also dismissed all the officials that protested that the move would fracture the country and make the political divide in Ukraine irreversible.

To rule Ukraine once more, the Orangists—the loosely-knit alliance of the governing parties that ran Ukraine under the Yushchenko-Tymoshenko governments, foreign-based Ukrainians, and the forces behind the Orange Revolution—and their foreign backers have used and manipulated the ultra-nationalist elements of the population—some of which are openly anti-European Union—as their foot soldiers in an application of force against their democratically-elected opponents.

Western Double-Standards and the Media War

The mainstream media selects which narratives prevail by deciding what voices to represent and the quantity and quality of coverage these voices get. Audiences should ask themselves some important questions about this. Whose voices are they hearing, and why? Why are certain voices excluded or deliberately ignored and other voices and points of view not excluded from the conversation? Why are some views deemed credible and others discredited?

Evaluation is needed. The voices and accounts that challenge the narratives that are being promoted as reality to the public are ignored or undermined so that they do not defy the message or vision that the mainstream media is framing for audiences. Circumstances are deliberately left out of the narratives being reported or transmitted in many cases because of the justifications they can provide and the perceptions they can create.

Not only has the role of the ultra-nationalists in executing the coup been ignored by the mainstream media in North America and the EU, the roots of the bloodshed in Kiev have been whitewashed to paint a narrative that suits the foreign policy goals of Washington and its EU allies. The shootings of protesters by snipers have simply been presented as the vile actions of the Ukrainian government, never taking into consideration the agitation of the armed ultra-nationalist gangs and the mainstream opposition leaders that promoted violent conflict.

According to a telephone conversation between Estonian Foreign Minister Urmas Paet and European Union Commissioner Catherine Ashton, which was leaked by the Security Service of Ukraine (SBU/SSU) on February 26, 2014, the snipers who shot at protesters and police in Kiev were allegedly hired by Ukrainian opposition leaders. Estonian Foreign Minister Paet made the statements on the basis of details he was given by one of the head doctors of the medical team of the anti-government protests, Olga Bogomolets, an opponent of Viktor Yanukovych's government who wanted it removed from power.

The Telegraph reported several days before the leaked conversation that "[a]t least three of the bodies displayed single bullet wounds to the heads," and "were shot in the head, the neck or the heart. None were shot anywhere else like in the legs." This means that the snipers were making kill shots by design, which seems like the last thing that the Ukrainian government would want to do when it was trying to appease the protesters and bring calm to Kiev.

The Ukrainian journalist Alexey Yaroshevsky's account of the sniper shootings is also worth noting, and it is backed up by footage taken by his RT crew in Kiev. Their footage shows armed opposition members running away from the scene of the shooting of anti-government protesters. What comes across as unusual is that the armed members of the opposition were constantly agitating to start firefights at every opportunity that they could get.

The commandant of the SBU/SSU, Major-General Oleksandr Yakimenko, has testified that his counter-intelligence forces were monitoring the CIA in Ukraine during the protests. According to the SSU, the CIA was active on the ground in Kiev and collaborating with a small circle of opposition figures. Yakimenko has also said that it was not the police or government forces that fired on the protesters, but snipers from the Philharmonic Building that was controlled by the opposition leader Andriy Parubiy, which he asserts was interacting with the CIA. Speaking to the Russian media, Yakimenko said that twenty men wearing "special combat clothes" and carrying "sniper rifle cases, as well as AKMs with scopes" ran out of the opposition-controlled Philharmonic Building and split into two groups of ten people, with one taking position at the Ukraine Hotel. The anti-government protesters even saw this and asked Ukrainian police to pursue them, and even figures from Right Sector and Svoboda asked Yakimenko's SSU to investigate and apprehend them, but Parubiy prevented it. Major-General Yakimenko has categorically stated that opposition leaders were behind the shootings.

Following the release of the conversation between Paet and Ashton, the Estonian Foreign Ministry confirmed that the leak was authentic, whereas the European Commission kept silent. The mainstream media in North America and the EU either ignored it or said very little. *The Telegraph* even claimed that Dr. Bogomolets told it that she had not treated any government forces even though she contradicts this directly in an interview with CNN where she says her team had treated military/security personnel during the anti-government riots.

Utter hypocrisy is at work. When similar protests and riots broke out in Britain and France, the positions taken and the tones used by the above actors were very different. These actors framed the protests and riots in Britain and France as issues of law and order, using language very favourable to the British and French governments. Where were the statements of concern about the rights and safety of protesters from the US government and the European Commission when force was used by the British and French governments or when protesters died?

While not overlooking, disregarding, or devaluing the loss of life in Kiev, the roots of the violence there need to be discussed honestly and traced back. On the same note, it has to be understood that members of the Ukrainian opposition and their supporters were agitating for a violent confrontation against the Ukrainian government. There is no argument here against the right of citizens to protest, but rioting or taking up arms with the intent to oust a democratically-elected government is something that no government in the US or the EU would accept on their own territory.

When the laws that the US and EU countries have in place are quickly glimpsed, gross double-standards are evident. Universally, the criminal codes of these governments forbid the assembly of their citizens for the purpose of discussing the overthrow of the government. Their criminal codes consider whoever advocates, aids, advises, or preaches for the overthrowing of the government by political subversion as a criminal and threat to the state. In the US individuals that fit into the following description are considered felons under the criminal code:

> anyone with intent to cause the overthrow or destruction
> of any such government, prints, publishes, edits, issues,
> circulates, sells, distributes, or publicly displays any written

or printed matter advocating, advising, or teaching the duty, necessity, desirability, or propriety of overthrowing or destroying any government in the United States by force or violence, or attempts to do so...

If two or more persons even meet to talk about removing the government in most these countries, they can be imprisoned. In the case of the United States, as the US Criminal Code states, these individuals "shall be fined under this title or imprisoned for not more than twenty years, or both, and shall be ineligible for employment by the United States or any department or agency thereof, for the five years next following his conviction."

Washington and the EU have aided and encouraged the above acts by openly supporting the campaign of the Ukrainian opposition and even sending officials and politicians to encourage the anti-government forces in Ukraine. The irony is that this is the exact type of behavior that the US and the European Union have outlawed on their own territories and would not tolerate against themselves whatsoever.

If it were merely a case of ethnocentrisim, this attitude could be called exceptionalism. It is not exceptionalism though. To be very candid, what is happening is heartless regime change perpetrated by governments that have a record of insincerely hiding behind democracy and humanitarianism.

How the European Union Brokered Agreement Enabled the Coup

What has taken place in Kiev is a coup that has unfolded through the manipulation of the emotions and hopes of a significant segment of the Ukrainian population by opposition leaders. It has to be emphasized that many opposition supporters are doing what they believe is right for their country and that they themselves are the victims of their own corrupt leaders and nationalist zeal. It must equally be emphasized, regardless of which side they support, that the Ukrainian people are all the victims of their corrupt politicians. Both the governing party and opposition parties have taken turns ruling the country and exploiting Ukraine for their personal gains.

The opposition leadership has basically usurped power while the European Union and the United States have given them their full support. This has been done via EU and US attempts to legitimize the opposition power grab through the portrayal of the coup in Kiev as the climax of a popular revolution in Ukraine. In reality, Washington's proxies have occupied the mantle of government in Ukraine.

While the mainstream opposition is not truly united, opposition leaders refused to fulfill any of their obligations after an agreement was brokered between them and the Ukrainian government by the European Union through mediation by the troika of France, Germany, and Poland. The Ukrainian government and Russia rightly accused the European Union mediating powers of refusing to fulfill their obligations to make sure that the opposition respected the EU-brokered agreement. Instead the European Union allowed the Ukrainian opposition leaders to ignore their commitments and to grossly violate the agreement whereas the Ukrainian government fulfilled its end of the agreement in what was effectively an act of capitulation.

While one faction of the opposition was negotiating, another faction of the opposition continued the pressure from the streets, refusing to relent until the government was ousted. The agreement signed between the Ukrainian government and the mainstream opposition on February 21, 2014 had no clause or terms that granted the opposition the right or power to take over the executive, legislative, and judicial branches of Ukraine or to unilaterally create new legislation. Any information that implies that the agreement allows for this to take place is false and misleading.

Instead the EU-brokered agreement has been used as a disguise for a putsch. The armed ultra-nationalist militias took over administrative bodies in Ukraine and fought until they managed to oust the Ukrainian government. Through violence the path was opened for a takeover by Arseniy Yatsenyuk's Fatherland Party and its associates. These same militias were already taking over government offices and regional governments in the western portion of Ukraine.

Put together with the murder of anti-government protesters by the snipers in Kiev, a successful coup was expected on February 20, 2014. When it looked like there was a possibility that the coup against the government in Kiev could fail, the mainstream media in North America and the EU started reporting how the western portion of Ukraine could break away without any traces of concern that they started to show later about the referendum in Crimea. *The Guardian* reported the following about the situation on February 21, 2014: "While protests continue on the streets of central Kiev, the cities in the west of Ukraine are slipping towards autonomy with new parallel governments and security forces that have openly admitted they have deserted to the side of protesters."

The EU brokered the agreement between the Ukrainian government and mainstream opposition as a means of empowering opposition leaders. The leaked phone conversation about the protests in Ukraine between the US Department of State's Victoria Nuland and Ambassador Geoffrey Pyatt, the US ambassador in Kiev, even indicated that the US and EU were planning on creating a new government in Ukraine. The Nuland tape reveals that Washington was working to inaugurate a new opposition-led government in

Ukraine with Ukrainian figures that would readily submit and acquiesce to US and EU demands.

What Nuland and Pyatt discussed is regime change in Ukraine, based not on what the Ukrainian people want but on what the US government and its allies need from Ukraine. If the US government really believed that the Ukrainian people have the right to determine their future, Washington would not be busy working to appoint political figures in the Ukrainian government or trying to configure how the Ukrainian government would be constructed. Instead the US government would leave the creation of government in Kiev to the Ukrainian people.

Hiding the Coup with Parliamentary Camouflage

The leaders of the opposition tried to cosmetically deceive Ukrainians and the world by hijacking the legislative branch of their country's government. To legitimize their takeover, the coup leaders used the Ukrainian Parliament or Verkhovna Rada. The Rada was already heavily corrupt with notoriously crooked and dishonest politicians dominating both the pro-government and opposition sides of the aisle. After the coup it became a rubber stamp legislature.

The Rada was not at full decorum for all the voting. The opposition initially used the instability and fleeing of the government to opportunistically declare its unchallenged Rada bills as legitimate. This happened while approximately half of Ukraine's parliamentarians were either absent or in hiding due to the violence in Kiev. In other words, opposition leaders used the absence of about half the parliamentarians in the Rada to falsely give a cover of legality to their coup by taking the opportunity to pass parliamentary legislation that would be defeated if all the Rada's members were present and voting.

Albeit under the management of the opposition the Rada retained a sufficient amount of parliamentarians or deputies to hold an emergency session, there were serious ethical, procedural, technical, legal, and constitutional questions about what happened. To hold an emergency session, the Rada needs at least two hundred and twenty-six of its parliamentarians to be present. Under opposition management there were initially two hundred and thirty-nine deputies, but this did not entitle the opposition to pass any type of legislative overhaul that it pleased or to pretend that the Rada was operating under a regular constitutional session. Rada deputies were also forced to vote under intimidation and coercion. Moreover, there were important and specific procedures that still needed to be followed that the opposition parties outright ignored and violated.

Ukraine's biggest political party, the Party of Regions, and the other pro-government parties or independent parliamentarians were not present for all the Rada votes taking place either. While an increasing number of pro-government deputies began to negotiate with the opposition and a faction of the deputies from the Party of Regions returned to the Rada to protect themselves, the absence of many of the Rada's deputies and the fact that all Ukrainian parliamentarians were not inside the Rada to challenge the opposition bills makes, at the very least, the radical legislation that has been passed questionable. Examining other factors, the laws passed in the Rada appear more constitutionally dubious.

The Rada's chairman (speaker or president), Volodymyr Rybak, has not been present for the reading of Rada bills. It was reported that Rybak has resigned from his post. Not only must the individual that has been elected as Rada chairperson by a full constitutional session of the Rada be present for the voting process to be legitimate, but the Rada chairperson must also approve the acts adopted by the Rada with their signature before they are sent to the executive branch of government for promulgation. Nor can Ukrainian bills be passed into law or promulgated after the Rada votes without a final presidential signature. The only way that a presidential veto can be overturned is if two-thirds of the Rada's deputies or members support a bill after the presidential veto, in which case either the president must sign it or the Rada's chairperson must sign the bill into law.

The opposition tried to circumvent the necessary presidential approval and the absence of a Rada chairperson. Instead opposition leaders got their parties to unilaterally select a new chairman, Oleksandr Turchynov, so that they could speedily push their political agendas forward without being challenged. Turchynov's appointment as Rada chairman was meant to give the Ukrainian opposition's parliamentary work the cover of legitimacy. The Turchynov appointment enabled the opposition to claim that constitutional procedures were being followed, because a Rada chairperson was overseeing their partisan bills and approving them. Moreover, Oleksandr Turchynov was not only overseeing and approving the unilateral bills of the Ukrainian opposition, but signing them into law as the acting president of Ukraine too.

This process, however, is illegal for a number of reasons. Firstly, at least one-third of the deputies or members of the Ukrainian Parliament, must convene before a new Rada chairman or speaker is selected to oversee parliamentary voting on bills. This did not taken place, because many of the Rada's members were missing when he was selected. Secondly, Turchynov could not assume the role of Rada chairperson while there was already a chairperson as well as a first vice-chairperson (first deputy chairperson) or assume the role of acting president until President Viktor Yanukovych resigned or was impeached by the Rada, which did not take place when Turchynov was appointed as acting president.

Outlawing Opposition

Regardless of whether the 2004 version or 2010 version of the Ukrainian Constitution was in operation at the time, the Rada was categorically used illicitly. Discriminatory laws against Russian and other regional languages were presented. Discussions also began about new media regulations and expelling the Russian media from Ukraine.

Using divisions inside the bewildered Party of Regions hierarchy, the opposition sought to cover its unconstitutional tracks. A splinter group in the Party of Regions was set up too. Days after Turchynov was appointed chairman of the Rada, the opposition got a faction of the Party of Regions deputies that had returned to the Rada and a series of independent Rada deputies to renounce President Yanukovych. These independent and Party of Regions deputies in the Rada are now working with the opposition in order to keep their places or to secure positions under the new political regime in Kiev.

The coup leaders exposed just how fake their democratic leanings were when they took over the Rada; they threatened to use the Rada to outlaw any of the political parties in Ukraine that opposed them. This included banning Viktor Yanukovych's Party of Regions. The Party of Regions was not only the most widely supported Ukrainian political party at the time; it also held nearly forty percent of the seats in the Rada. No other political party even came close to holding this degree of support in the Ukrainian political landscape or the Rada at the time. Excluding the parliamentary seats of its political allies in the unicameral Rada, which houses four hundred and forty-two seats in total, the Party of Regions alone had one hundred and sixty-five seats. The opposition political parties and coalitions comprised of Yulia Tymoshenko's Fatherland Party, the Ukrainian Democratic Alliance for Reform, and Svoboda only had a combined one hundred and sixty-seven seats. There is no question about which party the majority of Ukrainian voters supported at the time. Threatening to outlaw the Party of Regions was basically a threat to annul the electoral choice of the largest plurality of Ukrainian citizens.

Yet, the corrupt Party of Regions was not the only political party targeted by the putsch. Opposition leaders called for the outlawing of the Ukrainian Communist Party. The Ukrainian Communists have described the so-called "EuroMaidan protests" as a foreign-sponsored coup against Ukraine and its people. The threats in the Rada to outlaw it are meant to punish the Ukrainian Communist Party for the position it took during the riots in Kiev. Before the coup, the offices of the Ukrainian Communist Party were also being attacked because it refused to support the anti-government forces. The threats to outlaw the Ukrainian Communist Party have also been augmented by threats to hunt and kill its members.

The Balkanization of Ukraine: Following the Path of Yugoslavia

Ukraine is following the path of the former Yugoslavia. Questions about this began to be entertained with more and more seriousness after the coup. Andrei Vorobyov, a Russian diplomat in Kiev, much to the angst of the Ukrainian government, even commented that federalization was the best solution for Ukraine and that Ukraine was already in a de facto federal state that essentially needed to be institutionalized. The angst at the federalization comments at the time stemmed from the increasing anxieties of Ukrainian authorities and citizens about the possibility that their country could divide or fragment like Yugoslavia did.

Before the opposition takeover of Kiev, Ukraine was already a polarized country and society. Most of the western portion of Ukraine has been under the influence and control of the mainstream opposition whereas the eastern and southern portions were under the influence and control of the Party of Regions and its political allies, with the accretion of a few islands of support in the western portion of the country. The opposition's actions outside of the framework of constitutional democracy have opened the door for lawlessness and the devolution of governmental power.

Different areas of Ukraine have fallen into the hands of opposition militias. The militia of Aleksandr Muzychko, one of the ultra-nationalist opposition leaders and a fervent opponent of Russia who fought alongside Chechen separatists in Grozny against the Russian military, gained control over different towns in the western portion of Ukraine. Exposing the nature of the new putsch regime in Kiev, Aleksandr Muzychko was killed by his own EuroMiadan partners under orders from Arsen Avakov, the putsch's interior minister, on March 24, 2014. Political machinations from all sides are at work too. After the opposition takeover, officials from President Yanukovych's own Party of Regions laid responsibility for the deaths in Kiev squarely on his shoulder and condemned him as a coward and traitor to Ukraine, virtually ignoring the role that opposition leaders played in igniting the political crisis and the loss of life. Fearing the violent segments of the opposition, Party of Regions members additionally condemned the mainstream opposition's intimidation campaign and threats of violence against the Party of Regions and its supporters.

Rada deputies or parliamentarians from the Party of Regions seeking refuge in the eastern and southern portions of Ukraine started to revolt. There were reports that one or more parallel parliaments were being established somewhere in eastern or southern Ukraine. This would effectively divide the country like Bosnia was divided when the Bosnian Serbs created their own parallel parliament after the Bosnian Parliament in Sarajevo ignored Bosnia's communitarian formula that essentially guaranteed a veto to Bosnia's Bosniak, Croat, and Serb communities as a means of maintaining co-existence.

The silent or unheard of half of Ukraine, which the mainstream media in the US and the EU refuse to acknowledge, began preparing for an expansion of the violence. Ukrainians in the east and south feared the spread of violence being perpetrated by the militant segment of the opposition as they saw the violence reach Kharkov. This led to calls for secession from the predominately-Russophone Crimean Peninsula. The majority of Crimeans began to demand the annulment of the Soviet era decision of Nikita Khrushchev to detach the Crimean Peninsula from Soviet Russia as an award to Soviet Ukraine that symbolized the unity and kinship between Russia and Ukraine.

As calls for session in Crimean increased, there were suggestions made that Russia would intervene militarily in the Crimean Peninsula. The mainstream media in North America and the EU made it sound like the Russians were going to invade. The concern about Russian intervention was addressed with an indirect and ironically hypocritical warning from Susan Rice to the Kremlin not to sent troops into Ukraine. It was clear, however, that Russian military movements would take place through an invitation by Crimean officials and the Autonomous Rada (Duma or Parliament) of the Crimea. Moreover, the pre-coup Ukrainian government had sent the Kremlin a letter asking for Russian intervention that Vitaly Churkin, the Russian ambassador to the United Nations, presented to the UN Security Council.

The Autonomous Rada in Crimea has a history of independence that Kiev has worked to slowly erode. A movement to reunify Crimea with Russia has also always existed in Crimea with significant support from the much of its population. Crimean officials have clashed with the government in Kiev on many occasions too. The Autonomous Rada in Crimea even created anti-NATO legislation in 2006 banning North Atlantic Treaty Organization (NATO) forces from entering Crimean territory while its officials called Viktor Yushchenko, the pro-NATO president of Ukraine, a puppet of the US and the EU.

The Autonomous Republic of the Crimea, which is the historical home of Ukraine's Muslim minority, was not the only place in Ukraine that threatened to take action as a result of the coup in Kiev. As a precautionary reaction to the violent and armed segments of the Ukrainian opposition that destabilized Kiev, counter-militias were formed in places like the oblasts of Kharkov and Donetsk in the eastern and southern portions of Ukraine. Officials and Ukrainians from these eastern and southern parts of Ukraine have also said that they no longer recognize the Rada in Kiev as legitimate and that the legislation being passed by it is illegal and void. After the reunification of Crimea with Russia, these regions started demanding for increased autonomy under a federalization formula or union with the Russian Federation.

Not long after the ultra-nationalist Muzychko was eliminated, because he was a liability for the new regime in Kiev and its foreign backers in Washington and Brussels. Yatsenyuk ordered the Ukrainian military and security forces to move southwards and eastwards in armed operations against anti-EuroMaidan Ukrainian protesters that had been demanding that the putsch government step down and that either federalization be adopted or a referendum about the future of Novorossiya and their portions of Ukraine take place. Ironically, Yatsenyuk's government called the anti-EuroMaidan protesters terrorists for refusing to recognize his regime's appointees in their region and for taking over government offices. Yatsenyuk's government even presented the use of armed force against them as an "anti-terrorist operations." Meanwhile the US and EU supportively watched and blamed Russia for the anti-EuroMaidan protests.

Ukraine's polarized politics also overlap with the contours of organized religion. While the majority of Ukrainians are Christians who belong to the Russian Orthodox Church of Ukraine (simply called the Ukrainian Orthodox Church), there is also a division among them that is linked to nationalist politics. About half the followers of the Ukrainian Orthodox Church look to Patriarch Kirill in Moscow as their patriarch and as the supreme primate of the Ukrainian Orthodox Church, but another portion belongs to the breakaway Ukrainian Orthodox Church that follows Patriarch Filaret in Kiev. At least in nominal terms, ultra-nationalists and opposition supporters mostly follow the Kiev Patriarchate and those supporting the Party of Regions generally look to Moscow as their spiritual centre. These divisions also have the potential of being manipulated in a Yugoslavia-style scenario.

The picture gets more complicated when the minority faiths in Ukraine are examined. Ukrainian Catholic populations, both the Unites of the Greek Catholic Church and the Roman Catholics, generally seem to favor the opposition and integration with the EU. There has actually been growing resentment towards the Ukrainian Catholics, who are viewed as Polish agents, by some of the members of the Ukrainian Orthodox Church.

Despite the well-known and advertised dislike of Jews by a segment of opposition supporters (similar negative views about Jews, which have historically existed in Ukraine, also exist among some government supporters), Ukrainian Jews are divided between the pro-government and anti-government camps. According to the *Jerusalem Post* and the *Jewish Telegraphic Agency*, Ukrainian Jews have taken part in the anti-government protests alongside Ukrainian ultra-nationalists. Israel's government, which falsely hides behind the image of defending Jewish interests, has been silent on the issue.

Ukrainian Muslims, three-fifths of whom are Crimean Tartars, are silent. They seem to be divided between both camps. Like Ukrainian Jews, Ukrainian Muslims are cautious and fear clashes with either side. Most of the Crimean Tartars do not support the dissolution of Ukraine or separatist feelings that exist among the Russian community and the Mejlis of the Crimean Tartars called for a boycott of the March 16, 2014 referendum in Crimea.

The Blurred Lines that Exist between Ukrainians and Russians

Ukrainian politics are even more complicated by the fact that the Russian language is prevalent in the eastern and southern sections of Ukraine. There is an ongoing dispute about the exact numbers. Due to the closeness of both the Russian and Ukrainian languages, in some parts of Ukraine it is hard to identify if the local population is actually speaking a dialect of the Ukrainian language or of the Russian language. Even more confounding, the lines between Ukrainian and Russian identity are not clear cut.

Aside from the blurred language lines and the fact that both Ukrainian and Russian were once one language, there is a blurred line on who is ethnically Ukrainian and who is ethnically Russian. Approximately thirty percent of Ukrainians consider Russian as either their first or mother language and are Russophones according to the Ukrainian government, but only about half of these Russophone Ukrainian citizens are actually ethnically Russkiye (ethnic Russian). Sociological work conducted in 2004 asserts that the number of Russophones is actually much higher and that Russian and Ukrainian are actually used almost equally.

There is even a minority of ethnic Russians who speak Ukrainian as their first language and a much larger minority of ethnic Ukrainians that speak Russian as their first language. Most Ukrainian citizens are also bilingual and there is a preference for using Russian as a daily language and business language in many parts of Ukraine. As part of a historical and sociological process, ethnic Ukrainians have adopted the identity of ethnic Russians and vice-versa, ethnic Russians have adopted identities as ethnic Ukrainians. When asked, many Ukrainian citizens are not even sure if they are Russkiye or ethnic Ukrainian. Many of the Russophone ethnic Ukrainians in Crimea even voted for reunification with Russia alongside the ethnic Russians in Crimea.

If anything is to be remembered about the causes of the First World War and the Second World War, it should be that nationalism and feelings of exceptionalism were used like opiates to captivate and manipulate ordinary citizens into supporting war and the rise of opportunists. The Ukrainian opposition leadership has deliberately promoted and nurtured ultra-nationalist sentiments to blind and manipulate its followers. Ukrainian nationalism, specifically the Western-leaning pro-European Union type, has been formulated on the unhealthy basis of anti-Russian sentiments and a distorted notion of the cultural superiority of the European Union and the cultural inferiority of the Eastern Slavs (particularly Russians, but including Ukrainians and Belarusians).

It is the multiple convergences between Ukrainians and Russians and the complex relationship between the Ukrainian and Russian identities that make the decidedly anti-Russian attitudes of the mainstream opposition, some of whom openly glorify Adolph Hitler and the Third Reich and its invasion of the Soviet Union, so dangerous for solidarity in Ukrainian society and Kiev's future relations with Russia and the other countries bordering Ukraine.

Revolution for Democracy or Riots Promoting Subversion by the EU and US?

The crisis in Ukraine did not take place because the Ukrainian government was corrupt or used force against the protesters in Kiev's Independence Square. It started because the Ukrainian government refused to sign the European Union's EU-Ukraine Association Agreement in November 2013. This is why the violence in Kiev has not only unreservedly been given political cover by the political establishment in the United States and the European Union to give it public legitimacy internationally, but has also received media support in the form of biased reporting that favors the opposition.

Social media has been saturated by advertisements and questionable grassroots videos and footage, like the professionally-make "I Am a Ukrainian" YouTube video produced by Larry Summers of the Council for Foreign Relations, that paints a distorted narrative of the reasons behind the anti-government riots. Like the other propaganda ignoring the reasons behind the anti-government protests, the "I Am a Ukrainian" video totally ignores the fact that the protests in Kiev did not start on the basis of democratic demands, but started due to the Ukrainian government's refusal to sign an agreement with the European Union.

The Ukrainian government and the Party of Regions were initially very supportive of the association agreement with the European Union, but backed out after the EU refused to renegotiate the agreement or to give financial guarantees and economic relief to Kiev for the trade losses and higher gas prices that Ukraine would face as a result of signing the agreement. Moreover, the Ukrainian oligarchs aligned to President Yanukovich and his Party of Regions realized that the agreement would allow corporations from the EU to dismantle their own corporations and to replace their monopolies with EU corporate monopolies and control. The EU agreement would force Ukraine to change many of its trade laws and regulations that would disadvantage the Ukrainian oligarch's corporations and, in economic terms, allow for Ukraine to be gutted and essentially reduced to an Eastern European colony.

The Ukrainian government did not decide not to sign the EU agreement because it is pro-Russian. Albeit the Party of Regions politically caters to Ukrainians who view Russia favorably, anyone who says or thinks that the leadership in the Party of Regions is pro-Russian or that the Party of Regions is a pro-Russian political party is grossly misinformed or lying. For many years the leadership of the Party of Regions has even openly said that they are not hostile to NATO. Viktor Yanukovych, in the role of prime minister, even implemented the NATO integration policies that President Leonid Kuchma was pursuing. The Ukrainian government did not sign the European Union's EU-Ukraine Association Agreement because of its own interests and not on the basis of favorable sentiments towards Russia.

If the deal only targeted the Ukrainian economy without challenging the monopolies and privileges of the Ukrainian oligarchs, President Yanukovych and the Ukrainian government would have signed it without any hesitation. The EU deal, however, was simply unfeasible and suicidal for both the Ukrainian oligarchs and the economy. The agreement with the EU additionally would force Ukraine to cut its trade ties with its major economic partners, Russia and the other members of the Commonwealth of Independent States (CIS), without providing any alternative. It would have politically hurt the Party of Regions in the future too.

The Euro-Atlantic Drive into Eurasia: Targeting Moscow and Beyond...

The US and EU support for the Ukrainian opposition, even if in part, is aimed at bringing Ukraine into their orbit and to encircle, isolate, and eventual subvert the Russian Federation. Resurgent Orangists and a new coalition of opposition figures have formed a new front, which can be called a neo-Orangist front, which is intensely bent on shifting Ukraine into the

Euro-Atlantic orbit of Washington and the European Commission through eventual membership in such institutions and supranational structures as NATO and the European Union.

These opposition politicians made a mess of things after the earlier Orange Revolution when they ran Ukraine. It remains to be seen if they can re-orient Ukraine into the Euro-Atlantic zone (the word "Euro-Atlantic" camouflages the role that the US plays in Europe; more properly it should be called the Euro-American zone). When mainstream opposition leaders were ruling Ukraine, they were too busy embezzling and fighting one another to further the goals of the US and the EU. Yulia "Gas Princess" Tymoshenko, when she was in the position of prime minister, and the Orangist President Viktor Yushchenko were even busy accusing one another of corruption and betrayal. It is also worth noting that many of the EuroMaidan protesters booed her when she was freed from jail and arrived in Kiev. Some time later the "Gas Princess" would also be embarrassed by being exposed for angrily calling for the murder of all the ethnic Russian population in Ukraine, even saying that nuclear weapons should be used against them.

There is a simultaneous campaign to erase Ukraine's history and its deep and historic ties to Russia from the Soviet and pre-Soviet eras. Not only has the Russian Federation been demonized and the Russian language discriminated against in Ukraine by the mainstream opposition and the ultra-nationalist elements inside its ranks, but Ukrainian citizens with ethnic Russian background or favorable views towards Russia and Eurasian integration have also been portrayed as traitors, foreigners, or the enemies of Ukraine. Any reminders of a common history with Russia have been attacked, including monuments to the fallen soldiers that defended Ukraine and the Soviet Union from the Germans during the Second World War or, as it is called in Ukraine and Russia, the Great Patriot War.

Concerning Syria and Iran, it has been repeatedly stated that the road to Tehran goes through Damascus and that the US and its allies have targeted Syria as a means of going after Iran. In regards to Ukraine and Russia, a very similar axiom is also applicable. The road to Moscow goes through Kiev. The takeover of Ukraine is part and parcel of a geo-strategic campaign against the Russians, as is the regime change campaign against Damascus to a lesser degree.

Poland is already being watched with distrust from Belarus and Russia. The Polish government, in its interaction with Ukraine, has acted just like the Turkish government has acted towards Syria. With the backing of the governments of the US, Britain, Germany, and France, Warsaw has supported Ukrainian anti-government forces in multiple ways, just as Ankara has supported anti-government forces and regime change operations inside Syria in multiple ways.

Regime change in Ukraine is part of a covert and overt war against the Russian Federation. There has been a longstanding view that without Ukraine Russia cannot be an empire or great power. US strategist Zbigniew Brzezinski posits it thus: "Without Ukraine, Russia ceases to be a Eurasian empire." The installment of a puppet government in Ukraine will remove one of the most important partners that Moscow has. If Ukraine joins the EU and NATO, it will be a direct threat to the western borders of Russia and to the security of its ally Belarus.

Russia is not to be unaccompanied. The Russian Federation is not the only country concerned about what has happened in Ukraine. The EU and the US aim to prevent the entry of Ukraine into the Eurasian Union being formed being formed by Russia, Kazakhstan, and Belarus. The estrangement of Ukraine from Russia additionally aims to isolate Russia from Europe and to reduce the Eurasian Union into a predominately Asiatic project instead of a dually European and Asian project. Both the Belarusian and Kazakhstani government are worried too. Countries like Armenia, Kyrgyzstan, Tajikistan, Iran, and China are watching the events in Kiev with concern as well. Ukraine has been a partner to these countries and they all view the conflict in Syria and the anti-government riots in Ukraine and Venezuela as part of a multi-front global war that the US is waging against them and their allies.

The views of the Iranians are not much different from that of the Russians. Tehran considers Ukraine to be a part of the wider Eurasian region that includes the Iranians. Iran is also geographically much closer to Ukraine than countries like Britain and France. Iranian officials have voiced their concerns that what has been set in motion in Kiev will result in the eventual disintegration of Ukraine with far-reaching consequences that will destabilize the flanking Caucasus region, which shares the Black Sea with Ukraine, and will eventually reach Iran. The head of the Iranian military has even commented on the coup as a "move from independence to dependence."

Just to give an idea of the importance of the value that these Russian allies put on Ukraine, it should be noted that the Chinese signed a December 5, 2013 bilateral agreement announcing that Ukraine was Beijing's strategic partner. Included in the agreement was a Chinese pledge to provide Kiev with the military protection of a Chinese nuclear umbrella. The governments of Ukraine, China, and Russia had also discussed admitting Ukraine into the Shanghai Cooperation Agreement (SCO).

Even if it is denied that the opposition originally planned a coup, only when democratic means are exhausted can such a use of force be legitimate. While there is no question that Viktor Yanukovych and his ousted government were totally corrupt, the leaders of the US-supported coup-imposed regime are no better and equally as corrupt. These opposition leaders have hijacked the protests to serve their own agendas and made Ukraine a less democratic and secure place. They took power by mobilizing all their supporters to pour into Kiev and push for a violent escalation as the pro-government half of the country remained mostly immobilized. At the same time the EU and the US gave them full support because Brussels and Washington were afraid that Ukraine would join the Eurasian Union and strengthen its ties to the Russian Federation.

Furthermore, Washington and NATO have used the crisis in Ukraine as an opportunity to try to resurrect the image of Russia as a bogyman threatening European security and peace. NATO has capitalized on the situation to try to justify its existence and to give itself the meaning that it lost when the Cold War ended and the Soviet Union dissolved. Moreover, the EU agreement with Ukraine even included military dimensions in its fine print that aimed to integrate Kiev into NATO and to prevent Ukraine from remaining militarily neutral or from eventually joining the Moscow-led Collective Security Treaty Organization (CSTO).

During the start of the crisis in Ukraine, the US government and EU officials were explaining that the Ukrainians who had occupied government buildings were democrats, even as they waged a campaign of violence and destruction in the streets of Kiev. The tune of the US government and the EU has changed months later, when anti-EuroMaidan protesters began to protest, occupy government buildings, and react by arming themselves. The anti-EuroMaidan protesters in southern and eastern Ukraine began to be described as anti-democratic, militants, Russian agents, and terrorists instead. The US and EU said nothing as the politicians of this segment of the Ukrainian population were beaten and in the case of Oleg Tsarev, a presidential candidate, nearly killed by supporters of the new regime in Kiev. The use of force by Ukrainian authorities against EuroMaidan protesters was not acceptable then according to the US and EU, but now the use of force is acceptable against the anti-EuroMaidan protesters. The hypocrisy and deceit should be evident from the double standards.

RUSSIA EXTENDS ITS CONTROL OVER THE BLACK SEA AND STRATEGIC WATERWAYS

MICHEL CHOSSUDOVSKY

The decision of Crimea to join the Russian Federation has strategic and geopolitical implications.

The union of Crimea with Russia redefines both the geography as well as the geopolitical chessboard in the Black Sea basin. It constitutes a major setback for US-NATO, whose longstanding objective has been to integrate Ukraine into NATO with a view to undermining Russia, while extending Western military presence in the Black Sea basin.

With the March 18, 2014 Treaty signed between Russia and Crimea, the Russian Federation will extend its control over the Black Sea as well as over the Sea of Azov, the west coastline of which borders on Eastern Ukraine and the Donesk region. Under the agreement between Russia and Crimea announced by President Putin, two "constituent regions" of Crimea will join the Russian Federation: the "Republic of Crimea" and the "City of Sevastopol."

Both will have the status of "autonomous regions." The status of Sevastopol as an autonomous entity separate from Crimea is related to the location of Russia's naval base in Sevastopol.

Since the break-up of the Soviet Union, Russia retained its naval base in Sevastopol under a bilateral agreement with Ukraine. With the signing of the March 18th Treaty, that agreement is null and void. Sevastopol including the Russian naval base becomes part of an autonomous region within the Russian Federation.

The naval base is not within Ukraine under a lease agreement. Moreover, Crimea's territorial waters now belong to the Russian Federation.

Strategic Waterway: The Kerch Strait

Russia now formally controls a much larger portion of the Black Sea, which includes the entire coastline of the Crimean peninsula. The Eastern part of Crimea—including the Kerch Strait—is now under Russia's jurisdiction and control. On the Eastern side of the Kerch Strait is Russia's Krasnodar region and extending southwards are the port cities of Novorossiysk and Sochi. Novorossiysk is also strategic. It is Russia's largest commercial port on the Black Sea, at the cross-roads of major oil and gas pipelines between the Black Sea and Caspian Sea. Historically, the Kerch Strait has played a strategic role. It constitutes a gateway from the Black Sea to Russia's major waterways including the Don and the Volga.

During World War II, the Kerch peninsula occupied by Nazi Germany (taken back by the Red Army) was an important point of transit by land and water. In the coldest months of winter, it became an ice bridge linking Crimea to the Krasnodar region. The Kerch Strait is about 5 kilometers in length and 4.5 km. wide at the narrowest point between the tip of Eastern Crimea and the peninsula of Taman. Kerch is a major commercial port linked to railway, ferry and river routes.

The Sea of Azov: New Geopolitical Hub

Of significance, the integration of Crimea into the Russian Federation means that Moscow is now in full control of the Kerch Strait linking the Black Sea to the Sea of Azov. The Ukrainian authorities are no longer in control of the port of Kerch. The bilateral agreement between Russia and Ukraine governing the maritime route through the Kerch Strait has been scrapped.

The Strait constitutes an entry point into Russia's major river waterways. The Sea of Azov connects with the Don River and the Volga, through the Volga Don Canal. In turn, the Volga flows into the Caspian Sea. The Kerch Strait is strategic. The Kerch-Yenikalskiy Canal allows large (ocean) vessels to transit from the Black Sea to the Sea of Azov.

Moreover, the Kerch Strait links the Black Sea to the Volga which in turn connects to the Moscow river through the Volga-Moskva canal.

Full control of the narrow Kerch Strait by Russia ensures unimpeded maritime transit from the Black Sea to Russia's capital as well as the maritime route to the Caspian Sea.

In December 2013, Moscow signed a bilateral agreement with the Yanukovych government in Kiev pertaining to the construction of a bridge across the Kerch Strait, connecting Eastern Crimea (which was part of Ukraine) with Russia's Krasnodar region. This agreement was a follow-up to an initial agreement signed in April 2010 between the two governments.

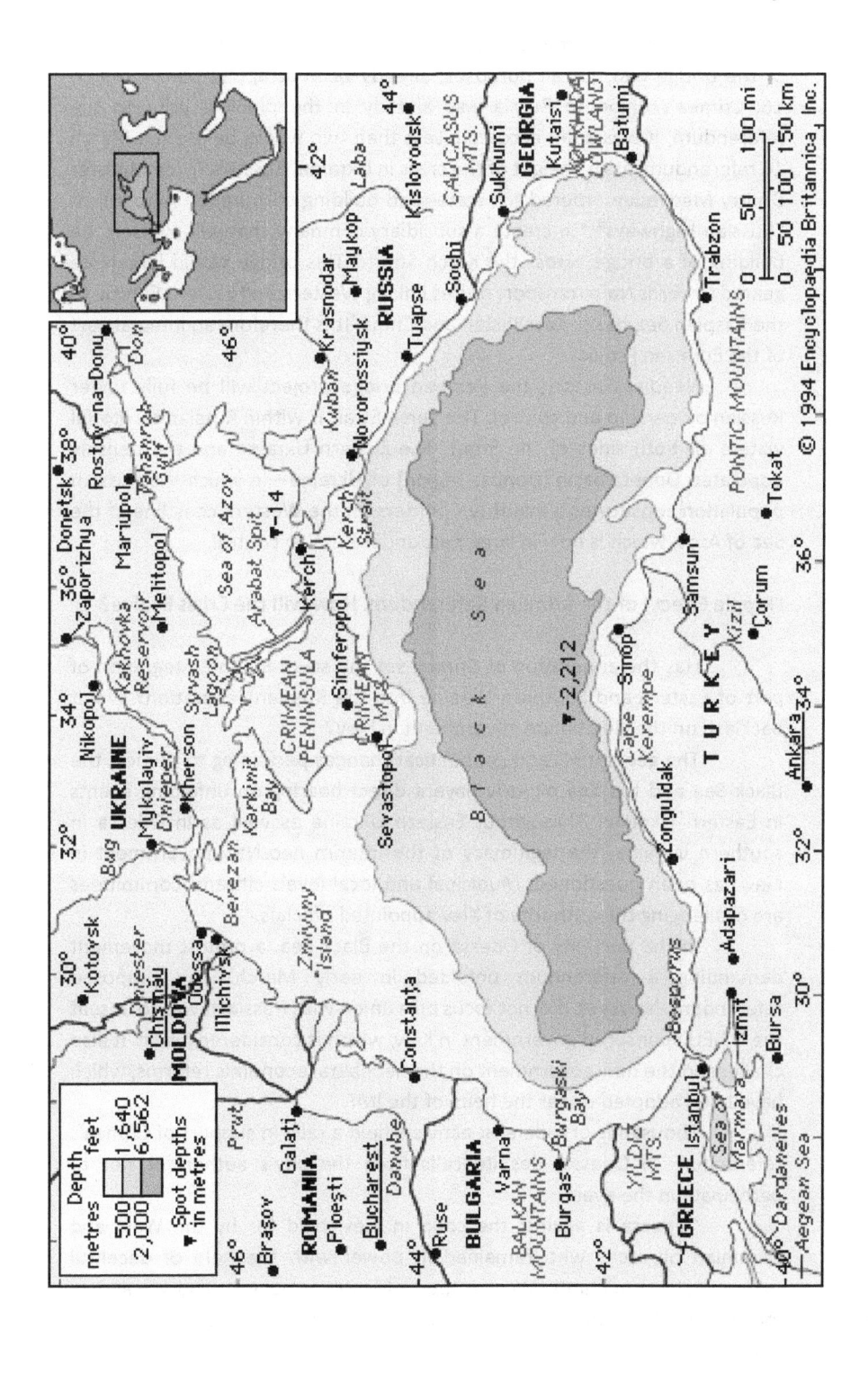

Russia Extends Its Control Over the Black Sea / Michel Chossudovsky

111

The Russia-Ukraine 2013 agreement pertaining to the construction of the bridge had, for all purposes, already been scrapped before March 16. Crimea's union to Russia was already in the pipeline prior to the referendum, it was a fait accompli. Less than two weeks before the March 16 referendum, at the height of the crisis in Ukraine, Russia's Prime Minister Dmitry Medvedev ordered the state-road building corporation Avtodor, or "Russian Highways" "to create a subsidiary company that will oversee the building of a bridge across the Kerch Strait." This bridge would largely be geared towards train transport routes linking Western and Eastern Europe to the Caspian Sea basin, Kazakhstan and China. It is therefore an integral part of the Eurasian Project.

Needless to say, the Kerchen bridge project will be fully under Russian ownership and control. The Kerch Strait is within Russian territorial waters on both sides of the Strait. The Eastern Ukraine and the densely populated Donetz basin (Donbas region) of Ukraine—in which the Russian population constitutes a majority - borders on the Western coastline of the Sea of Azov, which is now in large part under Russian control.

"Ripple Effect" of the Crimean Referendum. How will the Crisis Evolve?

Has the annexation of Crimea set the stage for the integration of part of Eastern and Southern Ukraine into the Russian Federation? Will it backlash on the illegitimate government in Kiev?

The geographic and geopolitical changes pertaining to Crimea, the Black Sea and the Sea of Azov have a direct bearing on unfolding events in Eastern Ukraine. Throughout Eastern Ukraine as well as in Odessa in southern Ukraine, the legitimacy of the interim neo-Nazi government in Kiev has been questioned. Municipal and local levels citizens' committees are challenging the authority of Kiev appointed officials.

In the port city of Odessa on the Black Sea, a protest movement demanding a referendum unfolded in early March. The proposed referendum, however, did not focus on a union with Russia. It was to unseat the US-EU sponsored government in Kiev, which is considered illegal. It also challenged the new government on the neoliberal economic reforms, which have been adopted under the helm of the IMF.

Thousands of federalist activists held a rally in support of Crimea's referendum in Odessa, despite calls from the city's authorities not to participate in the event.

"Odessa is against the coup in Kiev, paid for by the West and Ukrainian oligarchs who remained in power with the help of deceitful extremists and militants. We are tired of living in poverty and we are no longer going to tolerate the tyranny of oligarchs and officials..."

The people were chanting "Ukraine and Russia—one country," and "Odessa, be bold, drive the fascists out," as they gathered in the center of the city. In early May in Odessa, Right Sector thugs set fire to the city's Trade Union building leading to countless deaths of innocent civilians who were burnt alive within the building which had been set ablaze. The US-NATO sponsored Kiev coalition government is responsible for the killings perpetrated by Neo-Nazi Right Sector mobs and security forces in Odessa in which at least 43 people were killed.

"Such actions are reminiscent of the crimes of the Nazis," said Russia's Ambassador to the UN Vitaly Churkin.

Protests have developed in Kharkov and Donetsk demanding the holding of a referendum on the federalization of Ukraine. Protesters, on behalf of Kharkov's assembly, asked Putin to "guarantee their rights and freedoms" and pass to the United Nations their demands regarding a referendum on federalization. Additionally, activists asked to deploy Russian peacekeepers to Kharkov region, adding that they fear for their lives and property.

The demonstrators then marched to the nearby consulate of Poland, protesting against Western interference into Ukrainian affairs.

Kharkov protesters also looted the building housing offices of radical-nationalist organizations, including the Right Sector group, reported Interfax-Ukraine. The activists broke into the building, took out books and nationalist symbols and burnt them.

Pro-Russian activists held giant Russian flags during their rally in the eastern Ukrainian city of Donetsk on March 16, 2014. In Donetsk, pro-Russian protesters questioned the legitimacy of the interim coalition government.

Meanwhile, Kiev sent heavy military hardware to the borders with Russia. Activists in eastern Ukraine regions, including Donetsk and Lugansk, were reportedly blocking trains delivering military equipment from the central and western parts of Ukraine.

Similar rallies were held in Dnepropetrovsk and Lugansk. In Lugansk, the campaign focused on a 'people's referendum' directed against the Kiev interim government. In Lugansk, several thousand anti-coup activists were conducting a public poll by handing out "ballot papers" of "people's referendum" of Lugansk region. The poll raised questions of trust in the authorities in Kiev, the possibility of joining the Customs Union following the federalization of Ukraine.

One of the questions was about the international bailout: "Do you support reduction of social benefits and cancellation of benefits at the request of the IMF?"

"This is for all an opportunity to officially announce their choice. Now we have run out of 5,000 forms, we are rushing to print more," organizer Irina Gotman told UNIAN.

THE GEOSTRATEGIC SIGNIFICANCE OF UKRAINE IN NATO'S DRIVE TO THE EAST

RICK ROZOFF

With almost 1,500 miles of land and sea connecting the two nations, the border with Ukraine is the longest along the western frontier of Russia, with that of Finland next in length.

Until the end of the Cold War only one member of the North Atlantic Treaty Organization directly adjoined Russia: Norway, and that for only 135 miles, land and sea (though Turkey bordered other Soviet republics.)

The decade of NATO expansion beginning in 1999 brought four new members of the U.S.-dominated military bloc directly up to Russia territory: Estonia and Latvia to northwestern Russia proper and Poland and Lithuania to the non-contiguous Kaliningrad Oblast.

The acquisition of Ukraine as a full NATO member or even as it now is, a partner lending its territory, troops and general military assets to the alliance, would, with the likely prospect of Finland being enlisted in tow, cover the entire western flank of Russia from the Arctic Ocean and Barents Sea in the north to the Black Sea in the south with NATO air bases, naval docking facilities, firing ranges and training grounds, airfields, radar installations, storage compounds, cyber warfare centers, interceptor missile batteries, armored vehicles, troops and tactical nuclear weapons.

Ukraine is and for decades has been seen as the decisive linchpin in plans by the U.S. and its NATO allies to effect a military cordon sanitaire severing Russia from Europe.

In 1995, just four years after the dissolution of the Union of Soviet Socialist Republics, Ukraine became the first member of the post-Soviet Commonwealth of Independent States to join NATO's mechanism for the eventual absorption of all of Europe and the rest of f   er Soviet space not already in the bloc, the Partnership for Peace.

The twelve Eastern European nations t   NATO in 1999, 2004 and 2009 are all graduates of that program. (V   e wings are 22 more members of the transitional program for milita.   n and full NATO membership; all fourteen European countries not .   nbers, except for Russia, the three former Soviet republics in the   sus and the five in Central Asia.)

Two years later the military alliance established the a Distinctive Partnership, out of which was created the NATO Commission, which is active to this day; in fact more so than ever since the violent coup d'état in Ukraine in February of this year.

In December of 2008, four months after the Georgian government of Mikheil Saakashvili invaded South Ossetia and thereby triggered a five-day war with Russia, Ukraine and Georgia were both made the recipients of the first-ever Annual National Programs crafted by NATO. Earlier in the year, at the alliance summit in Bucharest, Romania, it was announced that, although the last stage before full NATO accession—the Membership Action Plan—would not immediately be granted to the two former Soviet republics, NATO was nevertheless committed to their eventual membership.

One of the Ukrainian public officials pushing for a Membership Action Plan was then-chairman of the nation's parliament, Arseniy Yatsenyuk, now the U.S.-selected (indeed, the U.S.-imposed) prime minister and effective head of the ruling junta.

In fact, the parliamentary opposition blocked the functioning of the Verkhovna Rada from January to March of 2008—ahead of the NATO summit in early April of that year—in protest against the nation being dragged into the bloc.

The main effort domestically to expedite the incorporation of Ukraine into NATO emanated from the duarchy emerging from the 2004-2005 "Orange Revolution," President Viktor Yushchenko and Prime Minister Yulia Tymoshenko.

Indeed, Washington and its European allies supported and directed the second so-called color revolution (after that in Georgia the preceding year) with just that intended effect in mind.

Ahead of the Bucharest summit President George W. Bush, fellow Republican and at the time candidate for his party's presidential nomination (which he later secured) John McCain, and Democratic rivals for their party's nomination, Barack Obama and Hillary Clinton, all fulsomely endorsed full NATO membership for Ukraine and Georgia.

A year ahead of the "Orange Revolution," Yushchenko's predecessor, Leonid Kuchma, had attempted to appease the U.S. and NATO by providing 1,650 troops for the NATO-supported Multi-National Force—Iraq.

A nominal contingent of Ukrainian troops has also been assigned to NATO's International Security Assistance Force in Afghanistan, part of an over 50-nation integrated command. But as not only Kuchma has learned, total subservience, abject submission alone are accepted by NATO "partners" in Washington and Brussels.

Georgia would later supply 2,000 (the third largest deployment after those of the U.S. and Britain at the time), which were airlifted home by American aircraft during the August 2008 war with Russia.

The "orange" regime of Viktor Yushchenko was accused of surreptitiously shipping weapons and allowing if not organizing the deployment of military and extremist nationalist paramilitary forces to Georgia during the fighting.

Immediately after the South Caucasus war ended, Yushchenko flew into the Georgian capital to join a rally with (and for) President Saakashvili and immediately upon returning to Kiev signed a decree demanding Russia notify his government of—in essence seek its authorization for—naval and air deployments from the Black Sea Fleet base in Sebastopol. He reserved the right to prevent Russian vessels from departing and returning to the complex; that is, to impose a de facto selective blockade.

Starting no later than 2006, at first covertly and then quite flagrantly, directors and other officials of the Pentagon's Missile Defense Agency visited Ukraine to discuss the stationing of interceptor missile components in the country, part of an initiative that has subsequently been embraced by all 28 members of NATO under the Barack Obama administration's European Phased Adaptive Approach land- and sea-based missile shield being deployed along Russia's western (and later southern) border.

Annual U.S.-led NATO Partnership for Peace military exercises code-named Sea Breeze have been held in Ukraine every year since 1996—in the Crimea, near the headquarters of Russia's Black Sea Fleet—except in 2006 when they were cancelled because of local protests.

Led by U.S. European Command, yearly Rapid Trident military exercises are also held in Ukraine with U.S., NATO and Partnership for Peace forces. In the words of U.S. Army Europe's account of last year's iteration, Rapid Trident "helps prepare participants to operate successfully in a joint, multinational, integrated environment with host-nation support ... designed to enhance joint combined interoperability with allied and partner nations" as well as "support[ing] Ukraine's Annual National Program to achieve interoperability with NATO and commitments made in the annual NATO-Ukraine work plan."

In the same month as NATO initiated its Annual National Program with Ukraine, December of 2008, Washington launched the United States-Ukraine Charter on Strategic Partnership, the founding document of which asserts and identifies among other objectives:

> Deepening Ukraine's integration into Euro-Atlantic institutions is a mutual priority. We plan to undertake a program of enhanced security cooperation intended to increase Ukrainian capabilities and to strengthen Ukraine's candidacy for NATO membership.
>
> Guided by the April 3, 2008 Bucharest Summit Declaration of the NATO North Atlantic Council and the April 4, 2008 Joint Statement of the NATO-Ukraine Commission, which affirmed that Ukraine will become a member of NATO.
>
> Recognizing the persistence of threats to global peace and stability, the United States and Ukraine intend to expand the scope of their ongoing programs of cooperation and assistance on defense and security issues to defeat these threats and to promote peace and stability. A defense and security cooperation partnership between the United States and Ukraine is of benefit to both nations and the region.
>
> Working within the framework of the NATO-Ukraine Commission, our goal is to gain agreement on a structured plan to increase interoperability and coordination of capabilities between NATO and Ukraine, including via enhanced training and equipment for Ukrainian armed forces.

In 2010 Ukraine became the first NATO partner state to provide a warship for the alliance's Operation Active Endeavor, a permanent naval surveillance and interdiction campaign throughout the entire Mediterranean Sea inaugurated in 2001 with the activation of NATO's Article 5 mutual military assistance provision.

In 2013 Ukraine complemented the above contribution by becoming the first NATO partner to assign a warship to the bloc's Operation Ocean Shield, a now five-year-old (and also intended to be indefinite) maritime mission off the Horn of Africa in the Arabian Sea and further into the Indian Ocean.

Before the onset of civil unrest in the country last November, NATO was already touting Ukraine as one of four partners to join the global NATO Response Force. (The other three being Georgia, Finland and Sweden.)

Flashpoint in Ukraine: How the US Drive for Hegemony Risks World War III

Now with a U.S.-NATO proxy regime in place in Kiev, the prospects for Ukraine being turned into a veritable gargantuan forward base for the Pentagon's and NATO's inexorable, now generation-long, drive to the east, overrun with Western military advisers and intelligence agents and hosting warplanes, warships, armor, troops and missiles, are being entertained by Western leaders with a degree of ambition and recklessness surpassing anything hitherto contemplated.

WHO BENEFITS FROM THE UKRAINE ECONOMIC CRISIS?

JACK RASMUS

Sunday March 16, 2014, 83% of the Crimea's eligible voters voted by 97% to secede from Ukraine and join Russia. Simultaneously, negotiations between the European Union and IMF with the interim government in the Ukraine, brought to power by a coup d'état on February 22, continue toward a conclusion set tentatively for a March 27 release of the IMF's final terms.

Extreme political uncertainty thus promises to continue for weeks and perhaps months given these events, while economic conditions consequently continue to deteriorate in the Ukraine from an already extremely precarious state.

Most accounts of the situation in the Ukraine and Crimea have focused to date on political events and conditions. Little has been said in the press about the economic consequences of the coup and subsequent events, or likely scenarios for the future.

What interests—in the Ukraine and global (i.e. western Europe, USA, Russia)—stand to benefit economically from recent and future events in the Ukraine? Who stands to lose?

There's a well-worn saying, if you want to find out who benefits, then follow the money trail. That trail will also lead to the inverse, who pays.

1. The IMF Deal of March 2014: Who Benefits, Who Pays

While the final version of the latest IMF package for the Ukraine is still in development, past relations and deals between the IMF and Ukraine indicate some likely characteristics of this latest IMF Ukraine deal due to come.

A tentative agreement was reached on February 21 between the IMF and the pre-coup government of President Yanukovich. While that tentative deal was agreed to on the 21st, it was upset within 12 hours by the violent street actions of proto-fascist forces and the sniper killings of more than 100 protestors and police forces in Kiev.

Former agreements between the IMF and Ukraine since the 'Orange Revolution' of 2004 resulted in IMF loans to the Ukraine as follows:

2005 IMF deal terms: $16.6 billion in loans to Ukraine

2010 IMF deal terms: $15.1 billion in loans to Ukraine

December 2013: Ukraine requests another $20 billion from IMF

The Orange Revolution of 2004 resulted in severing much (but not all) of the Ukrainian economy from Russia, causing a significant economic contraction for the Ukrainian economy for several years after.

Think of the similar effects of the severance as if the west coast economy of the US—California, Oregon, Washington—were stripped from the USA and joined Canada.

While the rest of the world economy, including Russia, enjoyed a moderate real economic recovery from 2004-07, Ukraine did not benefit much due to the economic severance from Russia that followed 2004 and the Orange Revolution. Ukrainian GDP declined or stagnated. In other words, the IMF deal of 2005 did little for the Ukrainian economy.

Then came the global economic collapse of 2008-09, generated largely by US, UK and western banks' over-speculation in financial securities. The Ukrainian economy and GDP, like many economies, collapsed by more than -15% during those two years.

That led to the second IMF deal of 2010. Ukraine believed the second deal would open its exports to western Europe and that would generate recovery. However, the European economy (EU) itself slipped into a second, 'double dip' recession in 2011-13, and demand for Ukrainian exports did not follow as anticipated.

Ukrainian GDP again stagnated after a short, modest recovery, and then slipped into a recession again in the second half of 2013. In short, the 2010 IMF deal did little for Ukraine as well.

In fact, the 2010 IMF deal probably slowed economic recovery, as it required a 50% increase in household gas prices and corresponding cuts in subsidies for the same. That significantly reduced aggregate consumption demand by Ukrainian households and slowed the economy. So did corresponding IMF demands for reductions in government spending, which were a precondition for the $15.1 billion 2010 IMF package.

One of the reasons no doubt that the Yanukovich government in December 2013 decided to forego another IMF deal where the reported requirement by the IMF was that household subsidies for gas be reduced by 50% once again.

Other onerous IMF requirements included cuts to pensions, government employment, and the privatization of (read: let western corporations purchase) government assets and property.

It is therefore likely that the most recent IMF deal currently in negotiation will include once again major reductions in gas subsidies, cuts in pensions, immediate government job cuts, as well as other reductions in social spending programs in the Ukraine.

This possibility does not seem to bother current interim prime minister, Arseny Yatsenyuk, who has publicly commented on the cuts, saying that «we have no other choice but to accept the IMF offer.»

In fact, Yatsenyuk and his post-coup government even stated before negotiations with the IMF began in early March that they would accept whatever offer the IMF and the EU made.

IMF/EU initially reported bailout terms provided a $2 billion immediate grant and subsequent $11 billion in loans. The European Investment Bank provided a couple billion more, for a total package of around $15 billion.

But there is no reason to believe that this $15 billion will prove any more economically stimulative to the Ukraine than did the 2010 deal of $15.1 billion. The Ukraine, European, and world economy is even weaker today than it was in 2010 when a brief, modest economic recovery globally was in progress. Today the trend is economic stagnation in Europe, significant slowing growth in China, and slowing growth emerging markets. Western Europe in general, and Germany in particular, will focus on subsidizing and expanding their own exports first, and will be little interested in encouraging Ukrainian exports to Europe at the expense of their own industries. Thus, as was the case with the post-2010 IMF deal, Western Europe in 2014-15 will not represent a major source of export demand to stimulate Ukraine's economy. More bailouts from the EU/IMF and the USA will quickly be required.

The $15 billion promised represents less than the $20 billion the Ukraine said it needed last December - i.e. before its currency fell 20% and its foreign exchange reserves fell to less than $10 billion. And less than the $35 billion the new interim prime minister, Yatsenyuk, admitted is needed. This writer in an earlier article has forecasted more than $50 billion will be required, given the projected 5% to 15% GDP decline expected for the Ukraine over the next two years.

Even if one assumes all the IMF's $15 billion will actually go into the Ukrainian economy directly the concurrent cuts to gas subsidies, pensions, government jobs and government spending demanded by the IMF/EU deal will almost certainly offset much, if not all, of the IMF/EU $15 billion.

Consider just the question of gas subsidies to households:

The latest Ukrainian GDP (2012) figures show its GDP was equivalent to $176 billion in nominal terms (and $335 billion if adjusted to global prices, or in 'PPP' purchasing power parity, terms).

Household gas subsidies reportedly amounted to 7.5% of GDP in 2012. That's about $13 billion in nominal terms. So if the IMF deal pending reportedly requires a cut of gas subsidies of 50%, that's about -$7.5 billion taken out of the Ukrainian economy. So the $15 billion IMF results in only half that in terms of real stimulus effects. The $15 billion becomes only a net $7.5 billion to the Ukrainian economy.

Cutting gas subsidies will not only result in removal of income for household spending who lose the subsidies, it will also result in sharp increases in gas prices that will reduce spending by nearly all households. Then there's the likely IMF demand for pension cuts. Particularly hard hit by the IMF deal will be elderly women households, who receive the majority of the pensions and which are spent to support children and grandchildren.

The cuts to gas subsidies and pensions, and rising gas prices, will reduce consumption immediately (and therefore GDP immediately) easily by more than $10 billion.

IMF-demanded cuts in other government spending will further offset the nominal IMF/EU $15 billion stimulus. Ukrainian government spending today represents 46% of GDP. The IMF will almost certainly therefore also demand a significant reduction in that 46%. That will mean in the short term even further GDP decline. That leaves a net real economic effect on the Ukrainian economy of well less than $5 billion. But there may not even be the $5 billion to begin with.

The lion's share of the $15 billion IMF loan will go to western banks (especially in Austria and Italy which are seriously exposed) to pay principal and interest on previous loans to the IMF and western banks (about $2 billion this year), will be used to finance future exports from the Ukraine (now running a $20 billion a year trade deficit), or will be used by the Ukrainian central bank to prop up the Ukrainian currency (now falling 20%).

How much of the $15 billion in the IMF/EU package will be initially diverted to cover bank loan interest, finance trade deficits, and for Ukraine's central bank efforts to slow the collapse of its currency remains to be seen.

If past IMF deals are an indicator, much of that $15 billion will be used as a first priority for the preceding purposes. What's left, if any, will go directly to the Ukraine economy. What's left will no doubt amount to far less going into the real economy than will be 'taken out' of the Ukraine economy as a result of cutting gas subsidies, government spending, and pensions.

Add in rising inflation from ending of gas subsidies and inevitable rising unemployment from cuts in government spending, it is not difficult to estimate that the latest IMF deal will have no more positive impact on the Ukrainian economy than did the prior 2010 and 2005 IMF deals. Indeed, it will most likely have an even greater negative impact on the economy in general, and the average Ukrainian in particular.

To briefly summarize in terms of just the net impacts of the EU/IMF deal, 'Who Benefits' includes: western European banks who will continue to receive principal and interest payments from the IMF that would have defaulted; global currency speculators who will be able to sell Ukrainian currency to the Ukrainian central bank at a subsidized price; Ukrainian companies that will be given export credits to continue selling to western Europe; and the western Europe companies that import the Ukrainian exports at a more attractive price.

Those who pay and who lose include: the majority of Ukrainian households that will have their real income reduced as they pay higher prices for gas, Ukrainian elderly who will have their pensions cut, Ukrainian government workers who will lose their jobs, and all Ukrainian households who will lose other government services.

But all the foregoing only refers to the negative net economic impacts from the pending March 2014 IMF deal. What about the general economy, apart from the IMF deal, which is predicted to contract by 5% to 15% over the next two years even assuming no worse development in political instability?

Who gains longer term from the Ukraine being more completely integrated into the western economy? Who loses longer term?

2. Russian Losses from the Crisis

The recent coup d'état of February 22 should be viewed as the continuation of the West's plan to sever the Ukraine economy from Russia, a plan that began in 2004 with the Orange Revolution but was not fully realized in 2004 by the West. The economic consequences of 2004 entailed a partial severing of the Russian and Ukrainian economies. The February 22 coup represents the beginning of the completion of that separation, a plan to totally strip off the Ukrainian economy from the Russian. 2004 and 2014 are thus not mutually exclusive events. They are linked and part of a continuum.

As a result of the 2004 'half revolution,' Russia and the European Union settled into a rough equal sharing of trade with the Ukraine, about a third of Ukrainian trade each. Post-coup that will no doubt shift dramatically, and Russia's trade balance will decline with the Ukraine as the West's rises significantly, to well over half of the Ukraine's total trade in the future.

In the immediate term, what Russia also stands to lose from the crisis economically is the $1-$2 billion of its previously offered 'deal' of February that has already been disbursed to the Ukraine and will likely not be repaid. It also stands to lose $2 billion in unpaid Ukrainian gas bills.

Longer term, there are the USA-EU economic sanctions that will be forthcoming. How extensive they will prove to be and how focused remains to be determined. However, this writer suspects western sanctions may prove more window dressing than serious, at least initially. The USA wants tough sanctions, since it has little to lose. The Europeans, on the other hand, are not as convinced and prefer token sanctions at first.

The UK in particular wants Russian wealthy investors' money to continue to flow to the UK to prop up its shaky property boomlet that artificially underlies its current fragile and weak economic recovery. France has recently gone to the USA, with hat in hand, requesting the USA help its economy. Its president, Hollande, will do whatever Washington wants.

Europe likes Russia's crony capitalists and oligarchs and will therefore be selective in its sanctions, focusing on Russian political figures and staunch Russian-Putin supporters rather than freezing of assets across the board, including for Oligarchs with investments in the west.

Germany is significantly dependent on Russian natural gas, but also has a large trade relationship with Russia, more than $75 billion a year. It will 'talk tough' to please the USA, but will not act so until it has assurances from the USA with regard to the latter supplying it with low cost USA natural gas -and that will take months if not years.

Concern about counter-sanctions from Russia targeting the extensive western corporate investments in Russia will also serve to reduce the severity of initial western 'sanctions.' Capitalists on both sides of the dispute, in Russia and in the West, will pressure their governments to not undertake serious sanctions precipitously. German companies with significant trade deals with Russia will especially resist strong EU trade sanctions. Opposition to EU sanctions from British companies, like the oil giant, BP, are also likely. Even American companies, like Exxon and credit card companies, will be lobbying Washington hard not to impose severe sanctions. Sanctions on individuals in Russia, especially those close to Putin, are more likely than across-the-board sanctions on Russian companies and industries. And then there is also the not insignificant threat of Russian counter-sanctions on EU and American companies.

EU business interests in particular will want to wait it out and hope the crisis blows over in time. Russian stock market and currency losses will prove relatively short term for Russia. To begin with, It is difficult to distinguish the declines in stock prices and currency from the political crisis, on the one hand, and the general decline in emerging markets that began last year and is accelerating today. Capital flight from Russia has already been significant, as it has from emerging markets in general in recent months. Should capital flight from Russia increase, there are countermeasures available to Russia to reduce it. Russia may raise interest rates to counter the effects of currency losses, and stock market price declines in Russia may eventually stimulate even more foreign investment into Russia.

Russian exports to the west in general, and to the Ukraine in particular, could take a more serious hit in the short run, and potentially in the longer run even more so. But Russia is likely able to offset losses longer term by turning east and selling more to China and Asia. Russian trade delegations are already heading east, to China and elsewhere in Asia to promote further energy trading.

In short, Russia will suffer some economic losses from the Ukrainian crisis but not nearly as severe as threats and claims made by the USA and European media and governments.

3. How the USA Benefits From the Crisis

In this Ukrainian crisis, the USA has the least economically to lose in the short run, and the most economically to gain in the longer run.

To begin with, the US Congress has committed a paltry $1 billion to the Ukrainian government so far. And it is not likely to commit significantly more, given the strategically critical USA mid-term Congressional elections coming up in November.

The neocons and Republicans have maneuvered the Obama administration into a box over the Ukraine crisis. If Obama comes down too strongly in terms of a military response, he loses the support of his liberal wing for the elections which already has turned against him in large part for his pro-corporate and pro-war policies to date.

If he doesn't come down hard with big financial commitments to the Ukraine, and is unwilling to implement significant economic sanctions, then the Republicans and political sociopaths like Senator John McCain in Congress will attack him severely.

Based on his past history, Obama will likely try to 'waffle' between the two poles of pressure, satisfying neither before the November elections.

What this means is that there is a strong political and economic element in the USA that would like a military confrontation with Russia, or at minimum a major economic break and attempt to totally isolate Russia economically.

There has been growing concern within the ranks of this element that Western Europe - and especially Germany - have forged too deep and too close economic ties with Russia. They want to break those ties and replace them with greater European dependency on the USA economically.

The long term objective is to have Germany and Europe dependent on US natural gas, at the expense of Russian gas. The USA now has a surplus of natural gas as a result of fracking and new exploration.

That surplus is reducing the price of natural gas in the US, and therefore profits. It wants to export the gas, which will raise prices and profits in the US while increasing profits from sales abroad.

However, current legislation prevents the export of that gas. A crisis in Europe and the latter's need for natural gas provides the perfect excuse for lifting US gas export controls. Oil and energy companies, facing lower demand for oil, want to boost profits by increased production of natural gas both domestically and to Europe. But the latter requires a breaking of Europe's dependency in the short run, for the next several years at minimum, on Russian natural gas.

US agribusiness also stands to gain from a Ukrainian crisis. A separating of Europe from Russia economically means an opportunity for increased US wheat exports to Europe. Not least, the US defense and military hardware industry stands to gain as well. With a projected $50 billion potential reduction in US arms production next year, a crisis in Europe will certainly provide a strong argument to restore those projected cuts.

4. The European Economy: Mixed Gains and Losses

The Ukrainian crisis poses a number of potential losses for the European economies. First, should the crisis deepen, it will mean a hike in natural gas and oil prices, food prices, and prices for certain raw materials. It could also mean a reduction in natural gas availability - not just from a Russian reduction, which is less likely, but from destruction of gas pipelines by the proto-fascist Ukrainian nationalists who have already threatened to blow up pipelines from Russia through the Ukraine to Western Europe.

Also this bodes negative consequences for the Euro currency and European stock markets. The Euro has already risen significantly, and is under pressure from global forces to rise further as well. That currency appreciation will make Euro products less competitive and more costly, in addition to the cost of energy. Euro exports, especially Germany's, to the rest of the world will slow and the Euro economic recovery, barely underway, could stall and even enter another recession, its third since 2008.

Shorter term, Euro stock markets have already begun to decline and that will accelerate should the Ukraine crisis worsen politically. Trade with

Russia dislocations in the short term will also reduce European economic growth, notwithstanding assurances from the USA that it will offset the differences.

In the short term, European banks will benefit from the IMF deal, which is crucial at a time that certain major banking institutions, like the big Italian Unicredit bank, have recently recorded huge losses. European multinational companies will do well, getting to buy up key Ukrainian companies and industries on the cheap.

But in the shorter run, the general crisis in the Ukraine and the latter's continued steep economic decline in coming months will result in European companies rushing to safe havens—currencies like the dollar, the Yen, and the Euro - as they move money to the sidelines until the crisis abates.

5. What USA-EU Multinational Corporations Want in the Ukraine

It is generally thought that the Ukrainian economy is largely uncompetitive and overly represented by outmoded basic industries like coal mining, steel, metals and other pre-information society industries. But that is a gross misrepresentation. The Ukraine offers an especially attractive economic plum ripe for picking by western multinational companies. Here's just some evidence of this latter point:

The Ukrainian economy is heavily invested in nuclear power generation and hydroelectric generation. This offers significant new investment opportunities for western nuclear power construction companies, which are facing growing public opposition to further nuclear plant construction in the west.

The Ukraine is the sixth largest exporter of aircraft military goods, especially transport equipment, and has an advanced rocket systems industry. It ranks fourth in the world in terms of IT technology professionals, behind only the USA, India and Russia, and has an exceptionally well educated technical workforce and tech-oriented education system that is growing by 20% a year.

Its tech market is more than $4 billion a year. Ninety percent of its populace is internet connected and there are 125 mobile phones per 100 population. Its shipbuilding industry is one of the most advanced, including natural gas tankers. It has a thriving automobile, truck, and public bus production industry. And it has 30% of the world's richest soil, producing grains, sugar and vegetable oils at costs well below Europe's. It also has its own proven, significant, but yet totally undeveloped shale gas reserves.

What the West wants is for its corporations to get their hands on these industries and their products and to integrate them into their multinational corporations' global expansion and production plans.

They will be aided by the IMF as part of its foreign direct investment requirements for any EU/IMF bailout deal. As these multinationals invest in the Ukraine, western banks will be paid significant fees (and allow Ukrainian banks to share as junior partners in the process).

Downsizing and restructuring of these Ukrainian industries will follow to integrate them into the global plans of the western multinationals. Ukrainians will lose jobs in these promising sectors, as their wages stagnate, and benefits are cut—as is the case going on globally for workers in all these industries today including the EU and USA.

6. Ukraine Crony Capitalists-USA Capitalists' Connections

Little has been written to date about the close connections between the Ukraine's crony capitalists' pro-western wing's connections to western capitalist interests, and USA capitalists in particular.

There are two wings of Ukrainian 'cronies'—the pro-western and the pro-Russian. Both are composed of opportunist bureaucrats of the Soviet era turned capitalist when the Soviet Union imploded more than 20 years ago. Both wings have been fighting it out openly since the Orange Revolution of 2004, now one in ascendancy, now the other.

The pro-western wing is loosely associated with the Fatherland Party, once led by Timoshenko and her predecessors, the other by Yanukovich and his predecessors, associated with the Party of Regions.

All the top politicians in both are multi-millionaires and billionaires, having alternated between themselves in raping the Ukraine economically for more than two decades now. Ukraine in the early 1990s had an economy and standard of living well above the other new ex-Soviet Republics. Today its' GDP and average income is less than Belarus and well below Russia's.

The Yanukovich cronies have been deposed in the recent coup of February 22, or are at least in retreat economically and trying to consolidate their economic forces. Ousted from political control are Yanukovich and Regions Party billionaire cronies like Rinat Akhmetov, richest man in the Ukraine worth $15 billion, with big holdings in energy and metals; Vadim Novinsky, the third richest; Dymtro Firtash, with billions in chemicals, banking and real estate, who was recently arrested in western Europe; and Sehiy Tihipko, former head of the Ukraine central bank.

The Fatherland party billionaires are now in control, with their very wealthy compatriot, newly minted prime minister, Arseniy Yatsenyuk, running the new government. But behind the scenes lurk the real new crony powerbrokers. At the top of this list is Victor Pinchuk, the second richest man in the Ukraine with an empire in Media and other business interests. His foundation has been central in funding NGOs (non-government organizations) in the Ukraine, which have been the conduits for western money to help destabilize the Ukraine for years.

Pinchuk's foundation works closely with Yatsenyuk's foundation. Pinchuk is also close to Wall Street and the Council on Foreign Relations in the USA, the premier foreign policy strategy organization of capitalists in the US. Pinchuk is also on the board of the Petersen Institute in the USA, another key organization influencing US economic and foreign policy. He interfaces frequently with the Clinton and Blair Foundations, and is a major participant in the annual gathering of big capitalists at the World Economic Forum in Davos, Switzerland. He is friends with Bill Gates and Warren Buffet.

Below Pinchuk are other key crony-billionaires like Igor Turchynov, interim President and Speaker of the Ukrainian parliament; Stepan Kuban, who heads the new Ukrainian central bank; Sergey Tartuta, billionaire coal and steel boss with extensive holdings in eastern Ukraine, who was just recently appointed the new governor of the Donetsk region in the east after the Yatsenyuk team fired its previous pro-Yanukovich governor.

Tartuta has close economic ties with Poland and Hungarian capitalists. Still another is Ihor Kolomysky, similarly appointed in recent weeks as new governor of the Dnepopetrovsk region in the eastern Ukraine.

These billionaires who are either themselves in the Ukrainian parliament, or who formerly and continue to control blocks of 30-50 votes each, were undoubtedly behind the inside strategy of the February 22 coup.

The outside strategy was driven by the proto-fascists on the street and in Maidan square. As the latter stepped up the attack outside the Parliament, on the inside the vote to depose Yanukovich took place, as some of his own cronies deserted him to join the Fatherland cronies - no doubt convinced in part by threats that arose simultaneously from the West that their assets in Swiss and Luxembourg banks would be frozen.

As for the Maidan proto-fascists—the elements of the Svoboda party, the Right Sector, the UPA, and others—they have been nicely rewarded for their assistance with no fewer than six key positions in the new post-coup government of Yatsenyuk.

These include formal positions of police and military power. It is clear the proto-fascists have chosen positions in the government that will allow them to build, arm and organize their street gangs better in the future, now under official government cover.

7. The Ukrainian Economy—The Big Loser

As noted earlier, the Ukrainian people will be the big economic losers from the crisis, after already having been so for more than two decades. The pending third round of IMF austerity will mean that gas subsidies will be reduced, pensions cut, jobs lost, services eliminated, and inflation will rise. The standard of living will fall still further, as predicted depression conditions of 5% to 15% drop in GDP in 2014-15 materialize.

As was estimated by Ukraine's prime minister last December 2013, Ukraine will need a minimum of $17 billion to prevent default on payments to banks for government debt already incurred. Ukraine's public debt as a percent of GDP was 39% in 2012. Measured in PPP terms, that's more than $13 billion still owed with interest. Its foreign exchange reserves are almost exhausted and it needs $20 billion a year just to finance its annual current trade deficit of that amount. But if its currency continues to decline, if its exports decline, and if the cost of imports rise—all of which are highly likely - then the IMF's pending $15 billion will prove grossly insufficient.

Ukraine will need $50 billion, and the question remains whether the EU-IMF and/or the USA will be willing to provide such a large sum. The answer to that is highly unlikely. That means the Ukrainian government will agree to whatever terms the IMF-EU offer in exchange for the $15 billion, and then more for follow-on additional loans as necessary.

It means the government will cut services and privatize public assets, selling them to billionaires and western interests at fire sale prices. And it means that foreign capitalists will scoop up Ukrainian companies and industries at historic low prices as those companies and industries desperately try to prevent their collapse and bankruptcy in the coming months of severe economic decline in the Ukraine.

Given the strong trends in the global economy in general toward slowdown, and the decline of currencies in emerging markets, it is likely as well that Ukraine's currency will continue to decline, further exacerbating all the above problems. The recent 20% drop in its value in relation to the dollar will continue, as the Ukraine is swept up in the general emerging markets crisis in addition to its own set of problems.

With the secession of the Crimea the Ukrainian crisis, economically and politically, now shifts to a new level. As the economic crisis deepens in the country, demands for secession will grow elsewhere in the eastern Ukraine as well. How the Ukraine government and the USA/EU choose to address that likelihood will be critical. Further political unrest and uncertainty will mean more economic crisis, as business investment and production stalls and employment and inflation rises.

The response to the growing economic problems by the post-coup government in Kiev will also prove critical. With its security forces now being led by proto-fascist elements that want above all a military conflict between the EU/USA and Russia, the great danger is that those proto-fascist forces may provoke a military conflict in an attempt to draw in NATO forces. Should that occur, then Ukraine's economic crisis will be the least of its problems.

MOTHER RUSSIA

AN ELUSIVE PRIZE

JOHN KOZY

Pyotr Ilyich Tchaikovsky's 1812 overture should be a constant reminder of what happens to those who have designs on Mother Russia. After defeating Tsarist armies in closely fought battles, Napoleon reached Moscow. Instead of surrendering, the Russians burned it down! Napoleon achieved no victory.

This Patriotic War of 1812 began on June 24 when Napoleon's Grande Armée crossed the Neman River. The official political excuse for the war was the elimination of the Russian threat to Poland.

Napoleon even named the campaign the Second Polish War to curry favor with the Poles and provide a political pretense for his actions. So, you see, Napoleon, too, carried a false flag in his knapsack. Politicians everywhere have no qualms about lying to cloak their true motives; they are all cut from the same cloth.

Now Americans and their Western allies want to save Ukraine from those same Russians. Don't you believe it. Ukrainians have been living with and beside Russians since the 9th century. Not only have they survived, they've maintained their identity very well. What the West really wants is something else, something else indeed!

In the Middle Ages, the 'Kievan Rus' became the center of East Slavic culture. It gave birth to both Russia and the Ukraine. But by the 13th century, the geographical part of Eastern Europe called Ukraine was divided and ruled by a variety of Western nations. A Ukrainian Cossack republic emerged during the 17th century, but otherwise the Ukraine remained divided until the Soviet Union consolidated it into a Soviet Republic in the 20th century. It only became an independent nation in 1991.

To illustrate how confused things in Eastern Europe became, my parents emigrated separately from there in the decade that preceded The Great War. They called themselves Ukrainians; they spoke Ukrainian; they carried on Ukrainian traditions; they regularly attended an Eastern Rite

Orthodox church. Two more Ukrainian people could not have been found. But! Neither of them ever lived in a country named Ukraine. Thousands of Ukrainians were just like them. Моя Україна (my Ukraine) was a mythical place.

Zbigniew Brzezinski's well known Polish family hailed from Brzeżany in Galicia in the Tarnopol region of Poland (now Ukraine). Zbigniew, along with his parents, emigrated to Canada from Galicia, the very region my parents emigrated from. But for the generational difference, they and the Brzezinskis could have been neighbors. Poles and Ukrainians living side by side! But my parents never called themselves Polish even though they were governed by Poland.

So when Arseniy Yatsenyuk says, "This is our land, our fathers and grandfathers have spilled their blood for this land, and we won't budge a single centimeter from Ukrainian land," he's blowing smoke. Much of the spilt blood was Russian.

The Ukrainians did not and could not have defeated the Germans in WWII. As a matter of fact, many fought on the side of Germany. So you see, the situation in Ukraine is very complicated, which makes the current events there very complicated too. Only fools and politicians describe them in simple terms.

There is about as much unity in Ukraine as there is in the American Republican Party. Dissent is rampant. To say that Ukrainians want this or that is pure nonsense. The country is home to 44.6 million people, 77% of whom are ethnic Ukrainians, 17% are ethnic Russians, and 6% are descendants of various other nationalities—Belarusians, Tatars, Romanians, Lithuanians, Poles, and others. And the Ukrainian opposition that caused President Viktor Yanukovych to flee consists of various groups that are by no means of one mind.

The pro-Russian Eastern Ukrainians can demonstrate just as easily as the anti-Russian Western Ukrainians did. An Egyptian scenario might very well ensue. A street revolution, an election, an unhappy losing opposition, more demonstrations, and finally a military intervention may be the ultimate result. Or Ukraine may be dismembered as it has been so many times in history. That is not what many of those who demonstrated in Kiev want.

"We want to change the system, not just the president," says Vitaliy Vygupaev, an auto mechanic and protest leader. "When we choose the president and change the system, we'll leave."

But that may not be possible. Ukraine has a problem it shares with many countries including the United States. Its Constitution allows the political system to become corrupted. That system is what created the problems and it is not likely to change.

Faulty economic policy, unwillingness to reform, and endemic corruption have destabilized the country. The currency, the hryvnia, was fixed at 8:1 to the dollar; at this writing in April 2014, it trades at about ten. The government recently issued short-term debt at interest rates as high as 15%; its bonds have done poorly, and many investors are worried that Ukraine will soon default.

Ukrainians hoping for a bailout will be shocked by the austerity any bailout will require. The European Union will treat the Ukrainians exactly as the Greeks were treated. Ukrainians may even have to begin singing the Porgy and Bess line, "nobody knows our sorrow".

Not only will they yield the pound of flesh demanded by any bailout, they will shed the blood spilt in its taking. The resolution of this economic problem will take many years. The Western concern is the repayment of Ukraine's sovereign debt, and to insure that, the EU must control Ukraine's economy as it controls the economies of Greece, Portugal, Italy, and Spain.

That's the economic problem, and except for Russia's owning some of Ukraine's sovereign debt, Russia has nothing to do with it. The Western world's political dispute with Russia is something else.

The West, especially Western Europe, has had its eye on Russia at least since the 1700s when it was invaded by Charles XII of Sweden. That invasion began with Charles' crossing of the Vistula on January 1, 1708 and effectively ended with the Swedish defeat in the Battle of Poltava on July 8, 1709 though Charles continued to pose a military threat to Russia for several years while under the protection of the Ottoman Turks. There, Charles persuaded Sultan Ahmed III to declare war on Russia. Backed by a Turkish army, Charles led the Turks into the Russo-Turkish War (1710–1711), but before he could engage in battle, Peter the Great bribed the Turks into ending the war. Charles' ambitions to conquer Russia were over.

As noted earlier, Napoleon invaded Russia in 1812. The Russian revolution brought the Union of Soviet Socialist Republics into existence in November 1917. The West intervened with a multi-national military force, an incipient NATO, in 1918. The stated goals were to help the Czechoslovakian Legions, secure supplies in Russian ports, and re-establish the Eastern front. But after winning the war in Western Europe, the allied powers militarily supported the anti-revolutionary forces hoping to reinstall Nicholas II to Russia's autocratic throne. The great defenders of democracy fought for an autocrat! Somehow or other, that doesn't sound right. The word 'democracy' does not go well with the word 'autocrat.' The Bolsheviks claimed correctly that their enemies were backed by Western capitalists.

A lack of public support and a deteriorating situation compelled the allies to withdraw in 1920. Mother Russia had again defeated a foreign invasion. The flags flown were proven to be false by the passage of time. The Western allies continued to fight on the side of the Tsarist forces for two years after the Great War ended and the Czechoslovakian Legions had withdrawn.

Then in June, 1941, German forces invaded the Soviet Union. Until the fall of 1942, the German army consistently prevailed. Europe had been conquered. The Germans reached Stalingrad. It proved to be the war's turning point. The Battle of Stalingrad lasted six months, from August 23, 1942 to February 2, 1943 when the German 6th army surrendered.

From then on, the Soviet army remained on the offensive, liberating most of the Ukraine, and virtually all of Russia and eastern Belorussia during 1943. In the battle of Kurst in 1943, the Germans were badly beaten again. The Soviets then liberated the rest of Belorussia and the Ukraine, most of the Baltic States, and eastern Poland. The war was effectively over. Another Western attempt to conquer Russia had failed. Had it not been for the Russians, the French and English would today be singing "Deutchland uber allies."

Yet the West's persistence is unreal. Not having learned that those who dismiss history are domed to repeat it, the West marches on. Immediately after the end of the Second World War, the United States began a strategy of global containment, extending military and financial aid to the countries of Western Europe, supporting the anti-Communist side in the Greek Civil War, and creating NATO.

Although by the 1970s, both sides expressed a desire to create more friendly relations, the United States organized, trained, and armed the American Mujahideen in Afghanistan to combat the Russians and the Russian backed Communist government. This was just one of many proxy wars fought between the two nations beginning with Korea. Western antagonism never ceased during this period. Although not explicitly American wars, they were fought mainly by Americans.

The American Mujahideen succeeded in expelling the Russians from Afghanistan, but the proxy wars fought in Korea, Vietnam, Iraq, and in Afghanistan when the Mujahideen turned on their American benefactors were largely failures. In the 1980s, the United States increased diplomatic, military, and economic pressures.

The USSR was suffering from economic stagnation. Mikhail Gorbachev introduced liberalizing reforms. In 1989, revolutions peacefully overthrew all of the Communist regimes of Central and Eastern Europe. The Communist Party of the Soviet Union itself was banned. This in turn led to the formal dissolution of the USSR in December 1991. It seemed that the West had won. But Mother Russia still existed, and the West still persisted.

The European Union launched what it calls "an initiative" concerning its relationship with the post-Soviet states of Eastern Europe called the Eastern Partnership on May 7, 2009. The EU claims the Partnership is intended to provide a venue for discussions of trade, economic strategy, travel agreements, and other issues between the EU and its eastern neighbors.

Since the Eastern Partnership was inaugurated, however, critical academic research has become available. Findings note both conceptual and physical problems. Firstly, the EU has scanty ideas about what it is trying to promote. The conceptions of 'shared values,' 'collective norms,' and 'joint ownership' are too imprecise to convey any real intentions. Secondly, the EU seems to favor a 'top-down' approach which is clearly inconsistent with the idea of voluntary partnership and explicitly limits the input of the partnering states which clearly means that anything agreed to will favor the EU. To the EU, the six Post-Soviet states have "strategic importance." That phrase usually has military implications.

The EU draft states, "Shared values including democracy, the rule of law, and respect for human rights will be at its core, as well as the principles of market economy, sustainable development, and good governance." Apart from values, the declaration says the EU has an "interest in developing an increasingly close relationship with its Eastern partners…" But the inclusion of Belarus in the partnership raises the question of whether values or geopolitics are paramount. EU diplomats agree that the country's authoritarian president, Alexander Lukashenko, has done little to merit inclusion but the EU fears that Russia will strengthen its grip Belarus if it is left out. So it is really Russia's grip that the EU is concerned about.

When Ukrainian President Viktor Yanukovych decided not to sign an agreement with the EU, demonstrations broke out in Kiev that ultimately forced him to flee. Within days, Russia took control of the Crimea. Russia had to do something to protect its political control over its only warm water naval base located at Sevastopol.

The Crimea itself was ceded to the Ukrainian Soviet Socialist Republic only on February 19, 1954 as a "symbolic gesture" to commentate the 300th anniversary of Ukraine's becoming a part of the Russian Empire. President Obama called Russia's action a 'provocation' and threatened consequences and costs.

But just think a moment about the word 'provocation.' If someone is dumping trash on my neighbor's property, I would be justified in being provoked. But a person living five miles across town would not. Washington is half a world east of the Crimea; Russia neighbors it. What justification has someone in Washington or even in the EU for being provoked? The real provocation was the EU's Eastern Partnership and its overtures to Ukraine. Russia's action stopped the EU from cooking the stew!

Flashpoint in Ukraine: How the US Drive for Hegemony Risks World War III

This more than three hundred years of animosity the West has had for Russia is something for which it is hard to find any justification. Except for some minor border wars, Russia has never attacked a Western nation. Western Civilization, however, has always been belligerent. Certainly since, and perhaps before, Alexander the Great, Western nations have been empire mad. Rome, England, France, Spain, Portugal, the Netherlands, Italy, Austria, Sweden, and Germany have all sought empires.

The history of Western Civilization is a history of war. This empire madness has not made life better for ordinary people. Not ever! No English commoner gained much from the empire on which the sun never set. And one by one, those empires expired. Western nations control less of the world's territory today than they did in 1939. To set out to conquer an empire is to chase a chimera!

This anti-Russianism has all the characteristics of a racial prejudice. It is just like anti-Semitism. The entire Jewish race was absurdly and collectively condemned for the death of Christ. Not even a similar fiction exists to justify anti-Russianism. Anti-Semitism is a product of Western Civilization; it is a Western European concept resulting in the slaughter of some six million Jews. Will Mr. Cameron and Mrs. Merkel be happy to see anti-Russianism result in the slaughter of six million Russians? It's certainly possible.

UN member states number 193. The Vatican and Palestine have observer status. The United States has deployed troops in more than 150 of them. Russia has deployed troops in three or four of its border states. Russia has one warm water naval base. The United States has several, one of which is in Diego Garcia. Why in Diego Garcia? Diego Garcia is in the middle of the Indian Ocean! The United States Navy operates a Naval Support Facility, a large naval ship and submarine support base, a military air base, a communications and space-tracking facility, and an anchorage for pre-positioned military supplies for regional operations aboard Military Sealift Command ships.

Between 1968 and 1973, the native Chagossians were forcibly resettled by the British government to Mauritius and the Seychelles to allow the United States to establish the base. Today, the exiled Chagossians are still trying to return, claiming that the forced expulsion was illegal. Does anyone really believe that the base exists for some benign purpose? Is anyone really that dumb? Claiming that Russia is out to rule the world is merely a case of pots calling the kettle black.

No one knows what the outcome of this current international imbroglio will be. I doubt that anyone wants to start another war. But if not now, someday someone will call the West's bluff, the result of which no one can predict.

Killing is not the way to make friends and influence people. Providing for their needs is. Things would be different if Western Civilization had become Shangri-La. But it hasn't! For a few, it has provided 'the good life,' for most, it has provided little. But poor people are eternally hopeful.

The peoples of Armenia, Azerbaijan, Belarus, Georgia, Moldova, and Ukraine are easily seduced by Western powers that offer bread and promises of butter. But these peoples need to look at Greece, Italy, Portugal, and Spain. When they do, they will see that the European Union has provided little bread for the peoples of these member countries.

The financiers and merchants of the West care nothing for people or nations. Jefferson knew it when he said that merchants have no country. The Western nations don't care how Ukrainians fare. They don't care how their own peoples fare.

The United States, the world's richest nation, cannot house, feed, or medicate its homeless, unemployed, or sick. Why does anyone believe that it will house, feed, and medicate Ukrainians? Chimeras can't be roasted on a spit! The West wants only Ukrainian flesh, blood, and wealth. You don't believe it? Well remember this: the Elgin Marbles, sculpted in Greece to be hung on the Parthenon, are now to be found in the British Museum.

Balzac is credited with saying, "Behind every great fortune lies a great crime." The Western world does make great fortunes for a very few. Western Civilization a very great crime! We are all guilty for endorsing it.

HANGOVER IN UKRAINE

TREATY OF VERSAILLE SPIRITS PACKAGED IN BRETTON WOODS BOTTLES

JEFFREY SOMMERS

The crisis in Ukraine was a hangover long in the making. The crash of this once Soviet industrial and agricultural powerhouse republic after its much heralded 'independence' was reminiscent of Tacitus' characterization of Rome's imperial military victories, put in the mouth of the Celtic chieftain Calgacus before the battle of Mons Graupius: "They make a desert and they call it peace." The treatment meted out to the former Soviet Union was presented benignly in packaging resembling the relative goodwill embodied in the post World War II Bretton Woods arrangement, but in content was closer to the toxic tonic administered at the Treaty of Versailles. The last glass poured that brought Ukraine to collapse was Viktor Yanukovych's rejection of the European Union's proposed Association Agreement. Yanukovych feared its austerity implications would topple his government, yet ironically it was the very rejection of the agreement that led to his downfall.

While the Association Agreement provided the last drink pushing Ukraine to collapse, its hangover resulted from binge drinking by opportunists in both the past and present. Both of, and apart, from Russia, Ukraine's history is inseparably part of Russia's past. Nested in Russia like a matryoshdoll while also maintaining a connection to Europe, its history reveals a fluid and ever-changing journey over the contours of East Europe, while also touched by West Asia. This pattern is repeated with Russia, which itself is nested inside both European and Asian worlds, simultaneously being of and apart from them.

Russia and Ukraine were quite literally born as one with Kiev Rus and through a kind of 'cell division,' to use a biological metaphor, started as twins, but eventually mutated into related but distinct cultures. They use the same written script passed down to them by the Byzantine monks Cyril and Methodius in the 9th century C.E. and share a culture forged in the Eastern

Orthodox Church. Ethnic Ukrainians think of themselves as a more pure 'Russia' by culture (and more disturbingly, increasingly by genetics) than the country of Russia itself. Eastern Orthodox Ukrainians see the latter as polyglot of ethnicities wrought into a nation by the force of imperial expansion over the centuries. Both, predictably, declare their branch of the founding Rurik (ironically Finnish) dynasty to be the legitimate heir to Kiev Rus.

Yet, Ukraine hardly represents static boundaries housing a homogenously preserved culture, pure or otherwise. Ukraine is largely a creation of the 20th century Soviet Union and Russian czarist contributions before it. In the mid 17th century Ukraine held a small territory about a tenth the size of the country's present-day borders. Russian czars over the centuries from Peter the Great onward tacked additional territories onto Ukraine's central and northern flanks. Catherine the Great also added territory in the south, with the Crimea Khanate annexed in 1783.[1] Vladimir Lenin pasted on the territories of what are today's industrial east (e.g., Donetsk, Kharkov, Luhansk, etc.) and historic cities to the south, such as Odessa. It is here where protests for more autonomy from Kiev, and even calls for independence, have been lodged. Meanwhile, Joseph Stalin carved Galicia out of Poland in 1939 with the Molotov-Ribbentrop Pact. In 1944 after driving the Nazis out in World War II, this oil and gas-producing region (at the time) was then formally annexed by the Stalin. Yet, it was in the ferment of WW II that Galician nationalists would fight the Soviets, and thus Galicia today has disproportionately provided leadership for Ukraine's rightwing radicals, such as *Pravy Sektor* (Right Sector) and *Svoboda* (Freedom). Nikita Khrushchev rounded out Ukraine's expansion by adding the Crimea in 1954, given it was assumed to be permanently part of the USSR. Ukraine, thus, had built in centrifugal forces that at any moment could tear it apart from within or in combination with external influences of Russia or the United States from without. The 'laws' of Historical Materialism in 1954 suggested the Soviet Union was the future, with its status both immutable and immortal. That 'future,' however, died in 1991.

NATO

Russia's incursion into Crimea, with their attention also fixed on eastern Ukraine, responded to the crescendo of US/NATO expansion since 1990. The unraveling of the USSR and its Soviet bloc (Warsaw Pact) dismantled the largest empire in modern history. Even more striking, it was the most peaceful dissolution of a major empire perhaps in world history. The fact that an empire stretching over a dozen time zones that included roughly a hundred ethnic groups, with concrete historical and contemporary grievances, broke up without a bloodbath[2] is nothing short of miraculous.

Part of the reason that this dismantling of empire went off with so little violence was the mutual desire of US President George H.W. Bush and Soviet General Secretary Mikhail Gorbachev to end the Cold War's threat of Mutually Assured Destruction (MAD). Gorbachev for his part recognized that the Warsaw Pact nations needed to be let go in order to free resources to deploy at home to reform the USSR. Meanwhile, second tier Soviet leaders merely wanted to take the USSR down so they could cash out as privatizers of state assets.[3] Demilitarization was to be achieved by disarmament, all the more remarkable in view of the largest human losses suffered in history from military invasion that occurred just two generations earlier. Germany became the focus, pending its reunification in 1990. It had invaded its neighbors every generation or so since the Franco-Prussian War of 1870. In World War II it laid waste to the USSR and left some 25 million of its people dead. Other East European states, including Romania, along with victims of Stalinist oppression (e.g., the Baltics and western Ukrainians) sometimes welcomed the Nazis in order fight against Russia.

As the USSR unraveled Russia had vital security concerns which could only be met by assurances that NATO would not move into the Warsaw Pact states, where so much Soviet blood had been shed in World War II. President George H. W. Bush pledged in 1990 that if the Soviets were to dissolve the Warsaw Pact, Russia must be assured that NATO would not fill the vacuum. As Bush's Secretary of State, James Baker, put the matter while at the Kremlin as the withdrawal of the Soviets from East Germany was being planned, there would be "no extension of NATO's jurisdiction for forces of NATO one inch to the east."[4] This promise was essential for getting the USSR to pull out of the Warsaw Pact.

Bush's successor, Bill Clinton, broke this promise by quickly taking former Warsaw Pact states into NATO. Clinton's successor, George W. Bush, moved into territory formerly annexed to the USSR with the Baltics, and folded them into NATO in 2004. It should have been foreseen—and probably was inevitable—that these new entrants wanted membership in NATO, given their own experience with Soviet oversight in the Warsaw Pact and direct rule in the Baltics. But the eagerness of a triumphalist United States to surround Russia militarily led Russian leaders to feel betrayed by the US.

Since the Soviet breakup, Russia has watched covert attempts from the US State Department to organizations such as the National Endowment for Democracy and NGOs, to increasingly anchor themselves in the former Soviet bloc. This threatened to remake Russia's 'near abroad' into a neoliberal periphery of the US. It is in this context that the Kiev Maidan government posed an existential threat for Russia, as previous NATO moves toward Georgia had already cut too close to the bone in 2008 and resulted in Russia's military intervention. Moreover, most Russians never forgave Gorbachev for the deal he made with NATO in 1990. Russian diplomats have stated clearly that Ukraine is a line that cannot be crossed regarding potential NATO expansion. The prospect of NATO assimilating Ukraine represents, from the perspective of Russia, the very ancestral home where Russia was founded and the ground on which it repelled the fascist invasion in the Great Patriotic War.

Given this background, the movement of Ukraine's Maidan government toward possible future NATO membership was inevitably going to produce a counter reaction from both Russia and Russian speakers in Ukraine. Naturally, this would occur in the region of Ukraine that had the most strategic significance to Russia and the greatest concentration of Russian speakers: Crimea. Russians in Crimea watched with alarm the rightwing nationalist violence in Kiev, which was over-represented by Russian media, but nonetheless real, while also under-reported in Western media. That said, contra Russian assertions, the Maidan was not only an ultra-nationalist movement. Chauvinist elements played a role, but the movement was broad based, representing elements across the political and even ethnic spectrum.[5]

Ukraine's President, Viktor Yanukovych, was as much a crook as Ukraine's previous kleptocratic leaders who wielded political power to rob the state and its public domain. Yet, many Russian speakers in the south and east viewed Yanukovych as 'their' president, given some of the ethnic separatist elements in the Maidan. The Crimean population and observers in Russia, however, feared that Yanukovych was illegally deposed not for his kleptocracy, but as part of a regional and ethnic divide and conquer identity politics. The only protection available, from the perspective of Russian speaking Crimeans, was from Russia. Moreover, the carrot of higher pensions and social supports from Russia generally also proved compelling for Crimeans wanting to join the more prosperous and stable Russia.

Economy

What precipitated the Ukrainian crisis in fall 2013 and into 2014? Many things, but foremost was Ukraine's failed economy. Ukraine has been a corrupt mess since its independence was secretly planned and then announced at the Belavezha Accords on December 8, 1991 in Belarus. Boris Yeltsin, never the sharpest tool in a shed full of leaders from the Soviet Union's gerontocracy, got the idea that breaking up the Soviet bloc would make Russia rich. His 'logic' went something like, 'since the USSR's balance of payments represented a net outflow of resources to the Warsaw Pact nations and to all but one Central Asian republic, Russia would get rich if it could merely offload them from its balance sheet.' Thus did Yeltsin organize with his Belarus and Ukrainian Soviet Republic party leaders the plan to spin them off from the USSR. Meanwhile, the US was keen to bust up the Soviet trading bloc known as the Council for Mutual Economic Assistance (COMECON), despite opposition from France, who correctly held that this would destroy industry and trade in the post-Soviet space.[6] From the perspective of US Eurasianists, busting up Russia's economy, and thus power, was precisely the point. The US was keen to break up Russia and prevent any future hegemon presiding over the great Eurasian space comprising the former Soviet bloc. Most specifically, as Zbigniew Brzezinski warned in his *Grand Chessboard*, Russian control of Ukraine would again make it a Eurasian-wide power.[7] Keeping them apart has been the motivating force for Eurasianists in the State Department ever since.

Most recently, the baton for this mission has passed to Victoria Nuland, the US Assistant Secretary of State for European and Eurasian Affairs. Nuland is spouse of Robert Kagan, who co-founded the Project for a New American Century (PNAC) in 1997. The PNAC brought together US 'hawks' that sought to preserve US empire and aggressively confront any challenges to it.[8] Most infamously, the PNAC were the chief proponents for the US war in Iraq. Nuland has referenced the United States spending $5 billion in Ukraine since 1991 to orient Ukraine in directions desirable to the US. While this may be desirable from the perspective of the US, for Russia it has not gone unnoticed, nor has it been welcome. Moreover, characteristic of the imperial hubris of the neocons and the US as the 'G1' nation, Nuland was noted for her remarks to "[expletive] the EU" when contemplating European considerations.[9] She also opined in winter 2014 on who should and should not be in a new Ukraine government.[10] The resulting head of Ukraine's new parliament was no surprise: the Nuland candidate, the former banker and leading member of Yulia Tymoshenko's corrupt former government. Arseniy Yatsenyuk, was selected as Prime Minister for Ukraine's new government and could be counted on to push through US desired neoliberal 'reforms.'

It should also be noted that Russia has its own Eurasianists, such as Alexander Dugin of Moscow State University who advises President Putin's United Russia party. Contra US State Department goals of splitting up Eurasia, figures like Dugin want to unite it. They wish to see Russia's power restored and its culture protected from external influence. They seek a 'Greater Russia' consolidated from majority Russian speaking areas. Their goal is to ultimately reincorporate much of Ukraine, Belarus and northern Kazakhstan into Russia.[11] For the moment, this means keeping these areas out of NATO. Their program, however, does not extend to the Baltic States, which they see as culturally separate from Russia. Thus, concerns over Russia entering the Baltics are likely misplaced, regardless of the past 1940 Soviet grab of the Baltics in the early stages of WW II and subsequent decades of Soviet rule, which largely had a historically specific defensive agenda.

We have seen two 'models' for treating a defeated great power over the past century. One was the Treaty of Versailles after World War I. It placed the blame squarely on Germany for the war and required that bankers be paid. This humiliated and bankrupted Germany, thus setting the stage for the next war. The other was the Bretton Woods system after World War II. While it was not nearly as progressive as John Maynard Keynes wanted[12] it still had the virtue of responding to Soviet economic and military power, not to mention its ideological challenge, by encouraging national economic development and social democracy in West Europe and Japan. Russia hoped to be treated as a partner after unilaterally dismantling the USSR in 1991. Instead, US treatment of Russia resembled more the Treaty of Versailles than Bretton Woods. Rather than building up the post-Soviet bloc, it was instead subjected, in cooperation with many of Russia's own oligarchs, to de-industrialization, structural adjustment and natural resource extraction in order to provide a 'spatial fix' to the global crisis of accumulation that extended back to the 1970s.[13] Poland proved somewhat of an exception as it was the first country to break with the Warsaw Pact, and thus given a much better aid package (more grants, fewer loans)[14] in order to entice the rest of the Warsaw Pact states into the West's embrace. This would have later significance for western Ukrainians, who thought relative prosperity there was a function of EU membership.

The result of the Soviet bloc's unraveling was an economic boom in the US and UK in the 1990s. It was fueled by cheap energy and raw materials from the Commonwealth of Independent States (CIS), with money paid to the post-Soviet economies for these commodities washing back to offshore bank accounts and equity markets in New York and London. For the post-Soviet space of the 1990s it was a mess, with demographic losses only surpassed by World War II. The post Soviet middle class collapsed. Some areas of the post-Warsaw Pact (bordering West Europe) economically saw recovery in the 21st century, but also faced huge bubbles and then busts of their property markets in 2008. Russia, with its copious quantities of oil, gas and metals prospered in the new millennium (at least compared to the Yeltsin disaster years of the 1990s). Buoyed by China and India's demand for resources, plus a US credit-fed global bubble in the Bush years, combined with Bush's Iraq War pushing up oil prices, there was enough 'trickle down' wealth for the condition of many Russians to improve despite still existing rampant corruption. Ukraine, however, never saw as much improvement. It experienced a property bubble like many other nations and it saw some money pour into its steel sector in the go-go years in the run up to the 2008 crash. But most of its people remained in a precarious state and after the 2008 crash it failed to fully recover. Moreover, corruption remained huge. Even by the standards of the post-Soviet bloc, Ukraine was an 'exemplar' of corruption, even to the point of being lectured on the topic by one of corruption's 'star' performers, Russia. As Putin noted in a March 3, 2014 press conference:

> Nothing or almost nothing has changed for the better. Corruption has reached dimensions that are unheard of here in Russia. Accumulation of wealth and social stratification—problems that are also acute in this country—are much worse in Ukraine, radically worse. Out there, they are beyond anything we can imagine imagine.[15]

The corruption and poverty was too much for Ukrainians, especially those with links to Europe where they frequently worked and visited. For example, Poland and parts of Ukraine share much history, with the latter having been at points in its history part of the former. Yet, today Poland has per capita incomes twice that of Ukraine. In part this is explained by the fact that a full third of Poland up to World War II was part of Germany. Sharing a large border with Germany and with much former German territory now part of Poland, has led to significant German investment. Moreover, Poland, as previously stated, got by far the best deal of Soviet bloc countries in terms of aid. Much of that aid extended was in the form of grants, rather than loans, which accelerated their development by reducing debt-service burdens. Ukraine, by contrast, enjoyed none of these benefits.

EU

The proposed EU/Ukraine Association Agreement extended the hope of European living standards and better governance for Ukraine. Oligarchs who privatized Soviet industry and frequently exported profits to offshore banks rather than re-investing in their own country have dominated Ukraine's economy since its independence. The desire for higher living standards and cleaner government by Ukrainians is understandable. The question is: would partnership with the EU improve the lives of Ukrainians?

EU expansion has largely produced disappointing results for people both East and West (although finance has profited handsomely). The aspiration by Ukrainians for prosperous, egalitarian societies once associated with Europe's social democracies is rational. The expectation of the EU bringing Europe's 'Social Model' to Ukraine, however, would be dashed by the reality of the EU's current neoliberalizing tides. While many hoped past EU expansion would represent an enlargement of the 'Social Europe' project, the actual experience has been one of it using (if not exploiting) East European labor that creates a 'precariat' of insecure migrant workers in West Europe. Thus, West European wages have been kept down by EU enlargement. Meanwhile, EU expansion into the former Warsaw Pact nations in the 1990s presented West European manufacturers with a veritable El Dorado market for its consumer goods. This worked to reduce West European unemployment created from the tight credit and fiscal policies of the Maastricht Agreement to create the euro. Furthermore, EU expansion has provided a bonanza for West European banks who loaded down previously debt-free East-European properties with big mortgages.[16] This provided windfall profits for banks and well-connected East European insiders. It represents a *de facto* tax, however, for common people who must then take on huge mortgages to get housing.

West Europe is looking to get another injection of economic vitality by reprising the same game of eastward expansion. The gains will not be as great with this attempted reprise. The markets east are poorer and smaller than those from the initial West Europe expansion into the former Warsaw Pact nations. Europe's eroding 'Social Model' is not for export, but its consumer goods and finance capital are. West Europe can expect in return to be on the receiving end of more social pathologies and crime from an increasingly unstable east that sees its local economy increasingly undercut by EU exports.

A better solution for Ukraine (and Russia alike) would be infrastructural investment at home, with roads being a top priority. This would require clamping down on corruption in order to reduce price gouging by well-connected insiders—easier said than done, of course. Identifying Soviet-era niche technologies (space, etc.) to develop in partnership with foreigners could also facilitate economic development. These industries represent an equity requiring decades of investment for newcomers to enter. Ukraine and CIS states generally would be wise to retain and exploit these advantages.

Ukrainians themselves (in federated regions) must decide on their best course of action. Current conditions in both Russia and Ukraine are no model to aspire to. Yet, Ukrainians will be sorely disappointed if they think partnership with the EU alone will deliver a Social European model (itself under serious attack in the West). The better option is to pursue an alternative based on local development and engagement with others from a position of autonomy. Many Ukrainians think partnership with the EU will provide a legal framework and enforcement of rules that will cleanse their economies of corruption and introduce European best practices. The reality, however, may be to lock them into neoliberal legal frameworks that diminish Ukraine's prospects for development, while flooding Ukraine with West European products and speculative bank capital. This could leave Ukrainians with uncertain employment prospects, thus reducing them to a cheap 'reserve army of labor' for West Europe. Their respective governments and economic elites have failed both Ukrainians and Russians to date. Expecting transformation to come from the EU, however, will prove disappointing and only further delay the major changes needed to transform their economies. Moreover, West European social democracies will be undermined by increased labor immigration from the east. If 'partnership' ever evolves into full EU membership, West Europeans will also find the East's rightwing politics further diluting the power of social democratic and green politics that have delivered such a high quality of life and stability in West Europe.

There was much to support in the protests of Maidan and, ironically, now much to protest against at the government emerging from Maidan. Yet, protesters should give more thought as to what alternatives will deliver the goals they strive for. Entanglement with EU free-trade areas is likely to bring about as much 'hope and change' as NAFTA did for Mexican labor and the election of Barack Obama did for progressives in the US.

Meanwhile, the EU seems bent on reprising its earlier eastward expansion of recent decades into the former Warsaw Pact to reap a windfall in exports of consumer goods. This helped alleviate the unemployment in West Europe resulting from the Maastricht Treaty's neoliberal fiscal and monetary austerity to create Eurozone's currency union. Yet, Ukraine's purchasing potential is much lower than that of the countries that bordered Germany and were integrated into EU markets with heavy European subsidy. No Euro-export boom is likely to occur with any likely proposed association agreement. About the only thing the EU can achieve is to ensure a strong enough austerity program gets implemented so that the holders of Ukrainian bonds get paid. Instead, the possible damage to Ukrainian markets from poorly executed trade liberalization and possible non-visa regimes may flood the EU with cheap labor.

Ukrainians looking to the EU as their savior have lost their sense of timing. They are seeing the last vestiges of a social model that has been sacrificed on the altar of neoliberalism. Yanukovych had been urged to raise the VAT, tax labor, and cut subsidies to energy and health. He resisted this in order to prevent earlier popular unrest, but got overthrown regardless. Now that Ukraine promises to move under Western neoliberal tutelage, the first policies that one can expect are higher taxes on labor and consumers—and an accelerated capital flight out of the country to Switzerland and to the eurozone (e.g., offshore banks in London and Riga).

Tymoshenko, Yushenko, et al. were all kleptocrats that neoliberals at points promised would enrich the post-Soviet states. The corrupt Yanukovych only really became the enemy when he committed the unforgivable sin of refusing to implement a EU/US-counseled austerity program. The aim of the EU and US is to transfer public wealth into the hands of private individuals who will be steered by the 'invisible hand' (presumably the hand behind the 'color revolutions') to seek their gains by selling what they have taken to Western investors. Finance is the new mode of warfare, as Michael Hudson has noted. We are seeing a grab for what military invasions in times past aimed at: land, natural resources and infrastructure monopolies.[17]

Prior to Yanukovych's overthrow, there was talk of a 'reset' as the United States and Russia seemed to be moving toward a mutual accommodation. His departure from the scene at first placed the United States and the EU back in a position of influence and emboldened hardline Eurasionists in the State Department. Meanwhile, the reappearance of Yulia Tymoshenko (who regained some stature in jail) represents the return of ethnic Ukrainian oligarchs. It is clear, however, as stated previously, the US prefers Arseniy Yatsenyuk as its neoliberal reformer. Yet, the blustery gusts blowing into the sails of US neconservatives and neoliberals with Maidan were quickly turned to doldrums by the Crimean secession from Ukraine and the protest movements in the industrial east, such as the proclaimed Donetsk People's Republic. As of April 2014 nothing is clear other than the days of the US's nearly unrestricted free hand on Russia's border are over.

Prospects

There is no greater source of 'shipwrecks' than the exercise of forecasting, ever thwarted by the introduction of new variables. What can appear a focused image of the future can quickly turn into a kaleidoscope as unforeseen events are introduced. That said, from the perspective of mid April 2014, we can hazard a guess at prospects and stretch to envision possibilities. The most interesting prospect would be if the Geneva Accords Agreement of April holds and a highly autonomous southeastern (and possible southern generally) region of Ukraine is recognized by the Maidan government in Kiev. At present this is being held up by a difference in opinion of the stakeholders regarding the meaning of those accords. For the Maidan government the accords mean more autonomy for regions in Ukraine, following protestors stepping down from occupying government buildings. For the protestors it means the Maidan government must also stop occupying government buildings in Kiev before a new accord can be reached. Resolution of that impasse will dictate the future course of events. Unfortunately, the Easter shootings of Donetsk protesters (Kiev claims Russians staged it, Donetsk protesters reject this view), to say the least, complicated matters.[18]

More interesting still, although less likely, is the chance of something like a national development model in east Ukraine that finally throws off the millstone of post-Soviet globalization and neoliberalism, and utilizes its inherited industrial infrastructure to develop. This could unfold something like Japan's development after WW II, where for geopolitical reasons the US extended it an 'invitation to develop' as Immanuel Wallerstein has termed it, but this time with Russia doing so to East Ukraine through extending preferential trading agreements and subsidies.

There is little likelihood of national economic development without new leadership in Ukraine. The aim of policymakers since 1991 has been to empty out the nation's resources, not create wealth. Structural adjustment (one of many euphemisms for austerity) will continue loading down Ukraine with debt, using it as a lever to control its economic policy. Meanwhile, Russia offers debt relief (or at least more loans) without development, because it too still partially remains under the thrall of neoliberalism. Until Russia fully rejects neoliberalism there will be no advance in either Ukraine or Russia. For Russia (and parts of Ukraine) to succeed it must pursue a national development model. Liberal critics will falsely decry this as a return to Soviet autarky, but to be successful it must be more like the past national development models in East Asia and West Europe, albeit with Russian characteristics.

Russia and Ukraine would benefit from an alternative economic policy based on regional capital investment in economic development. Both countries need to halt capital flight of their oligarchs to offshore banking sites in places such as London and Riga, and instead mobilize their natural resources, real estate and monopoly rents for domestic investment. Such moves would be denounced by the epicenters of "tax dumping" (London and New York). The IMF and the European Central Bank moved in and replaced the Soviet era Central Planners (GOSPLAN), but they only emptied their periphery of capital, rather than creating it. While these institutions have gotten much better than their mercenary days of the late 20th century, they have come nowhere near close to envisioning promotion of economic models based on the national economic development policies that created the world's rich countries.

Of course, the worst outcome would be a provocation or error that brings Russia and the United States into direct military conflict. A few hawks in the US saber rattle for military action. There are also the usual suspects from the former Warsaw Pact and Baltic states looking to settle scores even at the cost of action that might lead to a global nuclear holocaust. Fortunately, those voices are minorities even within their own countries. Moreover, most, even in the US Republican Party, have resisted the call for military action. Escalation into mutually assured destruction is unlikely, but given the possibility of even remote prospects materializing, highly disconcerting nonetheless, given what would be its result. The Baltics, given their small size and past forced incorporation into the USSR on the eve of WW II, are the most sensitive to assertive moves by Russia. Russia would be well served to ignore noisier Russophobe voices from that quarter, while also muting its own chauvinist choir. Russia would benefit by patiently engaging the Baltic states as partners, with all parties benefiting from increased cooperation, yet non-interference in each other's affairs. In short, a call for 'Finlandization,' if that is indeed Russia's sincere wish.

The other is for Ukraine's Russian dominated areas to be annexed, Crimea style. This outcome is possible, but less likely given that the concentration of Russian speakers in the region is less than exists in Crimea. Moreover, it may be that it was Crimea that 'annexed' Russia, and not vice versa.[19] Crimea's quick request for annexation seemed to catch Russia by surprise, albeit somewhat of a pleasant one from Russia's perspective, which was obviously on the ground with their special forces, despite their denials. Nonetheless, this annexation will cost Russia hundreds of billions of rubles to absorb in infrastructure costs (bridges, energy grids, social costs, etc.). It's unclear if Russia wishes to take another meal before digesting the large one still on its plate. More likely it prefers the federation of autonomous republics within Ukraine as an approach that serves its interests.

Another possibility is for the new Ukrainian government to assert full control over the south and east. Given events of April 2014, and what is clearly a popular rising from below (whatever outside influences might also be at work), it would prove difficult to impose control from Kiev over the entire southeast, either with or without a bloodbath. Moreover, early attempts at doing so in Donetsk proved embarrassing to Ukraine's government, when Donetsk protesters on April 6, 2014 captured six Ukrainian armored troop carriers, and saw Ukrainian troops 'defect' with protestors doing 'donuts' in their newly captured vehicles.[20] Moreover, the Maidan government's attempts at propaganda proved awkward and amateurish. At one point, rather ridiculously, the Maidan government claimed they intended their armored vehicles to get captured. Then, the Maidan government (or forces allied with them) attempted to smear the protesters by spreading anti-Semitic fliers and claiming they came from the Donetsk People's Republic.[21] Presumably, this was done to counter the public relations damage done by the very real (although exaggerated in scope by Russia) anti-Semitic extremism from *Pravy Sektor* and less so from *Svboda* of the Maidan.

Back to the most likely scenarios of an autonomous region within Ukraine. Such a region would be sandwiched between what are among the two most corrupt industrialized countries in the world: Ukraine & Russia. Smaller countries, or in this case autonomous regions, are more responsive to their citizens. People in power are more readily known to the people, and the people more readily known to their political leadership. Smaller industrialized countries have a history of more frequently forming national developmental states and sometimes social democracies. One in Ukraine made up of Russians speakers would be about the size of Sweden. Yet, other small post-Soviet states, such as Latvia, have been notorious centers of corruption, although less so than Russia in terms of its average citizen engagement with its governmental bureaucracies. That said, such an autonomous zone in Ukraine, unlike Latvia, is highly industrialized and would likely enjoy energy subsidies from Russia, thus helping to retain and perhaps grow that industry. This would be in contrast to a small post-Soviet state like Latvia, which rapidly de-industrialized and relied on transit (ports and rail) and offshore banking (both notoriously corrupt) to sustain its economy. Thus, perhaps a transition to local autonomy and real capital formation could occur from Donetsk People's Republic type movements across Ukraine's south and east.

The gravitational pull of corruption from all sides would be strong, but perhaps the workers and middle class recently engaged in a struggle for greater independence could create a national developmental state within Ukraine in which corruption was secondary to economic development. This could reprise the successes of national developmental states that existed in the century before the global crisis of accumulation of the 1970s and the neoliberalizing financialization and globalizing currents that followed. Those developmental states were forged under the pressures of external threats and national awakenings. It just may be that those forces have been unleashed again in the foundries of Ukraine's industrial south and east. Perhaps a new morning has indeed arrived? Alternatively, the seeming demise of the Geneva Agreement resulting from the violence observed in episodes such as the Odessa Massacre of May 2, 2104, threaten instability, terror and even war.

ENDNOTES

1   The Crimean Khanate being an archaic remnant of Turkish vassal states to the Mongol and later Ottoman Empire, of which Crimea ran the white slave trade. This extracted some 2 million people up through to the mid 18th century from what are today Ukraine and its bordering countries for sale to the Ottomans for use as galley and sex slaves.
2   Recalling that Yugoslavia was not part of the Soviet bloc.
3   David Kotz, with Fred Weir, *Revolution from Above: The Demise of the Soviet System* (London: Routledge Press, 1997; 2013).
4   Uwe Klussmann, Matthias Schepp and Klaus Wiegrefe, "NATO's Eastward Expansion: Did the West Break Its Promise to Moscow?" *Der Speigel*, Nov. 26, 2009, <http://www.spiegel.de/international/world/nato-s-eastward-expansion-did-the-west-break-its-promise-to-moscow-a-663315-2.html>.
5   For examples of 'left' participation in Maidan see interview with Volodymyr Ishchenko, deputy director of the Center for Society Research in Kiev from the International Journal of Socialist Renewal at: <http://links.org.au/node/3748>.
6   Peter Gowan, *The Global Gamble*, (London: Verso Press, 1999), 189-99.
7   Zbiginiew Brzezinski, *The Grand Chessboard: American Primacy And Its Geostrategic*

8   *Imperatives*, (New York: Basic Books), 1997.
8   Arno J. Mayer, "The Ukraine Imbroglio And The Decline Of The American Empire," *CounterPunch,* April 18-20, 2014, <http://www.counterpunch.org/2014/04/18/the-ukraine-imbroglio-and-the-decline-of-the-american-empire/>.
9   Anthony Faioloa, "Germans displeased by Victoria Nuland gaffe," *Washington Post,* <http://www.washingtonpost.com/world/germans-not-amused-by-nuland-gaffe/2014/02/07/66885a02-900d-11e3-878e-d76656564a01_story.html>.
10   Gavin Hewitt, "Victoria Nuland gaffe: Angela Merkel condemns EU insult," BBC News, February 7, 2014, <http://www.bbc.com/news/world-europe-26080715>.
11   For as summary of Dugin's 'Eurasianist' ideas rooted in his 'Fourth Political Theory,' see: <http://www.4pt.su/en/content/fourth-political-theory>.
12   Radhika Desai, *Geopolitical Economy: After US Hegemony, Globalization and Empire,* (London: Pluto Press, 2013 Kindle Edition). Kindle Locations 726-730.
13   David Harvey, *The New Imperialism* (Oxford: Oxford University Press, 2003), 43-4.
14   Jeffrey Sachs, "A New Post-Soviet Playbook: Why the West Should Tread Carefully in Ukraine," *Foreign Affairs*, March 4, 2014, <http://www.foreignaffairs.com/articles/140999/jeffrey-sachs/a-new-post-soviet-playbook>.
15   Baltic Course, "Putin answered journalists' questions on the situation in Ukraine," March 4, 2014, <http://www.baltic-course.com/eng/direct_speech/?doc=88562>.
16   Michael Hudson and Jeffrey Sommers, "Latvia's Road to Serfdom," *CounterPunch*, February 15, 2010, <http://www.counterpunch.org/2010/02/15/latvia-s-road-to-serfdom/>.
17   Jeffrey Sommers and Michael Hudson, "Russia, Crimea and the Consequences of NATO Policy: Ukrainian Hangovers," *CounterPunch*, March 14, 2014, <http://www.counterpunch.org/2014/03/03/ukrainian-hangovers/>.
18   Staff, "Russia accuses of Violating Geneva peace deal," *The Guardian*, April 21, 2014, <http://www.theguardian.com/world/2014/apr/21/russia-accuses-ukraine-violating-geneva-peace-deal>.
19   Boris Kagarlitsky, "Crimea Annexes Russia," *International Journal of Socialist Renewal*, March 24, 2014, <http://links.org.au/node/3790>.
20   "Ukraine Confirms Pro-Russians Seized Armored Vehicles," *Voice of America*, April 16, 2014, <http://www.voanews.com/content/putin-ukraine-at-brink-of-civil-war/1894430.html>
21   Alec Luhn, "Antisemitic flyer 'by Donetsk People's Republic' in Ukraine a hoax," *The Guardian*, April 18, 2014, <http://www.theguardian.com/world/2014/apr/18/antisemitic-donetsk-peoples-republic-ukraine-hoax>

THE LABYRINTH OF GEOGRAPHY IN A TIME OF IMPERIAL TERROR

MATTHEW WITT

Introduction: Consensus by Proclamation

Nineteen-eight-nine was a momentous year. The most storied symbol of the 70 Years War between the USSR and the United States—the Berlin Wall—came down that year. The exuberance and ebullience, the sense of openness that event occasioned is hard to gainsay even a quarter century later. Anything seemed possible.

In November of that year, while rubble from the Wall made its way to collectors across the globe, another enclosure was taking shape; emerging from an otherwise obscure Washington, D.C. think tank, a list of policy prescriptions ostensibly tailored to Latin America—but with clear implications for debt-ridden developing nations and "transition economies", particularly within orbit of former Soviet control—proposed what today passes for "austerity programs" directed at "under-performing" economies lured by the European Union, of which Ukraine is the latest flashpoint.

Dubbed by its author, economist John Williamson (fellow at the Institute for International Economics), "The Washington Consensus"[1] (WC), this set of policy presumptions quickly garnered gospel-like adherence across Washington policy echo-chambers.

Years later, its author demurred he ever intended to announce any kind of "manifesto" or "policy prescription", much less a fait accompli for muting dissent against one-best-way economics for an increasingly debt-ridden Global South.[2]

At the time he drafted the Consensus, the author considered its espoused postulates a "lowest common denominator" of agreed-to principles, "the common core of wisdom embraced by all serious economists".

Serious economists in this case he opposed to "cranks". Published a few years later in the journal *World Development*, the author's claims were anything but demure: "The proof may not be quite as conclusive as the proof that the world is not flat, but it is sufficiently well established as to give sensible people better things to do with their time than to challenge its veracity."[3]

Announcing intellectual formalisms simultaneously as consensus and unassailable wisdom is the luxury of think tank fellows that rank and file academics like me, subject to blind peer review, are not entitled to.

Williamson and his posse of economic Brahmins denounced those who dissented from the Consensus, claiming they were "politicizing" what ought (in their view) to be considered "a technocratic policy agenda". Writing in 2004, William Tabb put the counterpoint to Williamson's orthodoxy concisely, restoring the relevance of geopolitics to the posturing of Consensunistas:

> A globalization framework can explain the failure of the Washington Consensus by stressing the unacceptability of its central premise: that economic and social trends within a country were explainable in terms exclusively of the government's failure rather than power relations in the larger global political economy which constrained its options and was once again controlling its destiny.[4]

Nowhere examined dispassionately among the channels of the Consensunistas was evidence for the downsides of the medicine they called for, including: privatization of mineral rights and publicly held assets, including utilities and transit; dramatic cutback in state income supports and pensions; tax cuts to curb expenditures for redistribution; wage freezing on pretext of inflation control; dramatic deregulation of finance and industry keyed particularly to permitting foreign direct investment through free-floating currency exchange rates.

These and related measures assured that what was unassailable fact/wisdom in Washington would redraw the asset maps of the world by virtue of the repetitive incantation of "consensus" among the leading clearinghouse agencies of the International Financial Institutions (IFIs).

In this instance, "consensus" does semantic double-duty, simultaneously pronouncing policy piety while denouncing schooled skepticism, signaling like a weathervane to Beltway denizens the prevailing wind in Washington.

Noteworthy, also, is the bi-partisan, above-the-fray, anti-ideological pretensions of a "consensus" rung like a note of destiny rising above the din of egotistical divisions littering the most solipsistic geography on the planet.

The Consensus bore remarkable similarity to the economic "Shock Therapy" (rapid fire, synchronous reform from statist to monetarized governing and financial institutions shuttled under pretext of "crises"5) that the Chicago School of Economics had been advocating since the 1960s under intellectual imprimatur of arch-free-marketeer Friedrich von Hayek and his disciple, Milton Friedman. Hayek's 1946 manifesto, "Road to Serfdom", was an intellectualized mantra against centralized economic planning of any form, no matter how otherwise judicious such planning might be as a contingent response to economic instability and domestic vulnerability to powerful trading partners, as with the "development economics" adopted by vanguard of emerging economies of the Global South after WWII (and the United States in its infancy at turn of 19th Century).

During the post-War period, International Financial Institutions like the World Bank and the International Monetary Fund fully supported statist approaches to global development policy—intending thereby to head off genuinely independent regional powers and suppress trade unionism— adopting modest protectionism like tariffs to stimulate the substitution of costly imports with home-grown product innovations and mechanisms for curbing excessive inflation so long as the states in question adhered strictly to their subordinate, client state Cold War status.

With the collapse of the Soviet Union, these modest Keynesian approaches—under attack for decades by hard line monetarist orthodoxies like that advocated by the Chicago School—became increasingly vulnerable to intellectual gainsaying, culminating with the formalisms of the WC.

By the early 1990s, with the Soviet Union marginalized as military threat, the power and stature garnered by dependable strong men regimes across the Global South during the Cold War was deemed an unstable arrangement for the "Grand Chess Board" that sprawled across the Eurasian continent, where Washington-ensconced Cold Warrior policy wonks like Zbigniew Brzezinski (progeny of Mackinder's "World-Island and the Heartland" theory[6]) imagined the 21st Century showdown for global supremacy.

With its split ethnic allegiances, vast borderline with Russia and geo-strategic positioning, Ukraine plays a critical role in the grand visions of orthodox power players in Washington, viewed by them like an unstable molecule prone to the attractor forces of charged particles.

These aren't just files on a chessboard, grand or otherwise; they are like electromagnetic vortices, warping space and time; governed by formulaic prophecies like "the world is flat" and "the clash of civilizations", where otherwise "strange attractors" gather and propagate.

"Yats is the guy"

In late November, 2013, then Ukrainian President Viktor Yanukovych refused to sign an EU agreement forged at a trade summit in Lithuania to normalize trade relations and establish the policy framework for the incorporation of Ukraine into the EU.

Yanukovych hedged his refusal as stemming on the one hand from wariness of the EU austerity measures that would come with the agreement, on the other hand on pressure by Russia, adding that the offer of subsidy by the European Central Bank (ECB) was insufficient for gearing Ukraine's economy to EU standards.

Soon it materialized that Vladimir Putin was offering to Ukraine $15bn and discounted natural gas supplies.

Yanukovych's recalcitrance before the lords of European finance was duly noted, eliciting swift "unrest". Opposition was headed by leader of the All-Ukrainian Union "Fatherland" political party Batkivshchyna, Yulia Tymoshenko (gas industry magnate and close second in 2010 presidential run-off, claimed as among the world's most powerful women by *Forbes Magazine* in 2005), and Arseniy Yatsenyuk, lieutenant of Batkivshchyna and staunch supporter of EU austerity measures, who would be anointed with substantial pressure from Washington as interim Prime Minister (under protest by Russia and Venezuela).

With others, Tymoshenko and Yatsenyuk summoned large-scale protests in late November 2013 to commence in Independence Square, ground zero of the 2004 Orange Revolution over the disputed election between Yanukovych and Viktor Yushchenko, formerly Ukrainian central banker and briefly prime minister.

Yushchenko survived an assassination attempt in 2004 involving poisoning by a dioxin ingredient of Agent Orange – one indication of the high stakes playing out on this file of the Grand Chess Board and the symbolic pertinence of Independence Square (so named in 1991 after formal independence from the USSR).

United States Assistant Secretary of State for European and Eurasian Affairs, Victoria Nuland (wife of prominent neoconservative apostle Robert Kagan, sister-in-law of Frederick Kagan, adviser to CIA and Defense brass Robert Gates and David Petraeus), played a prominent role in the not-so-civil unrest since December 2013, including appearance under the banner of

Chevron at the National Press Club, proclaiming the billions given to Ukraine since 1991 for its "democratization"; and also passing out cookies to anti-government demonstrators in Independence Square, which featured at the time a backdrop of hoisted banners honoring Stepan Bandera, Ukrainian nationalist and collaborator with German Nazis during WWII in the militia roundup and mass murder of Jews and Poles.

Meanwhile, the National Endowment for Democracy (NED) (a clearinghouse set up by Ronald Reagan for psychological warfare and propaganda) claims scores of currently sponsored projects inside Ukraine. Putatively keyed to "protecting civil society" and promoting democracy and human rights, NED is believed to have staged neo-Nazi elements ideologically kindred to Bandera's legacy.[7]

Following Yanukovych's consent to speed up the 2014 elections and ordering police to stand down from crowd control of Kiev protests, neo-Nazi storm-troopers occupied government buildings, forcing Yanukovych and his aides out of the capital and country. From the vantage point of spycraft and espionage, the coincidence of these moves is noteworthy.

Was Nuland's demonstrably unstateswoman-like, partisan gesture—hyperbolically associated by her with encouraging "democracy"—at Independence Square in fact intended to signal an all-clear seized by Bandera's progeny of fascist storm-troopers?

For in fact: the neo-Nazis then proceeded to terrorize Ukrainian parliament members (who were otherwise democratically elected) into passing neo-liberalized laws geared, particularly, to punishing the Russian faithful among Ukraine's eastern and southern regions. Installed Prime Minister Arseniy Yatsenyuk subsequently signed the EU Trade Pact sought after by Washington.

From the notorious intercepted phone call from Nuland to U.S. Ambassador to Ukraine Geoffrey Pyatt, we know her choice for interim Prime Minister. "Yats [Arseniy Yatsenyuk] is the guy. He's got the economic experience, the governing experience. He's the guy you know".[8] During the conversation, Nuland indicated that Oleh Tyahnybok, representative of fascist-nationalist party Svoboda, otherwise under consideration for interim government post, might be a "problem" because of his party affiliation, but someone whom the State Department could nonetheless work with. As summarized by *Nation* correspondent Bob Dreyfuss:

> After noting that Ban Ki-moon of the United Nations and a UN envoy will be weighing in, Nuland expresses her disdain for the European Union (EU), which has been taking the lead on trying to bribe, cajole and persuade Ukraine to drop its dependence on Russia and start the process of

joining the EU. Although the United States has officially said that the EU ought to be out front, in Washington—and in Nuland's office—there is frustration over the fact that the EU won't move faster and more aggressively to undercut Russia. "F..k the EU!" says Nuland. Pyatt replies, rather hilariously, "No, exactly."[9]

In the Labyrinth of Consensus

Beginning in the mid-1990s, considerable academic debate ensued about to what extent the Washington Consensus (WC) was symbolic policy-speak actually intended to deliver Trojan Horse reforms across the globe favorable to the centralized financing interest of the IFIs. Nobel Prize Laureate Joseph Stiglitz has been leading figure of dissent from the WC, pointing to its demonstrable failures where its policy prescriptions have been applied across the globe as compared with successes where it has been resisted.

Stiglitz calls attention, in particular, to the claim among Consensunistas that government controls—particularly the import substitution model for development economics—were to blame for faltering economies in Latin America. According to consensus among dissenting economists, the rate of economic growth in those countries was double in the 1960s-70s what it was after the shock therapy imposed in the 1980s-90s. Debt crisis imposed by the IFIs was the cause of economic stagnation, Stiglitz argues. What successes accrued to shock therapy were short-lived, followed by dramatically worsening conditions as open capital markets exposed these regions to the dramatic financial volatility pre-staging the global financial crisis of 1997-1998.[10]

Counter claimants insist that the WC has been mistakenly conflated with policy prescriptions adhered to by Shock Therapy and neoliberalism,[11] leading to confusion about the origins, usefulness and intellectual probity of the WC.

The academic journal *Comparative Economic Studies* published in 2007 a piece (entitled, "Was Shock Therapy Consistent with the Washington Consensus?") sifting the policy orientations of the WC, comparing those with Shock Therapy and neoliberalism. Author John Marangos of Colorado State University concluded from his analysis that, while sharing some similarities, the WC "proper" differed in key areas with Shock Therapy and neoliberal principles.

Noteworthy, however, is Marangos' typological approach, splitting hairs where braiding them would be more revealing, abiding by an academic tactic of exaggerating distinctions between categories while downplaying the limited range of real difference across categories. Except for disagreement over utilizing foreign aid to finance budget deficits and how much to control labor markets, the author found overall "consistency" across the platforms of the WC, Shock Therapy, and the Neoliberal manifesto derived interpretation of the WC. Unspun and translated, the WC is for all intents and purposes every bit what its critics consider it to be: a blueprint for IFI domination of "transition economies".

The media drumbeat for U.S. military action in Ukraine limns contours of consensus that hew closely to IFI economic interests. At the National Press Club on December 13, 2013, Assistant Secretary of State Nuland announced that the U.S. had spent $5bn since 1991 "in the development of democratic institutions and skills in promoting civil society and a good form of government", emphasizing how much this effort has been keyed with a European future for Ukraine.

Five billion USD is a lot to spread around over 20 years in small grants for organizations with titles like "Center for Humane Technologies", "Association of Ukrainian Law Enforcement Monitors", "Center for Progressive Young People", and "Center for the Study of Social Processes and Humanitarian Issues".

Meanwhile, it's difficult to square Nuland's paeans to civil society with her curt dismissal early in February 2014 of the EU's measured deference to ousted President Yanukovych's hesitations about trade agreements. Again for the record: "F..k the EU!", said the U.S. Assistant Secretary of State for European and Eurasian Affairs in early February 2014.

In point of fact, "civil society" is a euphemism; a syntactic maneuver for covert operations requiring funneling of Treasury monies through CIA pay-out organizations (by "law" beyond the glare of Congressional oversight) that fund NED and kindred clearinghouses like National Democratic Institute for International Affairs, Freedom House, Millennium Challenge Corporation, International Center for Journalists, the Center for International Private Enterprise, and U.S. Agency for International Development (USAID), among scores of others.[12]

Seeding "civil society" organizations geared to an agitprop script requires, among other tactics, marginalizing or jeopardizing genuinely intentioned organizations (often initiating blowback against them) while simultaneously supplying radicalized opposition through black market depots with small arms and insurgent tactical training and support. At some point, apparatchiks like Nuland then take the podium to plea that "civil society" is being suppressed by tyrant regimes, applying a formula for "unrest" that is tried and true.

Informed reading of the Ukraine crisis finds that Nuland's position is consistent with the hyper aggressiveness of neoconservative posturing over Ukraine intermittently since the 1990s. Robert Parry[13] writes recently:

> The madness of the neocons has long been indicated by their extraordinary arrogance and their contempt for other nations' interests. They assume that U.S. military might and other coercive means must be brought to bear on any nation that doesn't bow before U.S. ultimatums or that resists U.S.-orchestrated coups.
>
> Whenever the neocons meet resistance, they don't rethink their strategy; they simply take it to the next level. Angered by Russia's role in heading off U.S. military attacks against Syria and Iran, the neocons escalated their geopolitical conflict by taking it to Russia's own border, by egging on the violent ouster of Ukraine's elected president.[14]

Parry calls out the *Washington Post*, in particular, as a reliable organ for neoconservative warmongering. But the syndication of CIA sponsored journalism has been well understood and documented for decades. For that matter, what isn't otherwise proclaimed in editorials is positioned through syndicated Op-Ed pieces staging mouthpieces that dependably hew to the approved "consensus".

What remains to be seen is to what extent Obama may actually be hostage to the neocon junta among State Department ranks. Parry continues:

> Obama's unorthodox foreign policy—essentially working in tandem with the Russian president and sometimes at odds with his own foreign policy bureaucracy—has forced Obama into faux outrage when he's faced with some perceived affront from Russia, such as its agreement to give temporary asylum to National Security Agency whistleblower Edward Snowden.
>
> For the record, Obama had to express strong disapproval of Snowden's asylum, though in many ways Putin was doing Obama a favor by sparing Obama from having to prosecute Snowden with the attendant complications for U.S. national security and the damaging political repercussions from Obama's liberal base.[15]

Besides Putin and the Snowden affair, Obama upended his Secretary of State, John Kerry, by announcing he would seek Congressional authorization while working out with Putin to defuse the Syrian crisis after Kerry's August 30, 2013 speech all but declaring war. This may have been indicative of deep divisions within Obama's Cabinet, or that other Chessboard divisions are in the mix.

Obama's 2008 victory was quickly followed by news reports touting his "team or rivals" strategy for cabinet level appointments that, as it turned out, included many top neocon officials from the Bush administration. Some (as with Robert Gates in his memoir, *Duty*) claim Obama was always wary of the aggressive posture of these neocon stalwarts, forcing him to draw a tightening circle around himself of trusted, seasoned wonks huddled around the preeminent democratic launderer of WC orthodoxy, Vice President Joe Biden.

Obama's touted claims for wishing to forge a team from "rivals" would seem more genuine if his rivals really differed substantially over U.S. foreign policy objectives. More likely, the tactic was intended to imply foreign policy dynamism where in fact there was overwhelming orthodoxy and to confer prestige transference from Abraham Lincoln to the United States' first "black" president (whose parentage is every bit as much "white" as it is "black", not to mention CIA affiliated[16]).

Meanwhile, major gas line installations carry Russian natural gas and oil to European markets, primary of which is Germany, for which democracy in Ukraine is entirely irrelevant if not a troublesome impediment.

Yats, indeed, is the "guy you know" for managing the flow from Russia of its energy exports, including 76% of its natural gas for Europe, which receives 15% of this flow through Ukraine. By contrast, Putin is "not our guy" for the kind of nationalism NED President Carl Gershman finds so distasteful but does not name in his Op-Ed piece in the *Washington Post* September 26, 2013: jailing billionaire oil oligarch Mikhail Khodorkovsky for maneuvering the sale of Yukos oil to Exxon in 2003. That kind of nationalism just won't do.

What's needed is IMF-styled nationalism, as with the recently announced plans by Ukraine's Washington-installed finance ministry to cut pensions by 50% in order to pay off Western bankers for their generous loans.

Beyond the Grand Chess Board proper, shale fracking now unleashed in the continental U.S. has profound Grand Chess Board implications as Washington faithful energy companies are poised to re-position the United States as lead energy exporter in the very near future.[17]

Chevron joins the usual suspects with clear and present motivations to hem in Russia's primary export, particularly now that China could replace Europe as leading importer of Russia's natural gas reserves. Under that scenario, alignment among the BRIC (Brazil, Russia, India, China) confederation would strengthen, further threatening an increasingly imperiled petro-dollar.[18]

If Ukrainian "nationalist" threats to blow up Russian gas lines leads to an "incident",[19] U.S. gas interests stand for a massive windfall in the short term, as a chilly Europe seeks its gas supplies elsewhere next winter. With these factors in perspective, it would seem the Grande Gambit being waged in Ukraine has more than the usual Consensus in mind.

If the petro-dollar teeters as precipitously as some observers believe, the dire threat everywhere will be if the impetuousness of Imperial Washington to throw over the chess board in favor of a "grand reset" at some point gains momentum in spite of any spoken consensus.

ENDNOTES

1. Paper title (presented at conference in November, 1989) was "What does Washington Mean by Policy Reform?" By "Washington", the author identified an interlocking set of key institutions and players, including: The International Monetary Fund, the World Bank, the Inter-American Development Bank, the US Executive Branch, Federal Reserve, Treasury Department, key Congressional members interested in Latin America, and economic policy think tanks. Notably missing from this list are the media organs that can be relied on to normalize and popularize a Washington agenda.
2. See J. Williamson, "The Washington Consensus as Policy Prescription for Development." Institute for International Economics. Paper delivered January 13, 2004 at the World Bank.
3. See J. Williamson (1993), "Democracy and the 'Washington Consensus'", World Development, Vol. 21, No. 8, pp. 1330, 1334.
4. See William Tabb (2004), *Economic Convergence in the Age of Globalization*. New York: Columbia University Press, p. 187.
5. Shock Therapy is given diligent account by author Naomi Klein in *The Shock Doctrine: The Rise of Disaster Capitalism* (Metropolitan Books, 2007). Klein argues persuasively that economic shock doctrine as espoused by the Chicago School of Economics derives startling congruence with and likely inspiration from electro-shock therapy experimentation of the mid-20th C. intended to test for the effects of high levels of electro-shock on patient memory recovery and personality structure.
6. Credited as founder of geopolitics and geostrategy, Sir Halford John Mackinder (1861-1947) synopsized his thoughts in the formulation: "Who rules East Europe commands the Heartland; who rules the Heartland commands the World-Island; who rules the World-Island controls the world (*Democratic Ideals and Reality: A Study in the Politics of Reconstruction* (Henry Holt & Co., 1919 p. 186).
7. President of NED, Carl Gershman, published Op-ed in the Washington Post, September 26, 2013, limning a litany of abuses against "civil society" he attributes exclusively to Putin, calling in not-so-civil terms for the Russian president's ouster. In his piece, Gershman links a "rise in nationalism" in Russia "not with a restoration of Russia's imperial greatness, which would be inconceivable if Ukraine joined Europe, but with fighting corruption and addressing the severe economic and social problems of the Russian people. Russians, too, face a choice, and Putin may find himself on the losing end not just in the near abroad but within Russia itself."
8. Robert Dreyfuss, "The Not-So-Secret Ukraine Phone Call", *The Nation*, Feb. 9, 2014.
9. ibid.
10. See J.E. Stiglitz, "Is There a Post Washington Consensus Consensus?" In The Washington Consensus Reconsidered (N. Serra and J.E. Stiglitz, eds.). New York: The Initiative for Policy Dialogue Series.
11. Neoliberalism is moniker adopted by what remains of the left spectrum in political science academia for putting into geopolitical and historic context the "technocratic"

	pretentions of the Washington Consensus. See David Harvey (2005), *A Brief History of Neoliberalism*, Oxford University Press.
12	CBS journalist Mike Wallace served as host for the series, *The 20th Century with Mike Wallace*, airing in 1967. In one segment—"The CIA: Fifty Years of Spying"—Wallace examines (with startling depth and candor, given the deep state affiliation with CBS), the extent of CIA infiltration of "civil society" in the U.S., naming names, as it were, of leading and venerated NGO institutions serving pay-out (laundering) functions for CIA operations at home and abroad.
13	Robert Parry was Associated Press journalist among others who exposed the Iran-Contra scandal of the second Reagan administration. He founded Consortiumnews.com in 1995, reputedly the first investigative news magazine on the internet.
14	See Robert Parry, "What Neocons Want from Ukraine Crisis," *Consortiumnews.com*. March 2, 2014.
15	ibid.
16	See William Blum, "Barack Obama, His Mother, and the CIA", Boiling Frogs Post, July 5, 2012.
17	See Glen Ford, "US Prepares to Gas Russia into Submission," *Black Agenda Report*, March 21, 2014.
18	See Matthias Chang, "The Global Tsunami End Game: The Petro-Dollar Regime is Finished?", Global Research, April 6, 2014.
19	See The Daily Caller, "World War III: Ukrainian leader threatens to blow up Russia's gas pipelines," March 17, 2004.

CONTAINING RUSSIA

STEPHEN LENDMAN

It's longstanding US policy. In his March 18 address on Crimea, Putin was right saying: "[W]e have every reason to assume that the infamous policy of containment, led in the 18th, 19th and 20th centuries, continues today." Western nations are "constantly trying to sweep us into a corner because we have an independent position, because we maintain it, and because we call things like they are and do not engage in hypocrisy."

"Everything has its limits," he added. "[I]n Ukraine, our Western partners crossed the red line." They "act[ed] irresponsibly and unprofessionally." Putin had courage to say what needs to be heard publicly. Containing Russia is longstanding US policy. It reflects US hegemonic ambitions. It risks a potential belligerent East/West confrontation.

As early as 1917, Washington and Britain wanted the new Soviet state destroyed. Three months before WW I ended, Britain led a multi-nation force. At the time, Lloyd George was Prime Minister. Churchill was UK Minister of War and Air. Woodrow Wilson was US president.Thousands of US marines were involved. They invaded Russia. They intervened against Bolshevik forces. They remained until April 1920.

So-called "preventive war" failed. At the same time, "Red Scare" propaganda was intense. Political scientist Murray Levin called it "a nationwide anti-radical hysteria provoked by a mounting fear and anxiety that a Bolshevik revolution in America was imminent - a revolution that would change church, home, marriage, civility, and the American way of Life."

Newspapers hyped fear. Xenophobia raged. Industrial Workers of the World (IWW Wobblies) were demonized. Latter-day media scoundrels called them "radical threats to American society" inspired by "left-wing, foreign agent provocateurs." Labor strikes they led were called "crimes against society," "conspiracies against the government," and "plots to establish communism." Dozens of Wobbly members were arrested. They were convicted. They got long prison terms. The IWW was never the same again.

The infamous 1917 Espionage Act and 1918 anti-anarchist Sedition Act were enacted. Law Professor David Cole said Wilson "targeted alien radicals." "[He] deported them for their speech or associations. [He] ma[de] little effort to distinguish true threats from ideological dissidents." In 1918, the abusive Palmer raids followed. They continued into 1921. Wilson's Attorney General Mitchell Palmer ordered them. He targeted Wobbly members and other left-wing groups.

He launched J. Edgar Hoover's FBI career. It began in the Department of Justice Bureau of Investigation's newly created General Intelligence Division. In 1935, it became the FBI. A year earlier, the Special Committee on Un-American Activities was established. The House Un-American Activities Committee (HUAC) succeeded it. From the mid-1950s through the early 1970s, Hoover's infamous COINTELPRO (counterintelligence) program targeted political dissidents, alleged communists, anti-war, human and civil rights activists, American Indian Movement members, and Black Panther Party ones, among others.

In their book, *Agents of Repression*, Ward Churchill and Jim Vander Wall said: "[T]he term came to signify the whole context of clandestine (usually illegal) political repression activities..." They included "a massive surveillance [program via] wiretaps, surreptitious entries and burglaries, electronic devices, live 'tails' and bogus mail." It was done to induce paranoia. It "foster[ed] 'splits' within or between organizations." Other tactics included:

- "black propaganda" through leaflets or other publications; it was "designed to discredit organizations and foster internal tensions;"

- "disinformation or 'gray propaganda'" for the same purpose;

- "bad-jacketing" to "creat[e] suspicion—through the spread of rumors, manufacture of evidence, etc." to turn some members against others violently;

- "harassment arrests [on bogus] charges;" and

- "assassinations [of] selected political leaders."

In November 1968, J. Edgar Hoover ordered FBI agents "to exploit all avenues of creating ... dissension within the ranks of the BPP (using) imaginative hard-hitting counterintelligence measures aimed at crippling" the organization. On December 4, 1969 Chicago police murdered Black Panther leaders Fred Hampton and Mark Clark while they slept. They did so in cold blood. Hoover targeted independent voices challenging America's imperial agenda. Soviet Russia supporters were prime targets.

Post-WW II, containing Russia became official US policy. US diplomat/ambassador to Soviet Russia/presidential advisor George Kennan (1904 - 2005) was "the father of containment." He was a core member of so-called foreign policy "Wise Men." His advice inspired the Truman Doctrine. More on it below.

His 1946 "Long Telegram" from Moscow and 1947 "Sources of Soviet Conduct" claimed its government was inherently expansionist. Containing its influence in strategic areas vitally important to America had to be prioritized, he argued. Cold War policies followed. Kennan was instrumentally involved. In February 1948, his "Memo PPS23" said:

> [W]e have 50% of the world's wealth but only 6.3% of its population ... [It makes us] the object of envy and resentment. Our real task in the coming period is to devise a pattern of relationships [to let us] maintain this position of disparity without positive detriment to our national society. To do so we will have to dispense with all sentimentality and daydreaming; and our attention will have to be concentrated everywhere on our immediate national objectives.We need not deceive ourselves that we can afford today the luxury of altruism and world benefaction....
>
> ... We should dispense with the aspiration to 'be liked' or to be regarded as the repository of a high-minded international altruism ... We should [stop talking about] unreal objectives such as human rights, the raising of the living standards, and democratization.The day is not far off when we are going to have to deal in straight power concepts. The less we are hampered by idealistic slogans (ideas and practices), the better.[1]

In July 1947, his so-called "X" article headlined "The Sources of Soviet Conduct." He urged "counter[ing] it "effectively." He stressed "containment", saying: "The main element of any United States policy toward the Soviet Union must be that of a long-term, patient but firm and vigilant containment of Russian expansive tendencies."[2]

He quoted Lenin as saying:

> Unevenness of economic and political development is the inflexible law of capitalism. It follows from this that the victory of Socialism may come originally in a few capitalist countries or even in a single capitalist country. The victorious proletariat of that country, having expropriated the capitalists and having organized Socialist production at home, would rise against the remaining capitalist world, drawing to itself in the process the oppressed classes of other countries.[3]

He said Soviet power reflects

> innate antagonism between capitalism and socialism. We have seen how deeply that concept has become imbedded in foundations of Soviet power. It has profound implications for Russia's conduct as a member of international society. It means that there can never be on Moscow's side a sincere assumption of a community of aims between the Soviet Union and powers which are regarded as capitalist. It must inevitably be assumed in Moscow that the aims of the capitalist world are antagonistic to the Soviet regime, and therefore to the interests of the peoples it controls.

Antagonism remains, said Kennan. "And from it flow many of the phenomena which we find disturbing in the Kremlin's conduct of foreign policy: the secretiveness, the lack of frankness, the duplicity, the wary suspiciousness, and the basic unfriendliness of purpose." Russians will be "difficult to deal with" for a long time, he stressed.

In November 1948, NSC 4 outlined "US Objectives with Respect to the USSR to Counter Soviet Threats to US Security." NSC 7 followed. It covered "The Position of the United States With Respect to Soviet Dominated World Communism." It said: "[A] defensive policy cannot be considered an effective means of checking the momentum of Soviet expansion."

"Defeat[ing]" communism was considered "vital to the security of the United States." It argued Washington should organize and lead a "counter-offensive" aimed at undermining Soviet strength. It should "develop, and at the appropriate time carry out, a coordinated program to support underground resistance movements in countries behind the iron curtain, including the USSR."

Kennan's 1948 "Inauguration of Political Warfare"[4] explained his ideas on how to conduct it. He discussed covert and overt strategies. He included political alliances, economic policies, and encouraging underground resistance initiatives. He encouraged establishing "Liberation Committees" across Europe. He supported policies short of war.

"In the long run," he wrote in Memo PPS23,[5] "there can be only three possibilities for the future of western and central Europe. One is German domination. Another is Russian domination."

> The third is a federated Europe, into which the parts of Germany are absorbed but in which the influence of the other countries is sufficient to hold Germany in her place.
>
> If there is no real European federation and if Germany is restored as a strong and independent country, we must expect another attempt at German domination. If there is no real European federation and if Germany is not restored as a strong and independent country, we invite Russian domination, for an unorganized Western Europe cannot indefinitely oppose an organized Eastern Europe. The only reasonably hopeful possibility for avoiding one of these two evils is some form of federation in western and central Europe.

In March 1946, Churchill spoke at Fulton, MO-based Westminster College. He delivered his famous "Iron Curtain" speech. He titled it "The Sinews of Peace."[6] He helped change the way Western nations viewed communist Eastern ones. In pointed language, he said:

> Nobody knows what Soviet Russia and its communist international organization intends to do in the immediate future, or what are its limits, if any, to their expansive and proselytizing tendencies...
>
> ... From Stettin in the Baltic to Trieste in the Adriatic, an iron curtain has descended across the Continent. Behind that line lie all the capitals of the ancient states of Central and Eastern Europe.Warsaw, Berlin, Prague, Vienna, Budapest, Belgrade, Bucharest and Sofia, all these famous cities and the populations around them lie in what I must call the Soviet sphere, and all are subject in one form or another, not only to Soviet influence but to a very

high and, in many cases, increasing measure of control from Moscow.

Many analysts consider his speech the beginning of the Cold War.

In March 1947, Truman's Doctrine pledged "support [for] free peoples who are resisting attempted subjugation by armed minorities or by outside pressures." He aimed to keep Greece and Turkey from going communist. His policy applied globally. He initiated America's National Security State strategy.

Establishing NATO followed. So did policy papers like Kennan wrote. Peace didn't last long. Truman attacked North Korea. More on this below.

In April 1950, a Paul Nitze-supervised Joint State-Defense Department Committee National Security Memorandum No. 68 (NSC-68)[7] was about containing Soviet Russia. Inflammatory language called it an enemy "unlike previous aspirants to hegemony ... animated by a new fanatic faith, antithetical to our own [wishing to] impose its absolute authority over the rest of the world."

It claimed it at a time America was the only global superpower. WW II devastated Soviet Russia. Many more years were needed to regain normality. It threatened no one.

IF Stone's *Hidden History of the Korean War*[8] explains a much different account than popularly believed. In 1952, *Monthly Review* co-founders Leo Huberman and Paul Sweezy wrote in the preface: "This book...paints a very different picture of the Korean War—one, in fact, which is at variance with the official version at almost every point." Stone's investigation into official discrepancies led him "to a full-scale reassessment of the whole" war.

Publisher Claude Bourdet wrote his own article titled "The Korean Mystery: Fight Against a Phantom?", saying: "If Stone's thesis corresponds to reality, we are in the presence of the greatest swindle in the whole of military history." It's "not a question of a harmless fraud but of a terrible maneuver in which deception is being consciously utilized to block peace at a time when it is possible."

Stone called it international aggression. Huberman and Sweezy agreed. In August 1951, they said: "[W]e have come to the conclusion that [South Korean president] Syngman Rhee deliberately provoked the North Koreans in the hope that they would retaliate by crossing the parallel in force."

He did so at Truman's behest. Multiple South Korean provocations gave him pretext for war. Millions perished. Northern areas were turned to rubble. More wars followed. "The northerners," said Huberman and Sweezy, wanted Korea unified, not war. They "fell neatly into the trap." Truman took full advantage. He instigated conflict.

Stone believed it saying: "[W]e said we were going to Korea to go back to the status quo before the war, but when the American armies reached the 38th parallel they didn't stop. They kept going, so there must be something else. We must have another agenda here, and what might that agenda be?"

The same one he later learned initiated Washington's Southeast Asian war and others. Permanent war is official US policy. Containing Russia continues today. More on this below.

Post-WW II, the Marshall Plan (European Recovery Program) had little to do with so-called "huge gestures of [US] benevolence." Economist Walt Rostow helped implement the plan. He called it one part of an "offensive to strengthen the area still outside Stalin's grasp." In December 1947, then Undersecretary of State for Economic Affairs William Clayton said if aid wasn't provided, "the Iron Curtain would then move westward at least to the English Channel." While implementation was being discussed, he said America "hold[s] in [its] hands the powerful weapon of discontinuance of aid if contrary to our expectations any country fails to live up to our expectations." Economic Stabilization Bureau head Chester Bowles was candid, saying: "The real argument for the Marshall Plan is a bolstering of the American system for future years."

The plan was named for popular General George Marshall. Post-war, Truman's popularity fell sharply. Putting his name on it risked public anger enough perhaps to get congressional rejection. Marshall played the game. He pitched the plan. He delivered canned speeches. He disingenuously claimed it was to relieve "hunger, poverty, desperation, and chaos." It was about saving capitalism from communism and Stalinist influence.

Containing Russia remains official US policy. It's back to the future. The Cold War never ended. It morphed into new form. Putin is public enemy number one. He's vilified more intensively than Soviet era leaders. In 2007, during his first term as president, Foreign Minister Sergei Lavrov discussed containing Russia, saying:

> The very issue of Russia's containment appeals to instincts of the past. It not so much attests to the lack of imagination, but rather that for some individuals almost nothing has changed since the end of the Cold War. These people propose imposing the structure of international relations which took shape long ago in the Western alliance, to the present moment.The motives that dictated this policy of containment are making themselves felt at this new historical stage, as well.[9]

"What kind of Russia should be contained," he asked? "What can be the goal of 'containing Russia' today?"

> A Russia that has renounced an ideology of imperial and other 'great plans' in favor of pragmatism and common sense. How can a nation, which has placed emphasis on its domestic development and is now progressing remarkably well, be contained? Russia's consolidation through creative work has naturally been translated into the strengthening of its international positions. Russia's foreign policy is nothing more than the continuation of its domestic policy. We have realistic and understandable aspirations, namely: the maintenance of international stability as a major condition for our further development together with the natural evolution of international relations with the goal of achieving freedom and democracy.

Washington and Moscow are geopolitical opposites, he added. Therein lies what's at issue. Russia's peace and respect for national sovereignty priorities are at odds with America's imperial agenda.

Heightened tensions risk an East/West confrontation. Irresponsible US policy risks possible global war. If initiated there's no turning back. Humanity's fate hangs in the balance.

ENDNOTES

1. See <http://en.wikisource.org/wiki/Memo_PPS23_by_George_Kennan>
2. See <https://www.mtholyoke.edu/acad/intrel/coldwar/x.htm>
3. ibid
4. See <http://academic.brooklyn.cuny.edu/history/johnson/65ciafounding3.htm>
5. Note 1, supra.
6. See <https://www.winstonchurchill.org/learn/speeches/speeches-of-winston-churchill/120-the-sinews-of-peace>
7. <http://legacy.wilsoncenter.org/coldwarfiles/files/Documents/nsc68.pdf>
8. <http://ifstone.org/hidden_history.php>
9. <http://eng.globalaffairs.ru/number/n_9792>

THE UKRAINE CRISIS AND THE PROPAGANDA SYSTEM IN OVERDRIVE

EDWARD S. HERMAN
DAVID PETERSON

From late November 2013, when the "Maidan" or Independence Square protests in Ukraine's capital city of Kiev first began, through the time of writing in late April, 2014, some five months later, we have been reminded almost daily how deeply ingrained Cold War ideology remains in Western capitals and their political and intellectual culture. Cold War ideology (or the Cold War system of propaganda) is best understood as a dichotomous or binary system: One side is "good," the other side is "evil." One side acts on behalf of universal values, the other acts out of narrow self-interests. One side helps other countries and peoples to build democratic institutions and good governance, and supports the rights to self-determination, sovereignty, and territorial integrity of all countries—the other side as a matter of principle rejects these rights and strives for power and territorial expansion.

The workings of such a binary system have been on full display through April 2014. As a major and still independent non-Western power, Russia, under challenge and threat by the United States and its NATO annex, has absorbed a piece of neighboring territory (Crimea), and removed it with minimal force from the jurisdiction of its neighbor (Ukraine), whose new coup-based government seeks to align with the United States and NATO. This is completely unacceptable to the Western power bloc, and arouses threats from it, flashes of feathers, and furious indignation from its media. Thus, the crisis in Ukraine has intensified, with close media collaboration. Which is our point of departure.

Flashpoint in Ukraine: How the US Drive for Hegemony Risks World War III

1. Dichotomy and Double-Standards

The misrepresentations of the U.S. media in dealing with the Ukraine crisis have been spectacular, reaching and perhaps surpassing their performance during the 50-year-long Cold War era, with the notion of "objectivity" buried beneath a landslide of biased tone and word usage, rewritten or suppressed history, use of selective evidence, and double-standards. In a striking example of such bias, an April 16, 2014 front-page article in *The New York Times* by David M. Herszenhorn repeated every cliché one would have expected 30 or more years ago. "Moscow's state-controlled news media outlets," Herszenhorn claimed, are engaging in "bluster and hyperbole,... misinformation, exaggerations, conspiracy theories, overheated rhetoric and, occasionally, outright lies about the political crisis in the Ukraine that have emanated from the highest echelons of the Kremlin and reverberated on state-controlled Russian television, hour after hour, day after day, week after week." He conceded that "There is no question that the new Ukrainian government and its Western allies, including the United States, have engaged in their own misinformation efforts at times." But, in contrast, "television news in Russia is ... a swirling 24-hour vortex of alarmist proclamations of Western aggression, sinister claims of rising fascism and breathless accounts of imminent hostilities by the 'illegal' Ukrainian government in Kiev..."[1]

Consider Herszenhorn's sardonic reference to "the 'illegal' Ukrainian government in Kiev." But the interim government, in fact, *was* unelected, coming to power through a Western-supported and increasingly violent street uprising. Reasonable word usage would therefore justify the description of that interim government as "unelected," and even going beyond this to call it a product of a "coup." But on the double-standard or binary rule of media performance, *The New York Times* is pleased to call the coup and unelected government merely the "government in Kiev." Had this "government in Kiev" been one that Washington disliked, the *Times* would have found it difficult to recognize that government even in the wake of a free and fair election, as with Hugo Chávez and now Nicolás Maduro in Venezuela. Similarly, during the aborted coup in Venezuela in 2002, the *Times* denounced the "ruinous demagogue" and "would-be-dictator" Chávez, even as it welcomed the military's anointed and short-lived successor, Pedro Carmona.[2] Such a dichotomous pattern is deeply entrenched and applied widely, both by the *Times* and the establishment U.S. media more generally.

Herszenhorn refers to the "breathless accounts of imminent hostilities" by this "illegal" government. His use of this rhetoric is humorous given that another article in the very same issue of the

Times contradicts his doubts about "imminent hostilities." The second article, written by Andrew Kramer and also appearing on the front page, was titled "Ukraine Sends Force to Stem Unrest in East,"[3] so by the title alone, imminent hostilities were already underway.

Robert Parry points out that Herszenhorn's "bizarre story" also missed the fact that Andriy Parubiy, head of the Ukrainian National Security Council, stated on Twitter that "a Reserve unit of National Guard formed [of] Maidan self-defense volunteers was sent to the front lines this morning."[4] Parry explained that "Parubiy was referring to the neo-Nazi militias that provided the organized muscle that overthrew Yanukovych forcing him to flee for his life." So not only is Herszenhorn's "Russian propaganda" true and therefore not propaganda, but his claim, plus his suppression of the role of the Maidan "self-defense volunteers" in the east, shows his own claims to be egregious propaganda on behalf of his own side. The *Times* and establishment U.S. media in general have downplayed the role of the far-right in the street protests and coup. Herszenhorn does mention Russian TV's "sinister claims of rising fascism," again deploying a put-down word like "sinister" to cover over the fact that strongly neo-Nazi, anti-Semitic elements had been important street-fighters during the protests, and even gained significant posts in the unelected interim government. Parry adds that the *Times* does occasionally let some unpleasant truths slip in. It quoted "Right Sector leader, Roman Koval, explaining the crucial role of his organization in carrying out the anti-Yanukovych coup. 'Ukraine's February revolution, said Mr. Koval, would never have happened without Right Sector and other militant groups', the *Times* wrote." But as Parry points out, "that reality—though actually reported in the *New York Times* [by Andrew Kramer and others]—has now become 'Russian propaganda', according to the *Times*."

2. Language and Tone

As suggested by the tone and word usage of reporter David Herszenhorn, there have been no holds barred in assailing and denigrating Russia and Vladimir Putin. Putin was of course demonized in the establishment media long before the Ukraine crisis, but the crisis unleashed an escalated torrent of abuse.[5] Just looking at the editorial pages of *The New York Times* in 2014, we find that Putin is:[6]

A "Russian strongman" (Thomas Friedman, 3-2); "bare-chested muscleman" (Roger Cohen, 3-14); a "villain" (Nicholas Kristof, 3-6); "unreconstructed Russian imperialist" (John McCain, 3-15); has "malign intent" and a "plan to enlarge his empire" (Alexey Navalny, 3-20); the "leader of a rogue state" (Ian Bremer, 3-17); an "authoritarian rule[r]" (the editors, 3-19); a "bully" (the editors, 4-5) who seeks a "Great Russia" in an "outrageous and highly dangerous power-play" (the editors, 4-16); and "revels in claiming American conspiracies" (the editors, 3-5), to give but a taste of the pejorative stream.

The contrast in the paper's treatment of Barack Obama and John Kerry is dramatic: During the same period, no editorial comment used a strongly derogatory term to describe them. They are almost always referred to as "President Obama" and "Secretary of State John Kerry," with no accompanying modification. In fact, the only slightly pejorative terms that had been used, no doubt reflecting frustration at the lack of strong retaliatory action by the United States in March and April, are Maureen Dowd's two references to Obama's "weakness," Nicholas Kristof's use of the word "disappointing," and Thomas Friedman's expression of regret over the president's "reluctance" to act. The bad guy and the good guys are as clear at the *Times* as they are in comic books.[7]

This language is common elsewhere in the media. CNN's Fareed Zakaria and Christiane Amanpour, for example, offer the same kind of vitriol towards Putin. For Zakaria, Putin is "neo-imperialist" (3-2), "thuggish" (3-9), and is "terrified of a democracy movement and will brutally oppose it" (3-2). For Amanpour, Putin is "Machiavellian" (3-3), "may not be in touch with reality" (3-3), is "engaged in rebuilding the Soviet empire" (3-3), and his "intervention is based on mythology and fabrications" (4-17).

These are manifestations of an establishment U.S. media in full propaganda mode. Nor were such comic book representations confined to *The New York Times* and CNN

3. Blocking-Out Historical Context

In the tirades against Russia and the parallel and supportive news selection it is taken as a given that Russia's action in Crimea is not defensive and responsive, but is a forward and unprovoked policy that justifies its being called aggression, imperialistic, and an attempt to reconstitute the Soviet empire. Most notable is the failure to give anything but passing reference to the expansion of NATO and to the fact that, since the Berlin Wall fell in November 1989, the Soviet bloc and Warsaw Pact broke apart, the Soviet Union dissolved in late 1991, and the nonaligned Socialist Federal Republic of Yugoslavia was dismantled from 1991 through 1995, the NATO bloc has grown from 16 member-states to 28 today, including 10 former Warsaw Pact members, and three former Soviet states.[8]

NATO's absorption of these former Eastern European satellites of the Soviet Union along with the three Baltic states and the placement of ground-based anti-missile interceptors and radar systems in Poland and the

Czech Republic, respectively, have all been done in violation of verbal but clear promises made to the former Soviet premier Mikhail Gorbachev by a succession of high-level U.S. and German figures in early 1990 that "there would be no extension of NATO's jurisdiction or NATO's forces one inch to the East," in Secretary of State's James Baker's words.[9] But, as Mary Sarotte has noted, "Gorbachev did something unwise—namely, fulfilling at least some of his part of the bargain [i.e., the withdrawal of 250,000 Soviet troops from East Germany, and accepting East and West German reunification] without getting written assurances that the other side would do the same [i.e., no expansion of NATO] ... But he did not, and by the end of February, it would be apparent that he would never get them."[10] That agreement was soon violated by the West, and the West's encouragement and support of a coup regime in the Ukraine in 2014 posed a still more acute security threat to Russia.

Although this is absolutely essential context to Russian action, it was mentioned only twice on the pages of The New York Times from January through April 15, 2014, and only once by a Times writer.[11] Indeed, Putin mentions it frequently. After recounting in his March 18, 2014 address before the Russian Parliament a litany of grievances with the United States and/or NATO that included their wars against the Federal Republic of Yugoslavia (1999), Afghanistan (2001-), Iraq (2003-), and Libya (2011), "color revolutions" among former Soviet states,[12] "NATO's expansion to the east, as well as the deployment of military infrastructure at our borders," the "deployment of missile defense systems" (properly understood to be offensive weapons systems), and, now, economic sanctions, Putin explained:

> ... there is a limit to everything. And with Ukraine, our western partners have crossed the line ... After all, they were fully aware that there are millions of Russians living in Ukraine and in Crimea. They must have really lacked political instinct and common sense not to foresee all the consequences of their actions. Russia found itself in a position it could not retreat from. If you compress the spring all the way to its limit, it will snap back hard. You must always remember this.[13]

Many Western analysts also understand the score. In the United States, Jack Matlock, a U.S. ambassador to the Soviet Union from 1987 to 1991, and author of *Reagan and Gorbachev: How the Cold War Ended*,[14] wrote in the *Washington Post* that since Putin was first elected the president of Russia in 2000, Russia has received from the United States the "diplomatic equivalent of swift kicks to the groin: further expansion of NATO in the Baltics and the Balkans, and plans for American bases there; withdrawal from the Anti-Ballistic Missile Treaty; invasion of Iraq without U.N. Security Council approval; overt participation in the 'color revolutions' in Ukraine, Georgia and Kyrgyzstan; and then, probing some of the firmest red lines any Russian leader would draw, talk of taking Georgia and Ukraine into NATO."[15]

John Mearsheimer, a University of Chicago political scientist and author of several important books on foreign affairs, wrote an op-ed column "Getting Ukraine Wrong," in which he argued that "Mr. Putin's behavior is motivated by the same geopolitical considerations that influence all great powers, including the United States … The taproot of the current crisis is NATO's expansion and Washington's commitment to move Ukraine out of Moscow's orbit and integrate it into the West … [T]he United States, which has been unable to leave the Cold War behind, has treated Russia as a potential threat since the early 1990s, and ignored its protests about NATO's expansion and its objections to America's plan to build missile defense systems in Eastern Europe … One might expect American policymakers to understand Russia's concerns about Ukraine joining a hostile alliance … Mr. Putin's view is understandable."[16] But Mearsheimer's message was too strong for *The New York Times*'s editors: Although this op-ed was published in the March 14 edition of the *International New York Times*, it never made it into the U.S. print edition.

Stephen Cohen, a distinguished academic authority on Russia, has also stressed the importance of NATO's expansion and threat to Russian national security, with the Western-supported coup regime in Ukraine serving as the last straw, compelling the kind of response that Putin has engineered. Very early in the Ukraine crisis, Cohen submitted a letter to *The New York Times* that responded to one of the paper's editorials, "The Cold War Should be Over,"[17] which urged Ukraine to resist Russia's "bullying" and go with the EU proposal. In addition to making the case that NATO was the aggressor and that Russia was threatened more than threatening, Cohen noted the editorial's resort to Cold War double-standards: "'Europe's use of trade leverage … is constructive and reasonable', but when Putin uses similar carrots—financial loans, discounted energy supplies, access to markets—to persuade Ukraine to join instead his fledgling Eurasian Customs Union, those are 'attempts to bludgeon.'" But Cohen's letter to the *Times* was rejected.[18] The bias-slate was kept clean.

Barack Obama, in his March 26 speech in Brussels, slithered past all of this history. "Since the end of the Cold War," he said, "we have worked with Russia under successive administrations to build ties of culture and commerce and international community."[19] But that was all. Obama made no mention of NATO's expansion, or the threat that it poses to Russia.

In his address before the Russian parliament eight days earlier, Putin had cited the "Kosovo precedent—a precedent our western colleagues created with their own hands in a very similar situation, when they agreed that the unilateral separation of Kosovo from Serbia, exactly what Crimea is doing now, was legitimate and did not require any permission from the country's central authorities ... This is not even double standards; this is amazing, primitive, blunt cynicism. One should not try so crudely to make everything suit their interests, calling the same thing white today and black tomorrow."[20]

Obama's response to Putin on Kosovo was risible. "NATO only intervened after the people of Kosovo were systematically brutalized and killed for years," he explained. "And Kosovo only left Serbia after a referendum was organized not outside the boundaries of international law, but in careful cooperation with the United Nations and with Kosovo's neighbors. None of that even came close to happening in Crimea."[21]

In fact, in 1999, NATO waged a two-and-a-half month long war of aggression against the Federal Republic of Yugoslavia (i.e., Serbia and Montenegro), with the goals of militarily occupying Kosovo province and prying Kosovo away from the FRY, thereby finishing the job of dismantling what was still left of the former Yugoslavia. Contrary to Obama, no referendum on Kosovo's separation from the FRY was ever held.

Obama also failed to mention the concurrent military exercises by NATO around the Russian border, and the continuous arming of these adjacent states, which Putin regards as hostile behavior and "building an empire," and Obama's dismissal itself as "based on mythology and fabrications." No such criticism of Our Leader can be found in the establishment media. As noted earlier, the almost exclusive criticism of Obama is that he is "weak" on foreign policy, and that his response to the Russian advance—and virtually nowhere is it suggested that Russia is responding to the U.S. and NATO advance—is not sufficiently forceful.

4. Double-Standards in Treatment of U.S.-NATO Intervention in Ukraine

Just as the establishment media have found it impossible to consider U.S. and NATO actions in encircling Russia as the threat that drives Russian policy in the Ukraine crisis, so that media underplays Western intervention in Ukraine and overplays and distorts that of Russia. The West is portrayed as simply supporting a democratic movement trying to displace corrupt leaders. That the ousted president of Ukraine, Viktor Yanukovych, was elected in 2010 and was replaced by a coup in the wake of a wave of violence is kept largely out of sight. The word "unelected" was rarely attached to the interim Kiev rulers, and the word "coup" was used almost entirely in quotes by Russian sources. The word coup appeared a total of 40 times in *The New York Times* between November 1, 2013 and March 31, 2014, to characterize the ouster of Yanukovych. But these were always citing statements by Putin and his camp (23), Yanukovych (10) and seven others (4 attributed to Russian citizens, 2 to Russian Ukrainians, and 1 by a letter writer the *Times* published on December 11). Significantly, at no time through March 31 did a *Times* reporter, op-ed writer, or editorial characterize the events of February 21-22 as a "coup" or "putsch."[22] The ouster of Yanukovych was a *good* coup, hence, not a "coup" in the loyal media.

Yanukovych fell into serious disfavor when on November 22, 2013, his government rejected a European Union proposal for closer engagement that also included International Monetary Fund conditionalities which the government concluded were too harsh to accept; shortly thereafter, his government accepted a Russian counteroffer. Opposition parties immediately began to stage protests in Kiev as well as other western cities. From prison, Yuliya Tymoshenko issued a statement urging Ukrainians to "react to this as they would a *coup d'état*." Within 48 hours, a tent city reminiscent of the 2004 "Orange Revolution" had been established in Independence Square, and U.S. Secretary of State John Kerry cancelled a visit that had been planned for Kiev in December.[23]

The Russian deal would have given Ukraine a much larger financial contribution and subsidized gas prices, but it did not forbid Ukraine from negotiating and entering into additional agreements with the E.U. The rejected EU proposal would not only have been financially less generous, it would have foreclosed any ability of Ukraine to enter into supplementary agreements with Russia, and it would have required Ukraine to affiliate militarily with NATO. This one-sided exclusivity and military agreement were ignored by the establishment media.

So also was the fact that the day before Yanukovych's ouster on February 22, 2014, he had signed an agreement with three main opposition party leaders (Vitali Klitschko, Oley Tiahnybok, and Arsenij Yatsenyuk), and with the foreign ministers of Germany, France, and Poland supporting the agreement, that called for the restoration of the 2004 Constitution within 48 hours, a presidential election no later than December 2014, an investigation into the Independence Square violence "under joint monitoring from the authorities, the opposition and the Council of Europe," and various measures to reduce tensions, including the turning-over of "illegal weapons" to the Ministry of the Interior.[24] This agreement was signed one day after the most intense street violence that Kiev had seen, when at least 51 protesters had been shot to death in a single day. The deaths in the streets were taken by the U.S. media to be the result of an intensified government crackdown. These killings helped discredit the government, and set the stage for the

February 22 vote by the Ukrainian parliament to "remove Viktor Yanukovych from the post of president," to schedule early presidential elections for May 25, and for the takeover by the interim government, quickly recognized by the United States and its close allies.

The timing of the increased street violence and the spike in sniper killing of protesters over the February 18-20 period, followed by an E.U.-sponsored agreement that might have defused the protests and allowed a slow transition of authority, but with an unpredictable outcome, suggests that the intensified violence may have been intended to prevent that transition from taking place, and to install a new government more attuned to U.S. interests. This is what gives the intercepted phone conversation between U.S. Assistant Secretary of State for European and Eurasian Affairs, Victoria Nuland, and Geoffrey Pyatt, the U.S. ambassador to Ukraine, some weeks earlier, so much significance. On February 6, 2014, someone posted to YouTube an audio recording of their conversation under the title "Puppets of Maidan."[25] No one has ever questioned the authenticity of the recording. It reveals Nuland telling Pyatt which Ukrainian political figure the United States wants to be included in any new government ("Yats is the guy," she says, using a nickname for Arseniy Yatsenyuk as if he were one of her pets) and which ones it doesn't ("Klitsch and Tiahnybok on the outside").

Later she raised "one more wrinkle" with Pyatt. Nuland told him that she had spoken with Jeffrey Feltman, a veteran of the U.S. foreign service and, since 2012, an Under-Secretary-General for Political Affairs at the UN. "[Fletman's] now gotten both [Robert] Serry and Ban Ki-moon to agree that Serry could come in Monday or Tuesday," she says. "That would be great ... to help glue this thing [together] and to have the UN help glue it and, you know, fuck the EU." Pyatt responded enthusiastically to this U.S. strategy for out-maneuvering the EU and short-circuiting a negotiated settlement, and added that "we want to try to get somebody with an international personality to come out here and help midwife this thing." As Stephen Cohen summed-up the significance of the Nuland-Pyatt exchange: "Any doubts about the Obama administration's real intentions in Ukraine should have been dispelled by the recently revealed taped conversation between a top State Department official, Victoria Nuland, and the US ambassador in Kiev. The media predictably focused on the source of the 'leak' and on Nuland's verbal 'gaffe'—'Fuck the E.U.'. But the essential revelation was that high-level US officials were plotting to 'midwife' a new, anti-Russian Ukrainian government by ousting or neutralizing its democratically elected president—that is, carrying out a coup."[26]

In the days that followed the posting of this four-minute phone conversation to YouTube, *The New York Times* used a series of six articles to cope with the insight it provided into U.S. policy towards Ukraine, and had mentioned it another three times as of the time of writing.²⁷ Not a single one of these items expressed outrage over heavy-handed U.S. meddling in the affairs of a sovereign state; and, of course, none of them characterized the Nuland-Pyatt exchange in terms of planning a coup, or as advocacy for the man who eventually went on to become prime minister in the interim government.

The result of the violence and coup was to produce a government different from the power-sharing one the E.U. members had tried to obtain in February, but hostile towards Russia and completely in NATO's back-pocket. The interim government's prime minister turned out to be "Yats"— Arseniy Yatsenyuk, a man who received 6.96% of the popular vote in the first round of the 2010 presidential election.²⁸ Shortly thereafter, Yatsenyuk was welcomed at NATO headquarters in Brussels and then at the White House in Washington.

Also notable in this context is the intercepted phone conversation between Estonia's Minister of Foreign Affairs Urmas Paet and EU Foreign Policy and Security Policy chief, Catherine Ashton. As with the Nuland-Pyatt exchange, someone posted an audio recording of their leaked conversation to YouTube. In one stunning revelation, Paet told Ashton ("Olga" refers to Olga Bogomolets, a physician who had treated protesters shot by snipers during the peak of violence February 18-20, and who joined the interim government after the coup): "[W]hat was quite disturbing, the same Olga told that, well, all the evidence shows that people who were killed by snipers, from both sides, among policemen and then people from the streets, that they were the same snipers, killing people from both sides ... [S]he also showed me some photos, she said that as medical doctor, she can say that it's the same hand-writing, the same type of bullets, and it's really disturbing that now the new coalition, that they don't want to investigate what exactly happened. So that there is now stronger and stronger understanding that behind snipers, it was not Yanukovych, but it was somebody from the new coalition."²⁹

> At this time of writing in late April 2014, *The New York Times* had not mentioned the Paet-Ashton exchange even once. In fact, according to a search of the NewsBank database, this exchange had been reported in the United States only 28 times.³⁰ We regard this as a stunning example not only of non-coverage of an important revelation (the truth of which requires verification, of course)—but of suppression of a disturbing story that simply cannot be reconciled with the dominant Western narrative on the Ukraine, and can

only be coped with through silence. *The New York Times* and establishment U.S. media had risen to the challenge.

5. Double-Standards in Treatment of Western and Eastern Ukraine Protesters

Although the anti-Yanukovich protesters included important rightwing factions (Svoboda, the Right-Sector, the Congress of Ukrainian Nationalists) that employed violent tactics and were possibly responsible for most of the killings in Maidan, they were treated by the establishment U.S. media as merely anti-government or anti-Yanukovych "protesters," and their possible links to and support by the U.S. and U.S.-allied political and military forces that their actions have advanced so well were essentially ignored. In sharp contrast, protesters in eastern Ukraine following the coup were regularly described as "pro-Russian militants," "pro-Russian civilian mobs," a "pro-Russian uprising," "pro-Russian separatists," "pro-Russian secessionists," and even pro-Russian insurgents," "pro-Russian extremists," and "pro-Russian terrorists."

Roughly since the date on which the NATO powers started accusing Russia of invading Ukraine on or about March 1, one of the commonest phases used by the Western media to describe those Ukrainians, particularly in the eastern provinces, who opposed the February 22 coup had been "pro-Russian militant" or the plural "militants." "Armed pro-Russian militants today stormed government buildings in Ukraine's Crimea as Russia's president Vladimir Putin put fighter jets on combat alert," a report in the February 27 *London Evening Standard* opened.[31] "Groups of pro-Russian militants, apparently unarmed but displaying a distinctively military sense of discipline, supported the militia in their deployment," Agence France Presse reported the following day.[32] A Factiva database search under the combined "Wires" and "Newspapers: All" categories for the period November 21, 2013 through April 23, 2014 (the date on which we carried out the search) found a total of 1,848 items that included descriptions of these protesters as "pro-Russian militants."[33]

Like "terrorist" and "extremist," "militant" is a term of derogation, and there is a great difference between being described as a "protester," and being described as a "militant." How did the same media that in the month of April described the eastern Ukrainian protesters as "pro-Russian militants" (and the like) describe the protesters in the western part of the country while the Yanukovych government still held power? Table 1 (below) depicts those results.

Table 1. Media treatment of the anti-Yanukovych government protesters.[34]

	"[...] protester[s]"	'[...] militant[s]"
"pro-democracy [...]"	107	0
"pro-European [...]"	438	0
"pro-E.U. [...]"	497	0
"pro-Western [...]"	350	0
"anti-government [...]"	4974	68
"anti-Yanukovych [...]"	415	6
"anti-Russian [...]"	172	0
Totals	6953	7

Table 1 shows that whereas a vast array of news media did in fact treat the Maidan protesters as *protesters*, that is, as people who possessed agency and had any number of motivations for taking to the streets (of course, the number exceeds the seven we've listed in column one), these same media very rarely characterized the Maidan protesters as "militants" rather than as protesters. In fact, Table 1 shows that the media characterized the people who took to the streets in Kiev and the western Ukraine while the Yanukovych government was still in power as "protesters" roughly 94 times as often as they characterized them as "militants." In contrast, as already noted, protesters in the eastern Ukraine since the ouster of Yanukovych were characterized as "pro-Russian militants" in 1,848 items during the slightly less than two month period from February 27 through April 23. Thus whereas the media had cast the protesters in Kiev and the west in an overwhelmingly positive light, the media had cast the protesters in the east in an overwhelmingly negative light. Once again, it was not the different nature of the protesters that the media were highlighting. It was the media's own biases that the media were highlighting, and their determination to hew to the dominant Western narrative on the Ukraine.

But even worse than this was the constant reference in media coverage to the eastern protesters' alleged links to Russia and their management or manipulation by Russian authorities. In his March 26 Brussels speech, Obama said "It's not America that filled the Maidan with protesters—it was Ukrainians."[35] In contrast, in her April 13, 2014 presentation before the UN Security Council, U.S. Ambassador Samantha Power said that in the eastern Ukraine, "instability was written and choreographed in and by Russia."[36] Three days later, Power continued to push this line. "[A] region," she said, referring to eastern Ukraine, has been transformed almost overnight from a state of relative calm to manufactured unrest. Over the last several days, heavily armed pro-Russian separatists have seized the city administration, police stations and other Government buildings in 11 cities in Donetsk oblast ... It is clear that those actions were not a set of spontaneous events or home-grown, but rather a well-orchestrated professional campaign of sabotage of the Ukrainian State. And there is substantial evidence of involvement from Russia, its own territorial expansion, its own fear-mongering, by trying to change the subject. Well, it will not work.[37]

Of course nobody had said America "filled the Maidan with protesters." However, serious analysts outside the mainstream had recognized a familiar pattern, and noted the resemblance with earlier "color revolutions" in countries such as the Federal Republic of Yugoslavia (2000), Georgia (2003), Ukraine (2004), Lebanon (2005), and Iran (2009—though this effort proved unsuccessful), and suggested that the United States and E.U. strongly encouraged the protesters and gave them various forms of aid. After all, it was the State Department's Victoria Nuland who reminded a forum sponsored by the U.S.-Ukraine Foundation in Washington on December 13, 2013 that, "Since Ukraine's independence in 1991,... we've invested over five billion dollars to assist Ukraine ... Today, there are senior officials in the Ukrainian government, in the business community, as well as in the opposition, civil society, and the religious community who believe in this democratic and European future for their country. And they've been working hard to move their country and their president in the right direction."[38]

But these issues remained outside the orbit of establishment media discourse, which by April 2014 had undergone its own escalations and lost touch with reality. And as it did with the intercepted Paet-Ashton phone conversation on the identity of the Maidan snipers, *The New York Times* never reported Nuland's admission that the United States had "invested over five billion dollars" in winning the kind of outcome it wants for Ukraine, even though she made it at a public event in Washington while the Maidan protests were underway.[39] At this time of writing, it looks as if a great switch had been flipped in the captive Western mind sometime over the weekend of February 21-23, from the "on" position, whereby the protesters in Maidan had been represented as democratic agents and makers of history, to the "off" position, whereby the protesters in the east were being represented, not as democratic agents and makers of history, but simply as Putin's puppets and henchmen. It was a trend that showed no sign of de-escalating.

6. Russia as Aggressor and Violator of International Law

The U.S. political and media establishment expressed both shock and indignation over two linked events inside the then-Ukrainian Autonomous Republic of Crimea during the first month after the coup. First, the establishment members became apoplectic over what John Kerry called Russia's alleged "invasion and occupation of Ukrainian territory" in the final days of February 2014, and Barack Obama a "clear violation" of "international laws."[40] And, later, over Russia's annexation of Crimea on March 17, following a referendum held the previous day that had asked voters whether they favored "Crimea becoming a subject of the Russian Federation" or "restoring Crimea's 1992 constitution and remaining part of Ukraine?" With voter turnout reported to have been 83.1% of Crimea's eligible voters, 96.77% of the votes were in favor of the first option.[41]

But the use of "aggression" and "violation of international law" in characterizing both of these events was also complicated by the fact that as of late February 2014, Russia had a large and long-term military presence on Crimean (i.e., Ukrainian) territory that at the time included its naval port at Sevastopol on the Black Sea, as well as army and air force bases with personnel totaling perhaps 22,000 in all. So in this sense, Russia already *was* in Crimea, and had been since the 18th century; what had changed was not the fact of the Russian military presence there, but the political disposition towards the Russian military presence among members of the coup regime back in Kiev, and Washington. Moreover, the March 17 annexation took place with minimal violence and with no evidence of coercion of its participants, even if events were moving rapidly and the situation full of uncertainty. Perhaps most important, the referendum was seemingly compatible with the related notions of "self-determination" and "remedial secession." Thus in its 2010 advisory opinion in the case of Kosovo, the International Court of Justice had noted that "During the second-half of the twentieth century, the international law on self-determination developed in such a way as to create a right to independence for the peoples of non-self-governing territories and peoples subject to alien subjugation, domination and exploitation."[42] Although not recognized by a majority of the world's states, Russia's annexation of Crimea may have pre-empted an effort by the coup regime and paramilitary forces from the western Ukraine to try to retake Crimea by force.

But the U.S. political and media establishment could debate none of this. "Russian Aggression," a *New York Times* editorial headlined just after the events of late February. John Kerry made the rounds of the Sunday morning broadcast TV news shows. "[I]t's an incredible act of aggression," Kerry told CBS TV's *Face The Nation*. "It is really a stunning, willful choice by President Putin to invade another country. Russia is in violation of the sovereignty of Ukraine. Russia is in violation of its international obligations. Russia is in violation of its obligations under the UN Charter, under the Helsinki Final Act. It's a violation of its obligations under the 1994 Budapest agreement. You just don't, in the 21st century, behave in 19th century fashion by invading another country on completely trumped up pretext."[43]

So hyped-up had the *Times* become on the notion of Russia's or Putin's "aggression" in Ukraine that between March 3 and April 15, it published 22 different items in which *Times* contributors (whether its own or outside writers) accused Russia of "aggression."[44] This number over a six-week period of time is all the more remarkable when we contrast it with how the *Times* coped with the U.S. aggression against Iraq in 2003. In that case, for the entire 52 week period of 2003, the *Times* published only three items in which a *Times* contributor used the word "aggression" in reference to the United States."[45] And these three were made in passing and were not remotely comparable to headlining "Russian Aggression."[46]

> *The New York Times* also noted in four different editorials and three Op-Eds that Russia's action in Crimea was a violation of "international law."[47] They may have been reluctant to use the phrase more lavishly, given that U.S. (and Israeli) violations of international law are standard operating procedure. The contrast in treatment with the U.S. invasion of Iraq in 2003 is dramatic. In this case, as Howard Friel and Richard Falk have written, neither "UN Charter" nor "international law" were mentioned once in any of the 70 editorials *The New York Times* published on Iraq between September 11, 2001 and March 21, 2003—"nor [had] it cited international law to date with respect to the invasion or occupation after March 21." As they continue: "Thus, the leading editorial voice in the United States simply declined to consider in print whether a major US military invasion and occupation of another country violated international law." [48] But there was no such hesitation in dealing with Russian actions in Crimea.

One important difference between the Iraq and Crimea cases is that at this time of writing, there were no or very few deaths caused by Russia in Crimea, whereas the U.S. aggression and occupation of Iraq resulted in hundreds of thousands of deaths or more. So the "international community" should have responded to the U.S. war on Iraq, and imposed serious penalties on the parties responsible for it. But of course that never happened, and in the Iraq case, it didn't take long for the United Nations and other Western powers to begin assisting the aggressor in pacifying its victim.[49]

In fact, while the U.S. war on Iraq was a "war of choice" and was eventually recognized everywhere to have been based on a big lie ("weapons of mass destruction"), Russian intervention in Crimea rested on a serious threat to Russian national security and was arguably defensive and virtually forced upon Russia. It was responding to a further step in a U.S.-led NATO-bloc encirclement policy that involved clear-cut U.S. subversion of a major state on Russia's borders. That subversion policy was arguably the real act of aggression, with Russian actions in Crimea a response and preventing military consequences that might have followed Russian inaction. Naturally, this line of thought remained unthinkable—beyond the orbit of possible debate within the U.S. political and media establishment.

7. Dichotomy and Double-Standards at the UN: A case study

David M. Herszenhorn's front-page article in *The New York Times* (see Section 1, above) also mentioned a report released in mid-April by the Office of the United Nations High Commissioner for Human Rights that, in his words, "said that threats to ethnic Russians in eastern Ukraine, cited repeatedly by Russian officials and in the Russian news media as a potential rationale for Russian military action, were exaggerated..."[50] He used this supposedly objective UN report to bolster his case for treating Russia as the fount of global disinformation on the Ukraine, in contrast to Western governments and media, which in terms of accuracy and reliability are presumably far superior. Indeed, after this report was released, Samantha Power praised its "independent and impartial reporting," and added that "After weeks of Russian disinformation and propaganda, the report gives us yet another opportunity to focus on facts."[51]

When the UN High Commissioner for Human Rights Navi Pillay released this report on April 15, based on the findings of a Human Rights Monitoring Mission (HRMMU) that had been dispatched to Ukraine one month earlier, she stated that "Facts on the ground need to be established to help reduce the risk of radically different narratives being exploited for political ends. People need a reliable point of view to counter what has been widespread misinformation and also speech that aims to incite hatred on national, religious or racial grounds."[52]

However, the April 15 report accomplished nothing of the kind. A stunningly biased document, it hews to the dominant Western narrative on the Ukraine, and is a textbook example of the double-standards involved.

Thus although it treats the March 16 referendum in Crimea as having "no validity"[53] (para. 6) and indeed as a source of human rights violations (para. 83), it never treats the February 21-22 coup in Kiev in a comparable manner, accepting the interim government as a *fait accompli*, rather than as a violation of the rights of millions of Ukrainians who accept neither the coup nor the interim government formed in its aftermath. The report decries the presence of "paramilitary and so called self-defense groups as well as soldiers without insignia" in Crimea (para. 6, 86, 98), but never raises this issue in relation to the Maidan protests or the armed paramilitary groups known to operate in the western provinces. Whereas no mention is ever made of the need to disarm such groups in the west, in Crimea, on the other hand, "authorities ... should immediately disarm and disband all paramilitary units operating outside of the law..." (para. 98).

The report decries violent acts committed by the Yanukovych government against the Maidan protesters (para. 2, 53-61), and it assails violent acts that occurred in relation to Crimea's referendum and secession (para. 80-92), but it never decries violent acts committed by armed forces working within the Maidan protesters, including the Right Sector, and the allegation that the lethal sniper incidents of February 18-20 were carried out by anti-Yanukovych forces. Although the report uses the interim Minister of Health Oleg Musii as a source on the 120 deaths that occurred during the Maidan protests (para. 57), Olga Bogomolets' name is never mentioned. (See Section 4, above.) And whereas it raises a complaint about "allegations according to which people were brought in buses and paid to take part in protests and conduct them according to specific scenarios" in Crimea (para. 68), it mentions nothing comparable about the Maidan protests, although many of these protesters came to Kiev from all over the western provinces, and some reputedly from other countries as well.

The report emphasizes the need for Crimean authorities to protect the rights of the Tatar minority (para. 88-89), but the need for the interim government to protect sizeable Russian and Jewish minorities throughout the entire Ukraine is never mentioned. Amazingly, the report even downplays ethnic Russian fears about their place in Ukraine's post-coup environment. Thus in what was perhaps this report's most oft-quoted passage, we read that attacks against ethnic Russians have been "neither systematic nor widespread" (para. 7), and that ethnic Russian fears are "greatly exaggerated" (para. 89). The implication of such findings is that the anti-interim government protests that were sweeping cities in the east as we write must be the result of a pro-Russian propaganda campaign and therefore lack legitimacy. The dominant Western narrative could not be stated more completely.

The report also covers the threat posed by well-known extremist groups (para. 73-76), and the Right Sector's fondness for the "principles set forth by [World War II] Ukrainian nationalist leader Stepan Bandera" is singled out (para. 73). But this threat is downplayed, and the report concludes that "according to all accounts heard by the OHCHR delegation, the fear against the 'Right Sector' is disproportionate..." (para. 76). And so on, and so on, with the report resorting to every double-standard conceivable.

Little known but worth noting here, the report states that two of the "high-level UN visits" to the Ukraine in February and March were taken by Under-Secretary-General for Political Affairs Jeffrey Feltman and by Robert Serry, a Senior Advisor to the Secretary-General (para. 28). As these two names were mentioned by Victoria Nuland in her phone conversation with Geoffrey Pyatt as part of the State Department strategy of resorting to the UN to out-maneuver the EU on Ukraine (and "fuck the EU"), we find it significant that they also turn up as key players in this biased UN Human Rights Monitoring Mission in Ukraine. (See Section 4, above.)

8. A Propaganda Miscellany

At this time of writing, the U.S. political and media establishment had engaged in a five-month-long propaganda assault centered on the Ukraine crisis, which had stirred up so much anger and fear towards Russia that a peaceful resolution of this crisis seemed unlikely. When high-ranking representatives of the United States, the E.U., Russia, and Ukraine's interim government reached an agreement in Geneva on April 17, the brief 234-word document listed the "initial concrete steps to de-escalate tensions and restore security for all citizens," but aside from the U.S., E.U., and Russia "commit[ing] to support" an OSCE Special Monitoring Mission, all other measures were the responsibility of Ukrainians, especially the disarming of "illegal armed groups." No further responsibility was assigned to Russia, the U.S., or the E.U.[54] Yet, during the first seven days after the agreement, Russia was singled out and subjected to a constant harangue by Western leaders and media for failing to live up to its alleged responsibilities. This culminated on April 24, when Secretary of State John Kerry delivered an attack on the Russian government and its "propaganda bullhorn that is the state-sponsored Russia Today [network]," accusing the Russian government of engaging in "distraction, deception, and destabilization," and RT of an "effort to propagandize and to distort what is happening or not happening in Ukraine." Running through a list of alleged Russian wrongdoing in eastern Ukraine that Kerry summarized with a quote from NATO Supreme Allied Commander Richard Breedlove—"What is happening in eastern Ukraine is a military operation that is well planned and organized and we assess that it is being carried out at the direction of Russia"—Kerry closed with a threat: "President Putin and Russia face a choice. If Russia chooses the path of de-escalation, the international community—all of us—will welcome it. If

Russia does not, the world will make sure that the cost for Russia will only grow."[55]

This late-April peak in anti-Russian propaganda and U.S. and NATO threats followed such a steady stream of insults and demonization of Russia that anything detrimental could be said about Russia and anybody denouncing Russia stood a good chance of being given a platform. Furthermore, the "propaganda bullhorn" of *The New York Times* and its confreres can outcompete RT and anything the Russians can muster. Their language in assailing the Russian "bully" makes RT look modest in comparison. And they frame the issues in exact accord with the party-lines laid down by Kerry, Breedlove, Obama and Samantha Power.

A pretty illustration is the fact that while Russia's alleged direction of protests in eastern Ukraine is claimed in a steady barrage by Kerry, Breedlove, and *The New York Times*, the U.S. role in guiding the "interim government" is buried. Thus the *Times*' David M. Herszenhorn satirized Russian Prime Minister Dmitri Medvedev's "conspiracy theories," referring to a Medvedev post to Facebook that mentioned "secret visits by the C.I.A. director" John Brennan to Kiev on the weekend of April 12-13,[56] but the *Times* itself did not report this visit until April 15, when it acknowledged that the "White House confirmed that John O. Brennan ... visited Kiev over the weekend," adding that his visit "provided propaganda ammunition to the Kremlin," not that Brennan's visit was significant and troubling in itself.[57] It is a sure bet that a secret visit by the head of the Russian Foreign Intelligence Service to Donetsk or Kharkiv in eastern Ukraine would be newsworthy at the *Times*. But in the Free Press, Kerry and Breedlove are not spouting "conspiracy theories," only Russian leaders are.

Among the stream of similar war propaganda we may note the *Times*' front-page push of the Washington-Kiev claim that a "dossier of photographs" passed to the OSCE by Ukraine's interim government and "endorsed by the Obama administration" showed clearly identifiable members of Russian special forces both in Russia and now in the eastern Ukraine.[58] The photos were fuzzy, the true identities of those pictured was uncertain, and, in the end, it turned out that the photo originally alleged to have been taken in Russia was in fact "shot in the Ukrainian town of Slovyansk, according to Maxim Dondyuk, the freelance photographer who took the picture and posted it on his Instagram account,"[59] leaving the *Times*' scoop a big flop. The *Times* was compelled to issue an evasive semi-admission of non-authenticity,[60] and Public Editor Margaret Sullivan's response to the *Times*' use of the fabrication was that "this article, with its reliance on an administration leak, was displayed too prominently and questioned too lightly."[61] What is important here is how this newspaper rushed to front-page coverage of such problematic but party-line servicing materials. In contrast, the *Times* barely mentioned Brennan's visit to Kiev, had never mentioned the claim that dozens of far-right Svoboda cadres were trained in street-fighting techniques in Poland, and that there was evidence that the killings in Maidan in February were carried out by the U.S.-supported protesters.

Another propaganda effort of interest was the passing out of leaflets by "masked men" outside the Bet Menakhem-Mendl synagogue in Donetsk and addressed to the "Jews of Donetsk," allegedly signed by Denis Pushilin, the leader of the Donetsk People's Republic, and "demanding that Jews register and pay a fine" or face deportation.[62] The authenticity of this document was quickly denied by Pushilin, and it was clearly a false-flag operation to divert attention from the anti-Jewish traditions of some of Ukraine's western political organizations, such as Svoboda, the Congress of Ukrainian Nationalists, and the Right Sector. But the Obama-Kerry-Power axis vigorously denounced this leaflet, without bothering to point out its fraudulent character, and thus gave it a place in their propaganda arsenal. *The New York Times* treated it "objectively," noting the denial of Pushilin and his colleagues, but not stressing its obvious propaganda role.

One of the best examples of the propaganda service of the Western media in this ongoing anti-Russian barrage has been their treatment of the Pussy Riot protest-artists. These women rose to prominence in the Western media in December 2011, in connection with street protests in Moscow claiming that the December 4 parliamentary elections were rigged in Putin's favor. "We are against Putin, against the regime," Pussy Riot member Garadzha told Agence France Presse.[63] "We believe that the Soviet Union's aggressive imperial politics is similar in many ways to Putin's course," the group told the *Moscow Times* in an email interview.[64] Clearly, this position conforms to the same overarching propaganda framework we've been analyzing throughout this chapter. But it wasn't until five Pussy Riot members staged an event on the altar of the Cathedral of Christ the Savior in Moscow in February 2012, leading to their arrest, conviction, and imprisonment for "hooliganism motivated by religious hatred," that their celebrity status skyrocketed in the West. Helping elevate their status, Pussy Riot never brought their culture of protest to the Pentagon or NATO headquarters in Brussels, demanding that NATO disarm and stop threatening the world. We also think it unlikely that they protested *The New York Times'* propaganda services for U.S. imperialism, when two former members of the group visited the paper's editorial board in early February 2014. When the Russian authorities locked up the Pussy Riot members, they became high-profile victims of an Official Enemy, and their cause was "cherry-picked"[65] by Amnesty International and Human Rights Watch and a whole legion of

Western celebrities to decry the badness of Putin's Russia. *The New York Times* published 23 articles featuring Pussy Riot from January 1 through March 31, 2014, and even awarded one of them, Maria Alyokhina, with op-ed space in the paper. "The reality of contemporary Russia, and Mr. Putin's goal, is to kill ... reflection, analysis and criticism...," she told us.[66] They may be lousy musicians, and do things that would land them in jail in the United States—but they denounce Putin. So their opinions are fit to print.

Another interesting case was that of the former RT America anchor Liz Wahl, who ended her telecast on March 5 by announcing her resignation from the channel. "My partner is a physician at a [U.S.] military base, where he sees every day the first-hand accounts of the ultimate prices people pay for this country," Wahl explained. "And that is why I personally cannot be part of a network funded by the Russian government that whitewashes the actions of Putin. I'm proud to be an American and believe in disseminating the truth. And that is why, after this newscast, I'm resigning."[67]

Wahl's resignation earned her an immediate guest appearance on CNN the same evening; and on the same program *New York Times* columnist Nicholas Kristof noted how much he "admire[s] those who fight against the system, who resist whether they be here at RT or those incredibly brave Russian newspaper reporters, reporting on corruption at the risk of their lives in Moscow...."[68] Her resignation was reported widely here (e.g., CBS, NBC, MSNBC, NPR, "The Colbert Report") and widely around the world.[69] Comparisons were even made between Wahl and the old Radio Moscow World Service announcer Vladimir Danchev, who in 1983 went "rogue" and began "inserting subversive messages into the official radio scripts" that named the Soviet invasion and occupation of Afghanistan as such.[70] Of course, such a comparison is nonsense, and an insult to Danchev, who was removed from his RMWS job, and sent to a psychiatric hospital in Tashkent. Wahl explicitly stated that her physician partner sees the human carnage suffered, not by Afghans and Iraqis, but by U.S. military personnel. Were Liz Wahl truly Danchev-like, it would be the victims of these U.S. military personnel on multiple continents with whom she expressed solidarity, not their U.S. killers and tormentors or the U.S. media, which whitewash U.S. actions. A subsequent investigation by Max Blumenthal and Rania Khalek found that Wahl had personally been unhappy with her prospects at RT, and had been approached by *The Daily Beast*'s right-wing, Neocon Russophobe James Kirchick to stage her on-air resignation as a way to embarrass RT.[71] In this melodrama, only anti-Danchevs took the stage.

One particularly important component in the new communications complex is the use of video platforms to "seed" propaganda into the public sphere. Propaganda videos can potentially be viewed by millions of people worldwide. It doesn't matter that the whole production may be a fabrication. What matters is that individuals propagate (i.e., share) them. "I Am a Ukrainian" was such a video.[72]

> A BBC News Trending report asked: "are we seeing the rise of the viral video protest?"[73] The answer is of course an emphatic no. The only videos that "go viral" are the ones that conform to the narratives of the dominant powers. "I Am a Ukrainian" quite clearly did this. Its speaker is a young woman standing amid the Maidan protesters. She purports to be a "native of Kiev," and wants us to "know why thousands of people all over my country are on the streets." "There is only one reason," she says: "They want to be free from a dictatorship ... That is why I ask you now to help us. ... And now I ask you to build this freedom in our country. You can help us only by telling this story to your friends, only by sharing this video. Please share it."

This is what the public relations industry calls "staying on message." There is not one sentence in this two-minute video that a State Department spokesperson or editorialist for The New York Times could not have uttered. "We are a civilized people," the young woman says at one point, "but our government are barbarians." With this, the dominant Western narrative on the Ukraine had been turned into a sharable video, and minds already captured by this narrative embraced the video and made it "go viral."

For the Western media in the five month period through April 2014, anything negative about Russia would do. The *Times* even gave front-page coverage to the claim that "Russia Failed to Share Data on Suspect, Report Says."[74] Of course, the Russians did provide several warnings about Tamerlan Tsarnaev to the FBI, which the FBI failed to follow up on successfully, so the FBI's own failure was converted into one more Russian put-down.

9. Concluding Note: The Captive Western Mind

When the United States, as the world's "hard" and "soft" hegemonic power, supports a campaign of regime destabilization and change, the establishment Western media will represent opposition protests and civil unrest in glowing colors as spontaneous, homegrown work at the grassroots level, and pro-democracy. Likewise, these same media will represent police actions against the protesters, not as police actions, no matter how violent the protests become, but simply as the regime's criminal attack on its own citizens, and as violations of their human rights. Concrete examples date back many decades, but over the past several decades, include ethnic Serbs in the former Yugoslavia 1991-1995, ethnic Serbs again in Kosovo 1998-1999, the government in Khartoum from 2003 on, Iran in 2009, Libya until the overthrow of Qaddafi in 2011, Syria from 2011 on, Venezuela in 2014, and the Ukraine as long as Viktor Yanukovych still held the presidency, but not after.

On the other hand, when the United States supports a regime and seeks to keep it in power, the establishment Western media will represent opposition protests and civil unrest as at best only partly spontaneous and homegrown, but also as manipulated if not wholly organized and controlled by a foreign power, hence having deeply anti-democratic credentials. Likewise, these same media will represent police actions against the protesters simply as police actions, that is, as the regime's defense of the rule of law and its constitutional authority. In turn, the media will represent the protesters, not in glowing colors, not as resulting from work at the grassroots and pro-democratic, but as hooligans, militants, extremists, even terrorists—above all, as lacking legitimacy, and deserving of being met with force. Three examples that come to mind are Israel in its relations with the Palestinians of the Occupied Territories (systematic and long-term), Egypt in the summer of 2013, after Gen. Abdul Fattah el-Sisi removed the elected government of Mohammed Morsi from power and the military dictatorship took over, and events in the eastern Ukraine since Yanukovych was overthrown the weekend of February 21-23, 2014, and replaced by the interim government.

The public statements of the Western political leadership during the period of the crisis in Ukraine that we have studied in this chapter, by Barack Obama, John Kerry, and Samantha Power through Anders Fogh Rasmussen and Gen. Richard Breedlove, Angela Merkel, David Cameron and William Hague, NATO- bloc representatives at the United Nations, high-ranking UN personnel, and the published discourse of the establishment Western media, all now readily searchable thanks to the Internet, overwhelmingly confirm the depths at which these principles operate.

Western discourse during months of February, March, and April 2014 had taken on a distinctly totalitarian character. Correcting for minor idiosyncrasies that result from local U.S. politics, on questions that pertained to Ukraine, it had become difficult to tell *The New York Times* and *Weekly Standard*, CNN and Fox News, from one another. What push-back against this single mindset that we could find came from genuinely independent websites and blogs and a few, small circulating traditional alternative sources, including *The Nation* and *Z Magazine*—and the RT America cable TV channel, singled-out by name by the U.S. Secretary of State for its intolerable deviations from the official creed.[75] Because RT remained the one source on American television (broadcast or cable) that kept up a constant critique of

Flashpoint in Ukraine: How the US Drive for Hegemony Risks World War III

the Western powers' expansion eastward and their exploitation of the crisis in Ukraine to carry this out, it was a natural target for NATO Party derogation. The political, intellectual, and media leaders of the Western Imperium know the Truth, and they struggle to ensure that theirs is the only voice that can be heard.

ENDNOTES

1. David M. Herszenhorn et al., "Russia Is Quick to Bend Truth About Ukraine," *New York Times*, April 16, 2014, <http://tinyurl.com/m766mkf>.
2. "Hugo Chavez Departs," Editorial, *New York Times*, April 13, 2002, <http://tinyurl.com/95wwz2j>.—For the record, Hugo Chávez returned within 48 hours, allowing the *Times* to denounce him yet again as "such a divisive and demagogic leader that his forced departure last week drew applause at home and in Washington." ("Venezuela's Political Turbulence," Editorial, *New York Times*, April 16, 2002, <http://tinyurl.com/agmjncd>).
3. Andrew Kramer, "Ukraine Sends Force to Stem Unrest in East," *New York Times*, April 16, 2014, <http://tinyurl.com/mqdkxqn>.
4. Robert Parry, "Ukraine: Through the U.S. Looking Glass," *ConsortiumNews.com*, April 16, 2014, <http://tinyurl.com/o67ghyl>.
5. See Robert Parry, "The 'We-Hate-Putin' Group Think," *ConsoriumNews.com*, March 7, 2014, <http://tinyurl.com/mndd23m>.
6. Nexis database search of *The New York Times* carried out on April 16, 2014 for the period January 1 – April 16, 2014. Our search parameters were: *Ukrain!* and *Putin* and *editorial*.
7. See David Cromwell and David Edwards, "The 'Professorial President' And The 'Small, Strutting Hard Man'," *Media Lens*, March 10, 2014, <http://tinyurl.com/l6m7k8e>.
8. When NATO was founded on April 4, 1949, its 12 member-states included the United States, Belgium, Canada, Denmark, France, Iceland, Italy, Luxembourg, Netherlands, Norway, Portugal, and the United Kingdom. In 1952, Greece and Turkey joined NATO. In 1955, West Germany. In 1982, Spain. Then no new members joined until 1999, when the Czech Republic, Hungary, and Poland were added. In 2004, Bulgarian, Estonia, Latvia, Lithuania, Romania, Slovakia, and Slovenia joined. NATO's last membership expansion was in 2009, when Albania and Croatia joined.—For more on NATO's relentless expansion, see Rick Rozoff, "NATO's Worldwide Expansion in the Post-Cold World Era," *Stop NATO*, October 12, 2013, <http://preview.tinyurl.com/m6d54gm>; Rick Rozoff, "NATO: 65 Years Later," *Stop NATO*, April 4, 2014, <http://tinyurl.com/mxvbzpn>; and Rick Rozoff, "NATO's Incremental But Inexorable Absorption of Ukraine," *Stop NATO*, April 25, 2014, <http://tinyurl.com/ljxx2ow>.
9. In Mark Kramer, "The Myth of a No-NATO-Enlargement Pledge to Russia," *Washington Quarterly*, Vol. 32, No. 2, April, 2009, p. 49, <http://tinyurl.com/kdacdzc>. Kramer's article is striking in that his conclusion, as reflected in his title, is contradicted by the evidence he examines.
10. Mary Elise Sarotte, *1989: The Struggle to Create Post-Cold War Europe* (Princeton, NJ: Princeton University Press, 2009), esp. "NATO's Jurisdiction Would Not Shift One Inch Eastward," pp. 107-115; here pp. 112-114. In the Conclusion to her book, Sarotte comments that, "Rather than bringing an end to the history that culminated in the Cold War, they had perpetuated key parts of it instead....As British Foreign Minister [Douglas] Hurd concluded, they did not remake the world. Rather, the struggle to recast Europe *after* the momentous upheaval of 1989 resulted in prefabricated structures from *before* the upheaval moving eastward and securing a future for themselves. Americans and West Germans had successfully entrenched the institutions born of the old geopolitics of the Cold War world—ones that they already dominated, most

	notably NATO—in the new era." (*Ibid.*, p. 201.) Also see Mary Elise Sarotte, "Not One Inch Eastward? Bush, Baker, Kohl, Genscher, Gorbachev, and the Origin of Russian Resentment toward NATO Enlargement in February 1990," *Diplomatic History*, Vol. 34, No. 1, January, 2010, pp. 119-140, <http://tinyurl.com/kjnh27a>.
11	Nexis database search of the New York Times carried out on April 15, 2014 for the period January 1, April 15, 2014. Our search parameters were: Gorbachev and NATO. The two items were: David M. Herszenhorn, "In Crimea, Russia Moved to Throw Off the Cloak of Defeat," *New York Times*, March 25, 2014, <http://tinyurl.com/ltp9eck>; and Melvin A. Goodman, Letter to the Editor, *New York Times*, March 26, 2014, <http://tinyurl.com/mgrnbr4>
12	See Gerald Sussman, *Branding Democracy: U.S. Regime Change in Post-Soviet Eastern Europe* (New York: Peter Lang International, 2010). Also see Gerald Sussman, "The Myths of 'Democracy Assistance': U.S. Political Intervention in Post-Soviet Eastern Europe," *Monthly Review*, December, 2006, <http://tinyurl.com/mg4jpa2>.
13	Vladimir Putin, "Address by President of the Russian Federation," Moscow, President of Russia website, March 18, 2014, <http://eng.kremlin.ru/news/6889>.
14	Jack F. Matlock, Jr., *Reagan and Gorbachev: How the Cold War Ended* (New York: Random House, 2005).
15	Jack F. Matlock, Jr., "Who won the Cold War? And who will win now?" *Washington Post*, March 16, 2014, <http://tinyurl.com/ma6vggn>.
16	John J. Mearsheimer, "Getting Ukraine Wrong," *The International New York Times*, March 14, 2014, <http://tinyurl.com/l9s9xaf>.
17	"Vadimir Putin Clings to the Past," Editorial, *New York Times*, November 20, 2014, <http://tinyurl.com/k6rnxvy>.
18	See Stephen F. Cohen, "The Grey Lady's recent editorial on Ukraine and Vladimir Putin was one-dimensional and ideological," *The Nation* (web only), December 2, 2013, <http://tinyurl.com/lq5jzva>.
19	Barack Obama, "Remarks by the President in Address to European Youth," Brussels, White House Office of the Press Secretary, March 26, 2014, <http://tinyurl.com/kjt7eq9>.
20	Putin, "Address by President of the Russian Federation," Moscow.
21	Obama, "Remarks by the President in Address to European Youth," Brussels.
22	Nexis database searches of the *New York Times* carried out on April 12, 2014 for the period November 1, 2013, through March 31, 2014. Our search parameters were: *Ukrain!* and (*coup or putsch*).
23	David M. Herszenhorn, "Ukraine Blames I.M.F. for Halt to Agreements with Europe," *New York Times*, November 23, 2013, <http://tinyurl.com/lb9ebjf>; Maria Danilova, "50,000 rally in Kiev calling on Ukraine's government to sign EU deal and turn away from Russia," Associated Press, November 24, 2013, <http://tinyurl.com/med2wd2>.
24	See the copy of the February 21, 2014 "Agreement on the Settlement of Crisis in Ukraine," as posted to the website of *The Guardian*, February 21, 2014, <http://tinyurl.com/myr9hf7>.
25	"Puppets of Maidan," YouTube, February 6, 2014, <http://tinyurl.com/kpwnjnk>. For a transcript of the Nuland-Pyatt phone conversation, see Dan Murphy, "Amid US-Russia tussle over Ukraine, a leaked tap of Victoria Nuland," Back Channel Blog, *Christian Science Monitor*, February 6, 2014, <http://tinyurl.com/m8q9ghw>.
26	Stephen F. Cohen, "Distorting Russia: How the American media misrepresent Putin, Sochi, and Ukraine," *The Nation*, March 3, 2014, <http://tinyurl.com/n2pnxdm>.
27	Nexis database search of the *New York Times* on April 20, 2014 for the period January 1 – April 20, 2014. Our search parameters were: *Ukrain!* and *Nuland*. This search retrieved 14 items in all, but upon checking them, we determined that only 9 were relevant to our search.
28	"Yanukovych Wins 35.32% of Votes, Tymoshenko 25.05% After 100% Of Original Protocols," *Ukrainian News*, January 25, 2010.
29	Michael Bergman, "Breaking: Estonian Foreign Minister Urmas Paet and Catherine Ashton discuss Ukraine over the phone," YouTube, March 5, 2014, our transcription,

30   beginning around the 8:22 mark, <http://tinyurl.com/n7g8uw8>.
30   Nexis database search of the New York Times carried out on April 21, 2013 for the period January 1 – April 21, 2014. NewsBank database search of the United States media (allegedly covering 3524 sources) carried out on April 21, 2013 for the period January 1 – April 21, 2014. Our search parameters were: Ukrain! and (Ashton and Paet) (Nexis) and Ukrain* and (Ashton and Paet) (NewsBank).
31   Joseph Watts and Will Stewart, "Militants raise Russian flag at Crimea's parliament," *London Evening Standard*, February 27, 2014, <http://tinyurl.com/m9cjfwl>.
32   Bertrand de Saisset, "Wave of pro-Russian sentiment hits Crimea capital," Agence France Presse, March 1, 2014, <http://tinyurl.com/mzloe2t>.
33   Factiva database search under the "Wires" and "Newspapers: All" categories carried out on April 23, 2014 for the period November 21, 2013 – April 23, 2014. Our search parameters were: rst=(twir or tnwp) and Ukrain* and (pro-Russian militant*). Factiva generated a total of 1,848 items that matched these parameters.
34   Factiva database search under the "Wires" and "Newspapers: All" categories carried out on April 23, 2014 for the period November 21, 2013 – April 23, 2014. Since the data depicted in Table 1 are the result of 14 different searches in all, our parameters for these 14 searches were as follows:

(Row 1) rst=(twir or tnwp) and Ukrain* and (pro-democracy protester*): 107.
(Row 1) rst=(twir or tnwp) and Ukrain* and (pro-democracy militant*): 0.
(Row 2) rst=(twir or tnwp) and Ukrain* and (pro-european protester*): 438.
(Row 2) rst=(twir or tnwp) and Ukrain* and (pro-european militant*): 0.
(Row 3) rst=(twir or tnwp) and Ukrain* and (pro-eu protester*): 497.
(Row 3) rst=(twir or tnwp) and Ukrain* and (pro-eu militant*): 0.
(Row 4) rst=(twir or tnwp) and Ukrain* and (pro-western protester*): 350.
(Row 4) rst=(twir or tnwp) and Ukrain* and (pro-western militant*): 0.
(Row 5) rst=(twir or tnwp) and Ukrain* and (anti-government protester*): 4,974.
(Row 5) rst=(twir or tnwp) and Ukrain* and (anti-government militant*): 68.
(Row 6) rst=(twir or tnwp) and Ukrain* and (anti-Yanukov?ch protester*): 415.
(Row 6) rst=(twir or tnwp) and Ukrain* and (anti-Yanukov?ch militant*): 6.
(Row 7) rst=(twir or tnwp) and Ukrain* and (anti-russian protester*): 172.
(Row 7) rst=(twir or tnwp) and Ukrain* and (anti-russian militant*): 0.

35   Obama, "Remarks by the President in Address to European Youth," Brussels.
36   Samantha Power, "Letter dated 13 April 2014 from the Permanent Representative of the Russian Federation to the United Nations addressed to the President of the Security Council (S/2014/264), UN Security Council, 7154th meeting (S/PV.7154), April 13, 2014, p. 5, < http://tinyurl.com/mvbscn3>.
37   Samantha Power, "Letter dated 28 February 2014 from the Permanent Representative of Ukraine to the United Nations addressed to the President of the Security Council (S/2014/136)," UN Security Council, 7157th meeting (S/PV.7157), April 16, 2014, p. 9, <http://tinyurl.com/m93e8oz>.— At this stage of her career on behalf U.S. expansionism, Power's depravity appears to be bottomless.
38   Victoria Nuland, Assistant Secretary of State for European and Eurasian Affairs, speaking before an event sponsored by the U.S.-Ukraine Foundation in Washington on December 13, 2013, our transcription, here picking-up the video from the 7:22 mark on, <http://tinyurl.com/knkxm7g>.
39   Nexis database search of *The New York Times* carried out on April 23, 2014 for the period January 1 – April 23, 2014. Our search parameters were: *Ukrain! and Nuland and ((five billion dollars) or ($5 billion))*. The results were zero.
40   John Kerry, "Situation in Ukraine," Press Statement, U.S. Department of State, Washington, March 1, 2014, <http://tinyurl.com/me8fuap>; and Barack Obama, "Statement by the President on Ukraine," White House Office of the Press Secretary, February 28, 2014, <http://tinyurl.com/ol2fst5>.

41. "Crimea declares independence, seeks UN recognition," RT, March 17, 2014, <http://tinyurl.com/kbv7rhb>.
42. *Accordance with International Law of the Unilateral Declaration of Independence in Respect of Kosovo*, Advisory Opinion, International Court of Justice, July 22, 2010, para. 79, <http://tinyurl.com/l85zw8x>.
43. John Kerry, "Interview with Bob Schieffer of CBS's Face the Nation," U.S. Department of State, March 2, 2014, <http://tinyurl.com/lfuzdcf>.
44. Nexis database search of the *New York Times* carried out on April 15, 2014 for the period January 1 – April 15, 2014. Our search parameters were: *Ukrain! and aggression and Russia!*. We found that in a total of 60 different items someone had accused Russia or Putin of "aggression" in Ukraine. But in 38 of these, it was typically a quote taken from someone outside the *Times*. However, in the 22 items in which writers for the *Times* leveled the charge, 10 of these were op-eds, 5 reports, 4 editorials, and 3 blogs. The 10 op-eds were written by Roger Cohen, Russ Douthat, Nicholas Kristof, Michael Wara, Oleksandr Turchynov, John McCain, Charles Blow, Jason Patrick and Brendan Simms, Slawomir Sierkowski, and Stephen Sestanovich.
45. Nexis database search of T*he New York Times* carried out on April 13, 2013 for the period January 1 - December 31, 2003. Our search parameters were: (United States or US) and (Iraq and aggression). Nexis retrieved a total of 139 items from this search. But after checking them, we determined that only 3 met our criterion of contributors to the Times accusing the United States of "aggression," rather than persons from outside the *Times* being quoted to the same effect. Namely: "This clash is epochal because it's beyond ego. It's about whether America will lead by fear, aggression and force of arms or by diplomacy, moderation and example."(Maureen Dowd, "He's Out with the In Crowd," *New York Times*, April 27, 2003, <http://tinyurl.com/moo6w8e >.) Like greed, aggression is good. Aggression has marked the upward surge of mankind. Aggression breeds patriotism, and patriotism curbs dissent. Aggression has made Democrats cower, the press purr and the world quake. Aggression, "you mark my words, "will not only save humanity, but it will soon color all the states Republican red. Mission accomplished." (Maureen Dowd, "The Iceman Cometh," *New York Times*, May 4, 2003, <http://tinyurl.com/k436bnv>) "Nothing makes human rights activists angrier than watching political leaders conscript human rights into a justification for aggression." (Michael Ignatieff, "Why Are We in Iraq? And Liberia? And Afghanistan?" *New York Times Magazine*, September 7, 2003, <http://tinyurl.com/lzg386q>.)
46. See Michael McGehee, "The *New York Times* Excoriates 'Aggression': The Washington Exception," *NYTimes eXaminer*, March 5, 2014, <http://tinyurl.com/knz9sze>.
47. Nexis database search of the *New York Times* carried out on April 15, 2014 for the period January 1 – April 15, 2014. Our search parameters were: *Ukrain! and international law*. Nexis retrieved a total of 37 relevant matches. But upon checking them, only seven met our criterion of actual contributors to the *Times* accusing Russia of violating "international law," rather than persons from outside the *Times* being quoted to the same effect. Besides the 4 editorials, 3 op-eds accused Russia of violating "international law." The op-eds were written by Roger Cohen, Michael A. McFaul, and Jason Pack and Brendan Simms. A fourth would have been by John Mearsheimer, but as we've already seen, the U.S. print edition of the *Times* failed to published his op-ed. (See Section 3, above.)
48. Howard Friel and Richard Falk, *The Record of the Paper: How the New York Times Misreports US Foreign Policy* (New York: Verso, 2004), p. 15.
49. See Edward S. Herman and David Peterson, *The Politics of Genocide* (New York: Monthly Review Press, 2nd. Ed., 2011), "The Iraq Invasion-Occupation," pp. 33-38.
50. Herszenhorn *et al.*, "Russia Is Quick to Bend Truth About Ukraine."
51. Samantha Power, "Letter dated 28 February 2014 from the Permanent Representative of Ukraine to the United Nations addressed to the President of the Security Council (S/2014/136), UN Security Council, 7157th meeting (S/PV.7157), April 16, 2014, p. 9, <http://tinyurl.com/m93e8oz>.
52. Navi Pillay, "Ukraine: Misinformation, propaganda and incitement to hatred need to

be urgently countered—UN human rights report," Office of the United Nations High Commissioner for Human Rights, April 15, 2014, <http://tinyurl.com/kcoojaf>. For the actual report, see Ivan Šimonović et al., Report on the human rights situation in Ukraine, Human Rights Monitoring Mission in Ukraine (HRMMU), Office of the United Nations High Commissioner for Human Rights, April 15, 2014, <http://tinyurl.com/ofp3qgf>.

53   Because Washington had been unable to push a resolution on Ukraine past the Russian veto in the Security Council, Washington turned to the General Assembly, a forum it usually scorns. On March 27, the General Assembly adopted a resolution sponsored by Washington on the "Territorial integrity of Ukraine," which states that the March 16 referendum in Crimea had "no validity," and therefore "cannot form the basis for any alteration of the status of the Autonomous Republic of Crimea or the city of Sevastopol...." ("Territorial integrity of Ukraine" (A/RES/68/262), March 27, 2014, para. 5, <http://tinyurl.com/lp522oj>.)

54   "Joint Geneva Statement on Ukraine from April 17: The full text," as posted to the website of the *Washington Post*, April 17, 2014, <http://tinyurl.com/l9xwmht>.

55   John Kerry, "Remarks on Ukraine," U.S. Department of State, Washington, April 24, 214, <http://tinyurl.com/kmtsut4>. Also see Supreme Allied Commander Philip Breedlove, "Ukraine 'Activists' Are Clearly A Professional Military Force under Russian Control," *Business Insider*, April 17, 2014, <http://tinyurl.com/kn4clxz>.

56   Herszenhorn et al., "Russia Is Quick to Bend Truth About Ukraine."

57   Peter Baker et al., "With Ukraine Tensions Mounting, U.S. Weighs New Sanctions Against Russia," *New York Times*, April 15, 2014, <http://tinyurl.com/mbnqpym>. The day before, the *Times* had merely reported that "Russian news media reported Sunday that the American C.I.A. director, John O. Brennan, had arrived in Kiev on a secret visit to advise Ukrainian officials in charge of domestic security and defense. The American Embassy in the Ukrainian capital declined to comment on the reports." (Andrew E. Kramer and Andrew Higgins, "Ukraine Forces Storm a Town, Defying Russia," *New York Times*, April 14, 2014, <http://tinyurl.com/n6nzlkj>.)

58   Andrew Higgins et al., "Photos Link Masked Men in East Ukraine to Russia," *New York Times*, April 21, 2014, <http://tinyurl.com/k3u365v>.

59   Robert Parry, "NYT Retracts Russian-Photo Scoop," *ConsortiumNews.com*, April 23, 2014, <http://tinyurl.com/kprsjkn>.

60   Michael R. Gordon and Andrew Kramer, "Scrutiny Over Photos Said to Tie Russia Units to Ukraine," *New York Times*, April 23, 2014, <http://tinyurl.com/kqpl3le>.

61   Margaret Sullivan, "Aftermath of Ukraine Photo Story Shows Need for More Caution," *New York Times*, April 24, 2014, <http://tinyurl.com/lbcz5kb>.

62   Andrew R. Kramer and Michael R. Gordon, "Demands That Jews Register in Eastern Ukraine Are Denounced, and Denied," *New York Times*, April 18, 2014, <http://tinyurl.com/mcb8gl8>.

63   Anna Malpas, "All-girl Russian punk band rages against Putin," Agence France Presse, January 26, 2012, <http://tinyurl.com/kgdtol7>.

64   Sergei Chernov, "Feminist Punk Band Become Unlikely Putin Foil," *Moscow Times*, February 2, 2012, <http://preview.tinyurl.com/87zm6b4>.

65   See Timothy Alexander Guzman, "The Pussy Riot Con Game," *Global Research*, December 14, 2012, <http://tinyurl.com/k6qqnbo>.

66   Maria Alyokhina, "Sochi Under Siege," *New York Times*, February 21, 2014, <http://tinyurl.com/kgvkcgf>.

67   "RT America's Liz Wahl resigns live on air," YouTube, March 5, 2014, <http://tinyurl.com/o9mna7t>. Also see RT editor-in-chief Margarita Simonyan's commentary on Wahl's resignation, "And here's what I have to say about it," March 5, 2014, <http://tinyurl.com/k368xvo>.

68   "New Cold War? Piers Morgan Live," CNN, March 5, 2014, <http://tinyurl.com/kj8jvan>.

69   A Factiva database search under the "Wires," "Newspapers: All," and "Transcripts" categories for the eight day period March 5-12, 2014, retrieved a total of 471 items

that had mentioned the name 'Liz Wahl'. Our search parameters were: *rst=(twir or tnwp or ttpt) and liz wahl*.

70   Stephen Ennis, "Vladimir Danchev: The broadcaster who defied Moscow," *BBC News Magazine*, March 7, 2014, <http://preview.tinyurl.com/lvoo5lu>.

71   Max Blumenthal and Rania Khalek, "How Cold War-Hungry Neocons Stage Managed RT Anchor Liz Wahl's Resignation," *Truthdig*, March 19, 2014, <http://tinyurl.com/lbb3qpr>.

72   "I Am a Ukrainian," YouTube, February 10, 2014, <http://tinyurl.com/ouzqfet>.

73   "#BBCtrending: 'I am a Ukrainian' protest video goes viral," BBC News Trending, February 20, 2014, <http://preview.tinyurl.com/k2dyt6r>.

74   Michael S. Schmidt and Eric Schmitt, "Russia Failed to Share Data on Suspect, Report Says," *New York Times*, April 10, 2014, <http://tinyurl.com/mubbpfa>.

75   For an outstanding expression of the official creed, see the symposium sponsored by the U.S.-based Heritage Foundation, "Propaganda, Disinformation, and Dirty Tricks: The Resurgence of Russian Political Warfare," Heritage Foundation, April 21, 2014, <http://preview.tinyurl.com/kwhaju2>.

THE NORMS OF JUSTICE, INTERNATIONAL LAW, AND THE 'DUTY TO PROTECT'

ROBERT ABELE

I. Introduction

Writing about Ukraine is like examining the trajectory of a speeding bullet. Events happen so quickly that by the time they are documented in writing, a whole new set of events are in motion.

Nevertheless, there are some aspects about the situation in the Ukraine that do not move so quickly, and through which we can analyze and critique the actions of the parties involved. They happen to be the normative (i.e. ethical) and legal aspects of international relations, neither of which changes as quickly as the events themselves, and by which one may arrive at a nuanced understanding of the events in Ukraine. These dimensions will be the focus of this chapter.

II. The Normative Foundations of Justice and the Basis of International Law

One thing that is nearly universal in discussions of justice is that the norm of equality is primary and intrinsic to the concept of justice. The importance of the norm of equality is demonstrated by the recognition that one cannot state any other principle of justice (e.g. fairness; dignity; self-determination; human rights) without presuming a notion of equality.

Furthermore, international law is itself based on the norm of the equality of nation-states. For example, the United Nations Charter states that the U.N. is "based on the principle of the sovereign equality of all its members." So we begin with the idea that a normative analysis must presume the value of equality as a starting condition.

From this point the positions regarding justice become complex and numerous. For that reason, we will opt for the use of a single model for normative concerns of justice: the political theory of John Rawls, professor of philosophy at Harvard University (1962-2002, the year of his death).

This is not to maintain that Rawls has the only workable set of social norms, or that Rawls' theory is unassailable. It simply stipulates as a heuristic device one of the fullest understandings of political justice as a model for our normative evaluation of the situation in Ukraine.

In 1971, Rawls published his most important work, *A Theory of Justice*, in which equality is the primary norm of both domestic and international relations. In Chapter VI, Rawls uses the principle of equality to establish international norms that are not contingent on social, political, or historical biases and advantages that would favor certain nation-states over others. The principle of equality implies the right to self-determination of peoples without external interference or intervention:

> The basic principle of the law of nations is a principle of equality. Independent peoples organized as states have certain fundamental equal rights. This principle is analogous to the equal rights of citizens in a constitutional regime. One consequence of this equality of nations is the principle of self-determination, the right of a people to settle its own affairs without the intervention of foreign powers.[1]

In *The Law of Peoples* (1993) Rawls reformulates his position in order to apply principles that would be morally acceptable to the foreign policies of truly liberal nation-states. These principles include the obligation of nations to respect the freedom of peoples by other peoples, the honoring of human rights, the duty to assist other people living in unfavorable conditions, and the duty of nonintervention.

The obvious conflict between the duty to assist and the duty of nonintervention is solved by stipulating that the latter overrides the former in cases of extreme human rights violations (p. 37). It is noteworthy that, as controversial as Rawls' text is, each item on the list of the foundational norms of justice that he provides has its direct correlate in contemporary international law today.

This basic normative analysis yields for us some specific political norms which are used not only for international law, but which provide a critical foundation for moral-political analyses. These norms include: equality of opportunity; self-determination; human dignity; and human rights, specifically the rights to security and human sovereignty.

III. International Law and the Rule of Law

A. Self-determination

Most definitions of self-determination revolve around the notion that all peoples have the right to determine their own economic and political development. This right legally came into existence in international law only in 1960, when, due to decolonizing concerns, the U.N. General Assembly adopted Resolution 1514 (XV), which stated that "all peoples have the right to self-determination; by virtue of that right they freely determine their political status and freely pursue their economic, social and cultural development."

Perhaps the most important formulation of self-determination from the United Nations was stated in U.N. General Assembly Resolution 2625, adopted on October 24, 1970, popularly known as the UN Declaration on Friendly Relations. Here are several crucial mandates from this resolution, each one salient for an international law analysis of the situation in Ukraine:

> No State or group of States has the right to intervene, directly or indirectly, for any reason whatsoever, in the internal or external affairs of another State. Consequently, armed intervention and all other forms of interference or attempted threats against the personality of the State or against its political, economic and cultural elements, are in violation of international law.
>
> No State may use or encourage the use of economic, political or any other type of measures to coerce another State in order to obtain from it the subordination of the exercise of its sovereign rights and to secure from it advantages of any kind. Also, no State shall organize, assist, foment, finance, incite or tolerate subversive, terrorist or armed activities directed towards the violent overthrow of the regime of another State, or interfere in civil strife in another State...
>
> Every State has the duty to refrain from organizing, instigating, assisting or participating in acts of civil strife or terrorist acts in another State or acquiescing in organized activities within its territory directed towards the commission of such acts, when the acts referred to ... involve a threat or use of force.

By virtue of the principle of equal rights and self-determination of peoples enshrined in the Charter of the United Nations, all peoples have the right freely to determine, without external interference, their political status and to pursue their economic, social and cultural development.

Each of these mandates involves the interaction of the principles of self-determination and intervention. The Resolution also condemns military intervention against the "territorial integrity or political independence of any State," referring to such incursions as "a war of aggression ... for which there is responsibility under international law."

Additionally, on January 3, 2006, the United States, Russia, and Ukraine, among many other nations, signed the International Covenant on Economic, Social and Cultural Rights, which guarantees, in Part I, Article 1, that "All people have the right of self-determination. By virtue of that right they freely determine their political status and freely pursue their economic, social and cultural development."

B. Intervention

Intervention into another country by a nation or group of nations can take one or all of several forms: military, economic, subversive (i.e. use of propaganda through media to foment civil unrest or revolution in another state), diplomatic (i.e. use of threats of military action by one state against another, in order to affect internal changes in the threatened state), and humanitarian.

Specific to our analysis here, the International Court of Justice (ICJ) has ruled that the right to national sovereignty and self-determination prohibit other nations from aiding insurgents with money, weapons, training, or logistic assistance (e.g. *Democratic Republic of Congo v. Uganda*, 2005).

Humanitarian intervention is frequently the pretext by which one nation claims to have the right to intervene in the affairs of another, especially militarily. By definition, humanitarian intervention is done in order to prevent or end human rights abuses by the state. Thus, the state government itself becomes the target for intervention.

This is the reason that humanitarian intervention tends to be of the military variety. Nonetheless, there is such a thing as non-military humanitarian intervention. The latter variety includes such things as economic sanctions, boycotts, withholding of loans and other aid, etc.

The international laws applicable to intervention may be taken from several sources, each of which is discussed below. The primary sources for such law include *jus cogens*, U.N. General Assembly Resolutions; various regional agreements between nations (e.g. Charter of the Organization of American States, Articles 16, 18, and 19); friendship and cooperation treaties between nations; the U.N. Charter (Article 2(7)), and various charters of international organizations (e.g. the World Bank).

Specifically, the ICJ has ruled (in *Nicaragua v. United States*, 1986) that intervention is prohibited when it bears on "the choice of a political, economic, social and cultural system, and the formulation of foreign policy. Intervention is wrongful when it uses methods of coercion in regard to such choices, which must remain free ones." Further, the definition of intervention includes "the indirect form of support for subversive or terrorist armed activities within another State" (para. 205).

Individual states are banned from unilateral intervention by Article 2(1, 3, and 4) of the U.N. Charter. It is a necessary condition of national sovereignty. Only the United Nations Security Council can make legal decisions regarding intervention (the authority of the UNSC to make such decisions was reiterated in the case *Yugoslavia v. United States of America*, 1999).

However, there is clearly a need in extreme cases for some type of intervention by the world into the affairs of another nation-state. This is demonstrated by the 1994 massacre in Rwanda, the ongoing war in Darfur (which some are calling a genocide), and the state failures of Sudan, Chad, and Somalia to prevent wars, disease and famine from breaking out among their populations.

Given this need, the U.N. adopted a report on the international law of humanitarian intervention, written by the International Commission on Intervention and State Sovereignty (ICISS), and entitled "The Responsibility to Protect." The report remains controversial because it lays out an "emerging consensus" on the limits of state sovereignty by individual human rights. Overall, it has become a widely quoted and used document outlining the main issues of humanitarian intervention.

State sovereignty is maintained as the norm in the Report, but it is limited: State sovereignty implies state responsibility to protect its citizens. When a population is suffering serious harm, and the state is unable or unwilling to halt or avert that civilian harm, "the principle of non-intervention yields to the international responsibility to protect." This international responsibility has three parts to it: prevent; protect; and rebuild. It limits military intervention to traditional Just War Theory, detailed below.

In sum, "what has been gradually emerging is a parallel transition from a culture of sovereign impunity to a culture of national and international accountability," based on "realizing the notion of universal justice—justice without borders" (2.18; 2.19).

C. International Laws of War (Military Intervention)

The ethical norms of warfare have not only been established for many centuries, but they are intrinsic to conceptions of justice (e.g. Rawls, *A Theory of Justice*, pages 378-382), and remain the foci of discussion of war today. Even though they have their detractors, the norms of war have entered not only into international law, but also into the lexicon of most citizens who discuss the justice of a war. The norms are traditionally divided into two categories, with subcategories under each.

The first category answers the question "Is the war justified?" In order to answer that question ethically, three subcategories must be addressed. First, is the cause just? In normative theory as well as in international law, the use of military force must only defensive—i.e. can only be in response to a current or obvious imminent threat to the use military force by another nation.

Second, ethics requires the use of a proportionality criterion, defined as a rational and reasonable calculation that the good resulting from going to war will exceed the evil produced by it.

Third, the military conflict must be the last resort as a means of achieving peace, after all reasonable options and alternatives have been exhausted.

The second category for use of military force must include considerations of discrimination (i.e. non-combatant immunity from direct attack) and proportionality. The latter requires that civilian casualties and infrastructure damage, termed as "collateral damage" by military planners, must not be intended, and must not exceed the overall objective of obtaining peace.

As ethical norms go, these are not detailed and allow in some cases for a robust debate regarding their applicability and even their fulfillment in a war.

The international law of military action by one country against another mandates that the U.N. Charter be followed. This requires a minimum of two things for a nation to be legally justified when using military force. First, the war must be in self-defense. According to the U.N. Charter, Article 51, defines self-defense as "if an armed attack occurs" or in response to a directly/immediately imminent attack. The second criterion is that, if it is not in immediate self-defense, then use of military force must be approved by the U.N. Security Council (Chapter VII, Articles 42 and 43).

There is a third norm in international law that nations are legally compelled to follow, and that is *jus cogens*—i.e. "compelling law," which is also seen to be a "higher law." These are arguably part of the "general legal principles" referred to by the ICJ, and include such laws as rejecting

Flashpoint in Ukraine: How the US Drive for Hegemony Risks World War III

genocide. Included in this type of law is a war of aggression (a.k.a. a crime against peace).

In international law, U.N. General Assembly Resolution 3314 defines aggression not only as military incursion into another state, but any actions engaged in by one state directed toward another "in any manner *inconsistent with* the Charter of the United Nations" (emphasis mine).

IV. Application to Ukraine

This now puts us in a position to assess, through normative justice and international law, the case of U.S., E.U., and NATO meddling in states such as the Ukraine.

A. Background information

It is important to recognize that all current events in Ukraine, particularly as they regard Russia, must be seen in the context of NATO encroachments on Russia since the 1989 fall of the USSR. They make little sense without this reference, especially since history does not operate without precedents, and since it is entirely plausible that the whole Ukrainian catastrophe is the direct result of NATO's ambitions regarding Russia.

For instance, immediately upon being installed, the new government called for "emergency aid" from NATO, and NATO immediately met to consider it. Ukraine is not a NATO member, so aid to Ukraine and the sending of military equipment, etc., are not legally prescribed.

Further, nearly every poll taken in Ukraine shows conclusively that the vast majority of Ukrainian citizens are opposed to NATO membership.[2] Yet NATO continues to encroach.

This is all part of a pattern established by the U.S. and NATO since at least the 1980s, under President Reagan. Reagan assured Gorbachev that NATO would not expand into the former Soviet satellites, but NATO at US direction then turned around and did precisely that. The U.S. also withdrew from the treaty that banned anti-ballistic missiles, and changed its nuclear doctrine to allow it to engage in a "first strike" option.

Second, NATO is and has been deploying troops all along Russia's western borders, not just in Ukraine, but in Poland, Latvia, Estonia, and Lithuania. That this is provocative to Russia can scarcely be denied.

Third, outgoing NATO General Secretary Anders Fogh Rasmussen crowed about the great success of NATO incursions to the East, and advocated a NATO takeover of Bosnia-Herzegovina, Macedonia, Georgia, and Montenegro.

Fourth, we have seen this NATO playbook opened before, as Rasmussen admits. Just since the fall of the Soviet Union in 1989, NATO has taken over the following former Soviet blocs: the Czech Republic, Hungary and Poland (1999), Bulgaria, Estonia, Latvia, Lithuania, Romania, Slovakia, Slovenia (2004), and Albania and Croatia (2009), and now has its eyes on Ukraine.

Finally, we may apply the ICISS report to the situation in Ukraine. The same norms the Report uses may be used to determine when state or NGO intervention in another state is inherently unjust—to wit, when such intervention causes harm to either the civilian population or to a government that has successfully protected its population, both domestically and internationally (e.g. ICISS, 2.25).

Thus, the ICISS recommendation that the normative limit to sovereignty occurs in the obligation of the international community to protect human rights ("responsibility to protect"), when taken in conjunction with current international law and practice on non-intervention (as shown above), can be given in its contrapositive form: when there is no protection of human rights needed, nations have a responsibility *not* to interfere in other nations, specifically when such interference harms that nation's population through human rights violations or is in violation of the right of self-determination and/or of the ability of a democratic government to protect human rights.

Call this the "responsibility not to harm" or even "the right to be left alone" principle (with reference to the dual notions of the people's sovereignty and state sovereignty, as stipulated in the ICISS report, 2.13). The same process has been essentially undertaken by other U.N. covenants regarding torture, etc.

B. The coup d'état in Ukraine

First, was there a coup d'état in the Ukraine? If it can be demonstrated that the U.S. and/or the E.U. played a significant role in the overthrow of the legitimately elected government then in power, then they are in violation of international law, which indisputably recognizes the right to state sovereignty from such interference.

The difficulty in making the case for the illegality of U.S. support for political protests in Ukraine comes from the fact that such intervention was not done militarily, but through economic and semi-subterranean U.S. support for the violent political protests in Ukraine. So one must play a "connect the dots" game to see who is behind the putsch in Ukraine. To that end, here are just a few of the facts we possess regarding U.S./E.U. actions in Ukraine that can make the case not just that the U.S./E.U. did in fact intervene in Ukraine, but did so in violation of basic norms of justice and international law:

Flashpoint in Ukraine: How the US Drive for Hegemony Risks World War III

1) The now-infamous leak of the phone conversation between U.S. State Department Assistant Secretary of State for European and Eurasian Affairs, Victoria Nuland, and Geoffrey Pyatt, U.S. Ambassador to Ukraine, revealed two important pieces of information concerning the degree of U.S. involvement in Ukraine: first, that the U.S. has spent upwards of five billion dollars to foment "regime change" in Ukraine; second, that the U.S. was actively planning who would be appointed to the top government posts in Ukraine, post-coup.[3]

2) Nuland herself, along with U.S. Senator John McCain, made no fewer than four independent trips to Ukraine to publicly hand out cookies to the right-wing, self-proclaimed neo-Nazi parties (i.e. Svoboda and Right Sector).

3) In early November, the E.U. demanded that the Ukrainian government decide one way or another to ally with either the E.U. or Russia. This forced the hand of Ukraine's president, Victor Yanukovych, who had strong and historical ties to Russia as well as to the E.U. The E.U. mandate was aggressive in intent, forcing another government to choose by means of an exclusive disjunction, even though Russia had proposed a tripartite agreement between Ukraine, Russia, and the E.U. The U.S./E.U. rejected such an agreement. This is the very definition of intervention, both in ethical norms and in international law, as we have seen.

4) In November, 2013, Yanukovych cancelled the signing of the Ukraine's association agreement with the E.U. in favor of maintaining and perhaps strengthening Ukraine's ties with Russia. By December, a few thousand organized protestors of the President's decision were in the streets. One must question the timing of the events in Ukraine in the light of this E.U. demand and the Yanukovych rejection of it.

5) As part of the fast-moving events that resulted in the dethroning of Yanukovych, officials from the E.U. and the IMF met with their newly-installed political leaders in order to discuss finances just a few days after they took office. The E.U. and IMF are now demanding that Ukraine establish "austerity measures," which will require deep slashes to state subsidies for the people, including subsidies for energy prices, a ten percent layoff of Ukraine's civil service workers, and a 50% increase in natural gas prices. This, of course, is a direct call for surrender of Ukraine's economy to capitalist hegemons, backed by the threat of being cut out of the global market currently controlled by Western, not Eastern, oligarchs.

6) The Constitution of Ukraine itself, in Article 2, clearly states that "the sovereignty of Ukraine shall extend throughout its entire territory," with Article 3 asserting the centrality of human rights "as the highest social value" in governing Ukraine under the Constitution. Article 5 guarantees popular sovereignty over their government, concluding with the sentence: "No one shall usurp the State power." That this reference is to self-determination is made clearer under Title III, Article 69 of the Constitution, which calls for elections with "direct democracy" concerning the government and governing. Finally, Article 10 protects the use of the Russian language in Ukraine.

When these facts are taken into account, a strong case can be made that the U.S./E.U. involvement in Ukraine constituted a coup d'état. Both the norms of justice and international law are clear in this regard: when other nation(s) interfere with the internal functions of another nation and then involve themselves in overthrowing that elected government, it directly infringes on self-determination and sovereignty, and thus constitutes a coup d'état.

The result of U.S./E.U. involvement in Ukraine was that a democratic form of government was effectively undermined by outside intervention. In its place is a band largely composed of violent fascists and racists who are not democratically oriented. Witness their first legislative act: banning the legal status of the Russian language, in violation the Constitution of Ukraine. Witness further their proclaimed goals of ridding Ukraine of Russians and Jews and stopping the "foreign" adoption of Ukraine children.[4]

As we have seen, there are clear and distinct ethical norms and international laws regarding intervention. To recapitulate a few of them: John Rawls; U.N. General Assembly Resolution 2625; ICJ ruling (*Nicaragua v. United States*, 1986); U.N. Charter (Article 2[1, 3, and 4]); *Yugoslavia v. United States of America*, 1999. Taken together, these norms and laws allow for a very plausible case to be made that U.S. and E.U. involvement in Ukraine is unjustified and unjustifiable.

C. Was the Crimean referendum legally justified?

The secession of Crimea presents a very thick and difficult case, both normatively and legally. We cannot develop that case in detail here, except to note a few salient issues regarding the debate on Crimean secession from the Ukraine. Contrary to the claims of conservative commentators (e.g. Ashley Deeks, "Here's What International Law Says About Russia's Intervention in Ukraine," *New Republic*, March 2, 2014; and Noah Feldman, "Crimea's Democracy Trampled its Constitution," *Bloomberg News*, March

20, 2014), neither ethical-political norms nor international law are clear regarding the issue of secession.

The parties the U.S./E.U. has been supporting and working with in Ukraine—Svoboda and Right Sector—have been widely reported to be deeply anti-Semitic and anti-Russian. In fact, the first act of the new, unelected government in Ukraine was to eliminate the right of Russian nationals to speak their native language, as noted above. But U.N. General Assembly Resolution 2625 permits secession from those States which do not "conduct themselves in compliance with the principle of equal rights and self-determination of peoples and possess a government representing the whole people, belonging to the territory without distinction as to race, creed, or color." When the first thing a new government does is to ban the speaking of the language of a section of the people belonging to the territory, in this case Russian, the case begins under 2625 for the right to secession.

While there is ample prima facie evidence that the Crimean secession was a violation of the Ukrainian Constitution, the arguments making this claim have all failed to take into account two important issues: the moral right to secede, and also legal precedence, such as the International Court of Justice (ICJ) decision concerning Kovoso.

Regarding the first issue, exactly when this moral right obtains and thus the right to secession may occur is highly contentious in normative thought. Some maintain that there must be ongoing and serious injustices and human rights abuses (referred to as "Remedial Right Only Theories), while others contend that the moral right to secession occurs even when no injustice has been experienced (called "Primary Right Theories").[5]

Nor do the arguments opposed to the secession take into account the significant and notable disagreement within international law regarding secession. For example, is the right to secession intertwined with or conceptually dependent on the principle of self-determination? Further, just how does one define secession, legally? There is no agreement between international lawyers on this.[6]

Finally, such arguments do not take note of the ICJ's decision regarding the secession of Kosovo, which stated, in ruling in favor of Kosovo's declaration of independence from Serbia, that "general international law contains no applicable prohibition of declarations of independence."

D. Was the Russian military intervention in Crimea legally justified?

Where Russia clearly can be faulted in its actions in Crimea is with its decision to move its troops outside of Russian bases on the Crimean peninsula and into the cities and civilian airports, and their disarming of Ukrainian troops, all of which are indisputable violations of the longstanding agreement between Russia and Crimea regarding Russian lease of Crimean territory for their military bases.

According to this 1977 agreement, Article 8.1 and 9.1 limit the activities and stationing of Russian troops and military equipment to agreed-upon territories (i.e. military bases). Additionally, according to the Budapest Memorandum of 1994 between Russia and Ukraine, Russia is bound to respect the national boundaries of Ukraine. So when Russian President Vladimir Putin expanded Russian troop movement in Crimea beyond their circumscribed bases, it seems hard to deny that this was, in legal terms, an act of military aggression.

But it seems inconsistent and unreasonable to condemn Russian actions in Crimea, while ignoring the facts that the U.S./E.U. had brought down a democratic government, installed their own government, that the new government then turned to the West and, in thanks, asked for NATO help, and NATO responded by its own de facto "annexation" of Ukraine as part of NATO and the E.U. Russia did it through military intervention; the U.S./E.U. did it through subversion, or as President Obama prefers to call it, "leading from behind," in essence by hiring a group of violent subversives to upset the order of the country it targets, just like the U.S. did in Libya and Syria. Both types of action are banned by international laws regarding intervention, as we have seen.

Regarding military intervention, the U.S. is once again using its military might as a direct threat to Russia, should Russia intervene in the U.S. intervention in Ukraine (beyond Crimea). Even more significant than the threats, the U.S. has substantially increased its military presence in the Baltic States, as of this writing sending six F-15C combat planes to Lithuania, holding Navy exercises in the Baltic Sea, and sending 300 military personnel and 12 warplanes to Poland. Additional U.S. troops are being sent to Latvia and Estonia. Germany and Britain have also committed to escalating their own military presence and maneuvers in the region.[7]

This is all being done under the pretext of an "existential threat" (although factually non-existent) of Russian military intervention in Ukraine. In reality, the U.S. is moving its military might into positions in Ukraine and surrounding areas in order to maintain their intervention in Ukraine and to prevent a military response from Russia. Where do such U.S. threats and potential military action in Ukraine stand regarding our normative and international law concerns?

The use of Western military force to occupy Ukraine or any other former Soviet territories surrounding Russia would violate not only the Just War Theory of "just cause" and "proper intention," but it would also be a direct violation of international law.

Once again, as in Iraq and Libya, the U.S. would be committing the crime of "aggression," the most supreme of all crimes, according Justice Robert Jackson, chief prosecutor for the United States at the Nuremburg Trials. The Nuremburg Tribunal itself stated: "To initiate a war of aggression ... is not only an international crime; it is the supreme international crime, differing only from other war crimes in that it contains within itself the accumulated evil of the whole."

However, Russia is also in violation of these criteria by its military takeover of Crimea, as we have just seen. In the case of the use of military force, Russia was not justified in taking over Crimea, and the U.S. would not be justified in militarily occupying Ukraine.

But if the U.S. agrees to a treaty with the new Ukraine government, and that government has not been democratically elected, then the treaty is illegitimate, since the right to sovereignty and to non-intervention has been both normatively and legally established. Thus, it could only be described as a legal fig leaf to cover what is in reality an occupation.

The military issue now becomes the use of threats to use force, as the U.S. has done repeatedly through the Obama administration pronouncements and through its military actions in and around Ukraine. But as we have seen, U.N. General Assembly Resolution 2625, adopted on October 24, 1970, prohibits it:

> ...armed intervention and all other forms of interference or attempted threats against the personality of the State or against its political, economic and cultural elements, are in violation of international law," and "every State has the duty to refrain from organizing, instigating, assisting or participating in acts of civil strife or terrorist acts in another State or acquiescing in organized activities within its territory directed towards the commission of such acts, when the acts referred to ... involve a threat or use of force.

V. Conclusion: Looking forward

The situation in the Ukraine calls for an analysis that extends beyond the immediate exigencies of the local events there, and involves a wider, global analysis that examines what portends for the future, given the rapacious greed and lust for power that pushes the U.S. to attempt hegemony in all directions. In answer to that, as we have seen, there is an emerging international discussion about, if not a consensus on, emphasizing norms that prioritize human rights, human dignity, and human security and sovereignty over state sovereignty.

Taken together with current historical movements, this renewed focus on norms that ensure human dignity could result in the diminishing of the power of states and most especially of empires, in favor of (and perhaps even being replaced by) an international order of peoples: a world order based on a community of citizens whose sovereignty means that, qua human, they are the locus of political arrangements, not state institutional arrangements or concerns.

This could be secured by an international arrangement seeking to guarantee the priority of human rights to state interests, thus fulfilling the democratic norm that power reside in the people, not in its leaders. In this light, sovereignty would be defined as the right to self-determination without internal or external pressures or interference from parties whose intentions are questionable in regards to increasing the right to self-determination for all persons involved, instead of just a few elites.

It is thus plausible that, as the U.S. and NATO forcefully push to the East in Ukraine (and the former Yugoslavia, and in Syria, and in Afghanistan) and to the West in the Pacific Rim (through Obama's "Asian pivot"), they are initiating a process of a change of world order to something far beyond the intended aim of Western dominance, to an era of reduced sovereignty of the nation-state due to the decided lack of security of those being either "hemmed in," isolated by, or taken over by, the world's hegemon. Ultimately, only two things will stop this (U.S.) superpower from expansion and world control: it meets its natural limitation (perhaps by over-extending its consumptive reach beyond its ability to finance it; or perhaps the depletion of the natural resources required to run the engine of Empire), or the people in the world, independently and with a recognition that they are all together in the struggle, begin to apply pressure on the superpower.

This "pushback" will entail an understanding and application of the very normative concepts we have discussed in this chapter: that power comes from and applies to the people, and that the sovereignty of the people is the value and commitment that unites them, not the artificial borders that separate them.

In any case, the implication for weakened or limited state sovereignty by human rights opens the way for a global democracy. It would be recognized under this new philosophy that institutions have their own distinct concerns; that those concerns are not in the interests of the individuals they ostensibly represent; that primary among those institutional interests is the growth of power toward the top levels of that institution; and that those institutional interests must be hemmed in by notions of individual autonomy, guaranteed by human rights.

One hope is that in a global democracy, the monolith of superpowers like the current U.S. Empire would become a thing of the past. If this is to happen, it remains up to the citizens of their governing institutions to initiate normative limitations to the natural upward power movements within ostensibly democratic government structures, so that interventions into other countries at the behest of such institutional drives for geo-political power and resource-control, such as is seen with the intervention of the U.S. and E.U. into Ukraine, will be both less likely to happen in the future, and will come with much a greater sanction against unwarranted intervening nations or municipalities and their agents.

ENDNOTES

1. John Rawls, *A Theory of Justice,* 1971, p. 378.
2. See Jonathan Steele, "The Ukraine Crisis: John Kerry and NATO must Calm Down and Back Off," *The Guardian*, March 2, 2014.
3. See Daya Gamage, "U.S. 'Regime Change' Plot in Ukraine Uncovered: How's Sri Lanka Destabilization?" *Asian Tribune*, February 12, 2014.
4. See "The Fascist Danger in Ukraine" [March 6, 2014], "The Real Face of Ukraine's Maidan "Democrats," [March 28, 2014], and "Western-backed Ukrainian Opposition Seizes Power in Fascist-let Putsch" [February 24, 2014], all from World Socialist Web Site.
5. For both types, see A. Buchanan, "Theories of Secession," *Philosophy and Public Affairs*, 1997, 261: 31-61).
6. See Ioana Cismas, "Secession in Theory and Practice: the Case of Kosovo and Beyond," *Goettingen Journal of International Law* 2, 2010, 531-587.
7. Stefan Steinberg and Peter Schwarz, "NATO Steps up Military Pressure on Russia," World Socialist Web Site, April 1, 2014.

THE ODESSA MASSACRE

STEPHEN LENDMAN

No-holds-barred barbarism explains it.

What happened in Odessa exceeded the horrors of early reports. Neo-Nazi Right Sector thugs set Odessa's Trade Union House ablaze. People were trapped inside. Dozens were massacred. Scores more were injured. Many remain missing. They're either dead or in neo-Nazi hands. Early reports way underestimated what happened. It's multiples worse than reported. If alive, they face torture and other forms of abuse. They won't survive. They might as well be dead.

On May 5, Live Journal (LJ)[1] headlined "How the thugs killed Odessa inhabitants in the Trade Union House (TUH) - the details of bloody scenario." Check out the horrific photographic evidence they provide.

Casualties far exceed early reports. Neo-Nazis trapped Odessans inside TUH. An unwitnessed massacre followed.

Setting the building ablaze was strategy. It was done to conceal mass murder. Ordinary Ukrainians were slaughtered in cold blood. Nearby tents were set on fire. Doing so preceded what followed.

"Federalism supporters had no Molotov cocktails prepared in advance," said LJ. "Where inside the building did fire erupt," it asked.

Right Sector thugs awaited there before slaughtering people began. They were armed and dangerous. They were well prepared in advance.

Police stood by and did nothing. They conspired with fascist killers. So did Odessa firefighters. They "only appeared when massive entrance doors were burned through," said LJ. "Only in a single room in the five-storey building with ceilings over 3 meters high had fire visible from outside."

Who had access to TUH's roof?

"Perhaps those who in advance got the keys to locked steel gratings protecting the roof doors," said LJ.

Charred bodies were shown on upper floors untouched by fire. How did they get there? Who's responsible? They were murdered in advance. Things were made to seem like fire consumed them. Again, check those LJ photos out. LJ photo captions read:

The same bodies from another viewpoint:

- Wooden battery panel, wooden railings on the stairs and chipboard sheet don't look burnt;

- Blue oval points to the barricade made of tables, chairs and cabinets. It hadn't even touched by fire, unlike the charred bodies lying nearby;

- From where has the barricade appeared? It was built by the Right Sector thugs in order to lock people trying to save themselves on the above floors.

Corpses were dragged from where they died. People perished inside from gunshot wounds, strangling and beatings. Some were thrown from windows. They didn't jump. It bears repeating. Setting TUH ablaze sought to mask what happened. Fire didn't kill activists inside. Neo-Nazi hoodlums did.

Another LJ caption: "Have you noticed that ... some dead people had burnt heads and shoulders only?"

Clothes they wore showed no signs of fire. Someone doused their shoulders and heads with "flammable stuff." Hands and wrists were burned to the bone.

Photos showed "a strange 'whitewash' " on the floor. It's "powder from extinguishers..." Right Sector thugs used it on people they killed. They did so to protect themselves from fire and carbon monoxide poisoning.

Hardwood floors show no signs of fire damage. Victims were killed by other means.

Note: according to one of the main versions of what happened on May 2 in Odessa, the Right Sector thugs performed a false flag operation."

They put St. George's Ribbons (symbols of anti-Maidan federalism supporters) and organized violent provocation against Maidan supporters (i.e. against their own allies), in order to later blame federalism supporters and make them look responsible for death of many people.

A dead woman was unclothed below her waist. "Most likely she was raped, then doused with a flammable mixture and set aflame."

Photographic evidence is damning. So are independent videos. They show mass murder by means other than fire and/or carbon monoxide poisoning. Some bodies had multiple gunshot wounds to the head. People were executed in cold blood at point blank range. A pregnant woman was strangled with an electric wire. She cried for help in vain. You can hear her cries on the video LJ provides

Numbers killed may be as many as 300, said LJ. "Most people, especially children and women, were hacked to death with axes and clubbed to death with wooden sticks in the (TUH) basement."

On May 7, RT International correspondent Alexey Yaroshevsky interviewed a survivor.[2] Tatyana Ivananko said pro-autonomy activists tried hiding from Right Sector thugs. They barricaded themselves for protection.

"On our way up the stairs, we were taking plywood sheets inside so that we could block the doors and prevent them from getting into the building," she said.

They were inside before fire started. They wouldn't let anyone out. They set parts of the first and third floors ablaze. Other floors weren't affected. Video evidence showed death by means other than fire.

"Have a look at the video," said Tatyanya. An "armed man in a vest is carrying a gun."

Shooting began outside. People tried to escape. They were trapped inside TUH. "(M)any were strangled" to death.

Others were shot at point blank range. Some were thrown from windows. It bears repeating. They didn't jump.

"17-year-old hooligans were finishing off people with bats," said Tatyanya.

Claiming they were foreign nationals didn't wash. They were Ukrainians. They were Odessan residents.

"They all loved their city deeply. We stood shoulder to shoulder from the very first day," Tatyanya stressed. "A regional council deputy, Vyacheslav Markin, is also known to have been killed" inside.

Victims "were innocent civilians who wanted to live a normal life rather than just 'survive'—s is now the case in Ukraine."

"The guilty party is the current government, which clearly seeks to divide Ukraine."

Flashpoint in Ukraine: How the US Drive for Hegemony Risks World War III

Videos circulating online are damning. One includes a woman atop TUH. She's screaming for help. Street-level thugs shout she's "not a woman. She's a separatist. Beat the s..t out of her, so that she finally shuts up!"

"Yeah, women sit at home with their children, and this one's an animal!"

Acting prosecuting general Oleg Makhnitsky lied. He claimed it's too early to know who set the building ablaze. Clear evidence is incontrovertible.

Coverup and lies conceal it. Mass murder is ignored. Kiev putschists praise it. Expect similar atrocities repeating. Expect much worse ones ahead.

Perhaps Eastern Ukraine will replicated earlier Cambodian Killing Fields. Maybe before things end.

Coverup and denial will try concealing it. The worst is yet to come.

ENDNOTES

1 <http://ersieesist.livejournal.com/813.html>
2 <http://rt.com/news/157256-odessa-witness-massacre-ukraine/>

UKRAINE: FROM COUP TO POLICE STATE

ANDREW KOLIN

The current crisis in the Ukraine: A brief timeline of the chain of events

The crisis unfolded in November 2013 when Ukraine's then-president Viktor Yanukovich rejected a trade deal with the European Union and accepted a $15 billion bailout from Moscow. This led to a three-month street protest and the overthrow of Yanukovich on Feb. 22, 2014. Moscow denounced the events as a coup and refused to recognize the new Ukrainian authorities.

- Nov. 21, 2013 -- Kiev announces suspension of trade and association talks with the EU and seeks to revive economic ties with Moscow.

- Nov. 24 -- One hundred thousand people rally in Kiev against spurning the EU.

- Nov. 29 -- Yanukovich does not sign the association agreement.

- Nov. 30 -- Riot police break up Kiev demonstration by force. Protest turns against Yanukovich.

- Dec. 1 – Three hundred and fifty thousand people protest in Kiev. Opposition leaders call for Yanukovich to resign.

- Dec. 4 – Senior EU officials and ministers start visiting the protest square.

Flashpoint in Ukraine: How the US Drive for Hegemony Risks World War III

- Dec. 6 – Yanukovich has unannounced talks with Putin.

- Dec. 13 – Yanukovich has first face-to-face talks with opposition with no breakthroughs.

- Dec. 15 – EU suspends talks with Ukraine on the pact.

- Dec. 18 – Tens of thousands in Kiev call for Yanukovich to resign over bailout period.

- January 15, 2014 – Ukrainian courts ban protest in central Kiev.

- January 17 – Yanukovich signs new laws, banning antigovernment protests.

- January 19 – Thousands protest in Kiev, in defiance of the ban.

- Jan. 26 – Police clash with protesters in Kiev. Yanukovich offers important government posts to the opposition.

- Jan. 27 – Yanukovich and opposition agree to scrap some of the anti-protest laws.

- Jan. 31 – Yanukovich signs into law a conditional amnesty for those detained.

- Feb. 7 – Moscow accuses US of trying to foment a coup in Ukraine.

- Feb. 14 – Russia accuses EU of seeking to make Ukraine a "sphere of influence."

- Feb. 21 – Opposition leaders sign EU-mediated peace pact.

- Feb. 22 – Ukraine's Parliament votes to remove Yanukovich. He denounces the removal as a coup.

- Feb. 26 – Ukraine names ministers for new government. Russia puts 150,000 troops on high alert.

- Feb. 27 – Armed men seize Crimean Parliament, raise Russian flag. Kiev's new rulers warn Moscow to keep troops within its naval base on the peninsula.

- March 1 – Putin wins Parliamentary approval to invade Ukraine. In Kiev, new government warns of war, puts troops on high alert and appeals to NATO.

- Mar. 2 – Russian forces tighten grip on the Crimea.

- Mar. 5 – Russia rebuffs calls to withdraw troops from Crimea.

- Mar. 6 – Crimea's pro-Russian leadership votes to join Russia and sets a referendum date for March 16.

The final results were historic. Crimean authorities showed how real democracy works. International observers praised the process. The voting went peacefully and smoothly. It was scrupulously open, free, and fair. No irregularities occurred. None were seen. There was no pressure, no intimidation. Not a single Russian soldier was in sight. None invaded; none occupy Crimea. Claims otherwise are false.

The turnout was impressive. It was unprecedented. It exceeded 83%. In Sevastopol, it was 89.5%.Over 1.274 million Crimeans voted. Plus Sevastopol residents excluded from this total. An astonishing 96.77% chose Russia—95.6% of Sevastopol voters. Russians comprise about 60% of Crimea's population. Ukrainians around 25%. Tatars 12%. Results show Crimeans overwhelmingly reject the Kiev putschists. Russians, Ukrainians and Tatars agree. Claims otherwise are false.

On March 17, Vladimir Putin endorsed Crimea's union with Russia. On March 18, he signed a reunification treaty. Both Russian houses of parliament approved it overwhelmingly. On March 21, reunification became official. Crimeans are going home.

Given the preceding chain of events, its starting point to examine how the United States and the EU present the nature of the crisis. German Chancellor Angela Merkel claimed in Parliament that the Kremlin's actions could "massively" damage Russia. Merkel urged economic sanctions. Her tone has since become more blunt, warning that further "steps would contribute to escalation to an assessment that the current crisis is a very serious conflict in Europe." During the Obama-Merkel phone call, they agreed that Russia has committed a "clear violation of Ukrainian sovereignty and territorial integrity."

The issue, which Obama and Merkel have sidestepped, is that the

Russian response to send troops as the crisis unfolded could be understood as a reflexive response on the part of Putin, in which he regarded the protests and the Ukrainian Parliament's removal of Yanukovich as all part of a coup d'état. One must consider the significance of Obama's meeting with the Ukrainian interim prime minister, Arseniy Yatsenyuk. After his meeting with Obama, Yatsenyuk made an interesting remark: "We fight for our sovereignty and will never surrender.» He also remarked that Ukraine «is and will be a part of the Western world." Even more significant is Yatsenyuk's intention to meet with members of Congress, the World Bank and the International Monetary Fund, indicative of his efforts to establish international support for a new Ukrainian government.

A number of underlying assumptions can be deduced from Yatsenyuk›s actions. One is that the US and the EU are expressing support for the coup d'état. Another is passage of the expected Senate foreign relations committee package of loans and aid for Ukraine. The aid package contains $1 billion in loan guarantees, $50 million for democracy-building and another $400 million for security in the Ukraine.

Most of all, one can interpret US and EU support as based on the assertion that this was a democratic coup d'tat. The US and the EU characterize this democratic coup d'état as mobilizing segments of the population that destabilized the existing government by calling into question its legitimacy and expressing a willingness to use force or the threat of force to replace those in power. With a successful democratic coup, other policy options would be put in place.

The assertion that this is a democratic coup d'état masks the official US-EU support for regime change in the Ukraine and follows a pattern of policy elsewhere. For example, the Egyptian military coup of 2011 was at first presented as a democratic coup d›état with the removal of Mubarak. A mass-based movement supported the ruling military, which was supposed to transfer legislative authority to the Parliament after parliamentary elections. As events unfolded in 2012-2013, the military was unwilling to surrender its control over the government to the Egyptian people.

Another example of a so-called democratic coup d'état occurred in 1974 when the Portuguese military with popular support, overthrew the Estada Novo (New State), a creation of Antonio de Oliveria Salazar dating back to 1930. Until the overthrow of Estada Novo, the regime in power manifested authoritarian traits of elite rule. There was an absence of procedural democracy, political parties were illegal and voting for state-sponsored candidates took place only immediately prior to an impending election. The political police PIDE (Polica Internacionalle de Defesa do Estado) suppressed civil liberties, assailed dissent through preventive detention, and tortured those in detention.

The sole source of resistance to the regime emerged from the military. With many Portuguese having served in the military, it was an integral part of Portuguese society. As the standard of living and job prospects continued to decline, widespread resistance grew, spearheaded by a revolt of two hundred junior military officers, elements of the armed forces movement, which prepared and staged a coup on April 25, 1974. Mass support for the coup appeared as many thousands took to the streets.

A third example of a democratic coup is the Turkish coup of 1960. The one party rule in Turkey put in place in 1923 the Republican People's Party (Cumhuriyet Halk Partisi) or CHP. In 1946, the Democrat Party (Domokrat Purti) or DP appeared on the scene and in 1950 came to power in Parliament and ousted CHP. Even though CHP was out of power, it maintained support from the military and the bureaucracy for the CHP ideology of "Kemalism," the belief in the political values of modernization, national unity and secularism.

The DP was well aware of the social support for CHP ideology and from 1950 to 1960, took measures to target social segments supportive of CHP. These measures amounted to diminishing political diversity. In response to DP initiatives, protesters took to the streets to demonstrate in September 1955. In response, the DP declared martial law. To further cement DP authority, the prime minister, Adnan Menderes, proposed a "new type of democracy" in which he outlined a blanket policy of wholesale repression to any opposition to DP policy under the guise of national security.

One aspect of this policy authorized the Turkish Parliament to investigate subversive activity. The effect was to create a DP commission with the authority to criminalize thought and action so as to imprison violators. In response to the activities of this commission, mass protests unfolded in April 1960. In an act of defiance, the DP passed a law, which augmented the powers of the commission. Nonetheless, the wave of protests intensified. Once again, the DP declared martial law, authorizing the military to shoot protesters.

As was the case in Egypt, the Turkish military's refusal to fire on protesters set the stage for the coup d'état of May 1960. These examples of democratic coups are exceptions and not the norm. The overwhelming majority of coups are carried out to overthrow a democratic-based government.

Returning to the current crisis in Ukraine, there are two essential elements that define the nature of the crisis. One is the official cover story presented by the United States and the European union of a democratic coup d'état.

The second crucial element is the underlying motives as to why the US and the EU have such an interest in the Ukraine. Upon close examination, the so-called democratic coup is not so democratic after all. For one thing, Ukraine could not be characterized as a homogenous democracy. There are two Ukraines: one half wants to remain associated with Russia while the other half seeks association with the West.

As one segment articulates closer ties with the West, the US and the EU have provided rationalizations and encouragement for the protesters who throw homemade bombs and use weapons to shoot at the police and government officials.

One reason for western support of this destabilizing violence is the two-decade old policy of efforts to expand NATO during the Clinton-Bush-Obama regimes. In addition, there was support for non-governmental organizations, NGOs, to set up shop inside Russia.

Other indicators point to western interests in pursuing military expansion near Russian borders, such as the US military installations and the establishment of a military base in the former Soviet Republic of Georgia.

From the past to the present, the mindset of the US and EU amounts to a divide and conquer strategy for the Ukraine, putting it in the position of having to choose between Europe and Russia.

When Obama remarked that "President Yanukovich and the Ukranian government have the primary responsibility to prevent the violence," it amounted in actuality to justifying the actions of those committing the violent acts.

Western involvement in and support for the coup appeared in a leaked conversation between the US ambassador to the Ukraine Geoffrey Pyatt and Victoria Nuland, the top US diplomat to Europe, who indicated their preference for the then leaders of the opposition movement, Klitschko and Yatsenyuk. The other name mentioned, Tyagnybok, is the leader of the extremist Freedom Party.

Another factor contributing to the current crisis is the fact that former President Yanukovich, like his predecessors, had, since Ukrainian independence in 1992, been pursuing policies to enact economic austerity measures in conformity to those articulated by the IMF. These measures included the privatization of services, various spending cuts, and the reduction of government subsidies.

Underlying this democratic coup d'état are western capitalist financial interests gaining access to public monies for an upward redistribution to the one percent. With the imposition of IMF austerity measures, the seeds were planted for social unrest. With the decline of social services and with it the standard of living, a westward turn gained traction as the road to economic mobility.

Consider the likely result of embracing western style capitalism. For one thing, the Ukranian economy would be hard pressed to fulfill the conditions imposed by the IMF in order to receive the aid. The economic squeeze on the Ukraine would amount to the shouldering of long-term debt.

In order to adhere to IMF mandates, the Ukrainian economy would have to initiate policies that support a capitalist market economy. Such a policy would widen social inequality in part by giving extensive tax breaks to the top one percent.

Contributing to the problem, since independence Ukraine has been governed by corrupt party officials who also supported privatization, which oriented the benefits of such policies to the upper one percent.

While all this is taking place, western interests seek to exploit the situation. Behind the scenes, prior to the outbreak of protests, US public and private organizations, such as the National Endowment for Democracy, Freedom House, the Democratic Institutes of the Democratic and Republican parties and various NGOs, have provided funding, ideology and training for segments of the Ukrainian populace to incite an uprising.

Given the fact that the crisis in Ukraine continues to evolve, it is difficult to predict how it will be resolved. If past history is a guide, US and European interests in shaping the form of government in Ukraine are a troubling factor. Consider the end result of past US policy toward Iran, Iraq and Chile: once all the elements were put in place, the overthrow of the governments in power by a coup was supported by a manufactured uprising. After the facade of a democratic coup, the US proceeded to assist in putting in place a police state. The absolute powers of the Shah, Hussain and Pinochet were implemented through a police state, the common features of which included an ideology of extreme crisis and threat so as to place the country in an ongoing state of national emergency.

Next, clear structural changes in the functioning of state power emerge; for example, a division of labor appears wherein a specialized part of the state monopolizes security functions. Following this development, a political police is created to investigate political crimes, which include thoughts and actions enabling the state to exercise mind-body control and suppress diverse viewpoints, including the elimination of free association. The flow of information (propaganda) from the state centers on generating unquestioned support for the regime in power.

In the absence of legal restraints on the exercise of state power, there is neither due process nor civil liberties. From thence, state power is used to exercise body-control, which in one form manifests as preventive detention in relation to political crimes.

With body seizure and control, confinement is in principle unlimited. Once processes of confinement and Interrogation are established, torture unfolds as another form of body control, using and abusing peoples› bodies as a demonstration of state power.

Flashpoint in Ukraine: How the US Drive for Hegemony Risks World War III

If a prediction is possible at this time for how the crisis will be resolved through Western involvement, it is the formation of a police state in Ukraine.

THE KIEV PUTSCH

REBEL WORKERS TAKE POWER IN THE EAST

JAMES PETRAS

Introduction

Not since the US and EU took over Eastern Europe, including the Baltic countries, East Germany, Poland and the Balkans and converted them into military outposts of NATO and economic vassals, have the Western powers moved so aggressively to seize a strategic country, such as the Ukraine, which poses an existential threat to Russia.

Up until 2013 the Ukraine was a "buffer state", basically a non-aligned country, with economic ties to both the EU and Russia. Ruled by a regime closely tied to local, European, Israeli and Russian based oligarchs, the political elite was a product of a political upheaval in 2004, (the so-called "Orange Revolution") funded by the US. Subsequently, for the better part of a decade the Ukraine underwent a failed experiment in Western backed 'neo-liberal' economic policies. After nearly two decades of political penetration the US and EU were deeply entrenched in the political system via long-standing funding of so-called non-governmental organizations, political parties and paramilitary groups. The strategy of the US and EU was to install a pliant regime which would join the European Common Market and NATO as a subordinate client state. Negotiations between the EU and the Ukraine government proceeded slowly. They eventually faltered because of the onerous conditions demanded by the EU and the more favorable economic concessions offered by Russia. Having failed to negotiate the annexation of the Ukraine to the EU, and not willing to await scheduled constitutional elections, the NATO powers activated their well-financed and organized NGOs, client political leaders and armed paramilitary groups to violently overthrow the elected government. The violent putsch succeeded and a US appointed civilian-military junta was imposed.

The junta was composed of pliant neoliberal and chauvinist neo-fascist 'ministers'. The former were selected by the US, to administer and enforce a new political and economic order: privatization of public firms and resources; a break in trade and investment ties with Russia; the elimination of Russian military bases in Crimea and the end of military exports. The neo-fascists and sectors of the military and police repressed the pro-democracy opposition in the West and East. They oversaw the repression of bilingual speakers (Russian-Ukrainian), institutions and practices. They purged opposition office holders in the West and East and imposed local governors by fiat—essentially creating a martial law regime.

The Strategic Targets of the NATO-Junta

NATO's violent, high risk seizure of the Ukraine was driven by several strategic military objectives. These included:

1. The ousting of Russia from its military bases in Crimea—and turning them into NATO bases facing Russia,

2. The conversion of the Ukraine into a springboard for penetrating Southern Russia and the Caucasus, a forward position to politically support liberal pro-NATO parties and NGOs within Russia.

3. The disruption of sectors of the Russian military defense industry linked to the Ukrainian production chain, by ending the export of crucial engines and parts to Russia.

The Ukraine was an important part of the Soviet Union's military industrial complex. NATO strategists, planning the putsch, were aware that one-third of the Soviet defense industry remained in the Ukraine after the break-up of the USSR and that forty percent of the Ukraine's exports to Russia, until recently, were armaments and machinery. More specifically the Motor-Sikh plant, manufactured the engines for most Russian military helicopters including the engines for one thousand attack helicopters—on order. NATO strategists directed their political stooges in Kiev to suspend all military deliveries to Russia, including medium range air to air missiles, inter-continental ballistic missiles, transport planes and space rockets, as the *Financial Times* pointed out on April 21 (p. 3.) US and EU military strategists saw their putsch as a way to undermine Russian air, sea and border defenses. President Putin has acknowledged the blow but insists that Russia will be able to substitute domestic in-house production in less than two years.

4) The extension of the military encirclement of Russia with forward military bases in the Ukraine matching those from the Baltic to

the Balkans, from Turkey to the Caucasus and then onward from Georgia into the autonomous Russian Federation.

The US-EU encirclement of Russia is designed to end Russian access to the North Sea, the Black Sea and the Mediterranean. By encircling and confining Russia to an isolated land mass without 'outlets to the sea', US-EU empire builders seek to limit Russia's role as a rival power center and possible counter-weight in the Middle East, North Africa, Southwest Asia and the North Atlantic.

Ukraine Putsch: Integral to Imperial Expansion

The US and the EU are intent on destroying independent, nationalist and non-aligned governments throughout the world and converting them into imperial satellites by whatever means are effective. For example, the NATO armed mercenary invasion of Syria is directed at overthrowing the nationalist Assad government and establishing a pro-NATO vassal state. The attack on Syria serves multi-purposes: eliminating a Russian ally and maritime base; undermining a supporter of Palestine and adversary of Israel; encircling Iran and Hezbollah in Lebanon and establishing new military bases on Syrian soil.

The NATO seizure of the Ukraine has a multiplier effect that reaches 'upward' toward Russia and 'downward' toward the Middle East and control over its oil wealth.

The recent NATO wars against Russian allies or trading partners confirms this prognosis. In Libya, the Qaddafi regime stood out as a partisan of a non-aligned policies amidst Western satellites like Morocco, Egypt and Tunisia. Qaddafi was overthrown via a massive NATO air assault. Egypt's mass anti-Mubarak rebellion and emerging democracy was subverted by a military coup and eventually returned to the US-Israeli-NATO orbit. Armed incursions by NATO proxy Israel against Hamas-Gaza, Lebanon-Hezbollah and US-EU sanctions against Iran are all directed against potential allies or trading partners of Russia.

The US has moved forcefully from encircling Russia via 'elections and free markets' in Eastern Europe to relying on military force and economic sanctions in the Ukraine, Middle East and Asia.

Regime Change in Russia: From Global Power to Vassal State

The strategic objective is to isolate Russia from without, undermine its military capability and erode its economy, in order to strengthen NATO's political and economic collaborators inside Russia. The imperial strategic goal is to return to power the neoliberal political proxies, who facilitated the pillage and destruction of Russia during the infamous Yeltsin decade. The US-EU power grab in the Ukraine is a big step in that direction.

Evaluating the Encirclement and Conquest Strategy

So far, the NATO seizure of the Ukraine has not moved forward as planned. First of all the violent seizure of power by overtly pro-NATO elites, explicitly intent on breaking military agreements over Russian bases in Crimea, forced Russia to intervene in support of the local population. Following a free and open referendum, Russia annexed the region and secured its strategic military presence.

While Russia retained its naval presence on the Black Sea ... the NATO junta in Kiev unleashed a large-scale military offensive against the pro-democracy, anti-coup Russian-speaking majority in the eastern half of the Ukraine who have been demanding a federal form of government reflecting Ukraine's cultural diversity. The US-EU promoted a "military response" to mass popular dissent and encouraged the coup-regime to eliminate the civil rights of the Russian speaking majority through neo-Nazi terror and to force the population to accept junta-appointed regional rulers in place of their elected leaders.

In response to this repression, popular self-defense committees and local militias quickly sprang up and the Ukrainian army was initially forced back with thousands of soldiers refusing to shoot their own compatriots on behalf of the Western-installed regime in Kiev. For a while, the NATO-backed neoliberal-neo-fascist coalition junta had to contend with the disintegration of its 'power base'. At the same time, 'aid' from the EU, IMF and the US failed to compensate for the cut-off of Russian trade and energy subsidies. Under the advice of visiting US CIA Director, John Brennan, the Kiev Junta then dispatched its elite "special forces" trained by the CIA and FBI to carry out massacres against pro-democracy civilians and popular militias. They bussed in armed thugs to the diverse city of Odessa who staged an 'exemplary' massacre: Burning the city's major trade union headquarters and slaughtering 41, mostly unarmed civilians who were trapped in the building with its exits blocked by neo-Nazis. The dead included many women and teenagers who had sought shelter from the rampaging neo-Nazis. The survivors were brutally beaten and imprisoned by the 'police' who had passively watched while the building burned.

The Coming Collapse of the Putsch-Junta

Obama's Ukraine power grab and efforts to isolate Russia has provoked opposition in the EU. US sanctions prejudice major multinationals with deep ties in Russia. The US military buildup in Eastern Europe, the Balkans and the Black Sea raises tensions and threatens a large scale military conflagration. US-EU threats on Russia's border has increased popular support and strengthened the Russian leadership. The strategic power grab in the Ukraine has radicalized and deepened the polarization of Ukrainian politics-between neo-fascist and pro-democracy forces.

While the imperial strategists are extending and escalating their military build-up in Estonia and Poland and pouring arms into the Ukraine, the entire power grab rests on very precarious political and economic foundations—which could collapse within the year—amidst a bloody civil war/inter-ethnic slaughter.

The Ukraine junta has already lost political control over a third of the country to pro-democracy movements and self-defense militias. Secondly, by cutting off strategic exports to Russia to serve US military interests, the Ukraine lost a major market which cannot be replaced, as its military exports are geared to Russian specifications. The loss of Russian markets is leading to mass unemployment, especially among skilled industrial workers who may immigrate to Russia. Ballooning trade deficits and the erosion of state revenues is leading to economic collapse. Thirdly, as a result of the Kiev junta's submission to NATO it has lost billions of dollars in subsidized energy from Russia. High energy costs make Ukrainian industries non-competitive in global markets. Fourthly, in securing loans from the IMF and the EU, the junta agreed to eliminate food and energy subsidies, severely depressing household incomes. Bankruptcies are on the rise, as imports from the EU and elsewhere displace formerly protected local industries.

No *new* investments are flowing in because of the violence, instability and conflicts between neo-fascists and neoliberals in the junta. Just to stabilize the day to day operations of government, the junta needs a no-interest $30 billion dollar hand-out—from its NATO patrons, an amount which is not forthcoming now or in the immediate future.

It is clear that NATO 'strategists' who planned the putsch were only thinking about weakening Russia militarily and gave no thought to the political, economic and social costs of sustaining a puppet regime in Kiev dependent on Russian markets and energy. Moreover, they overlooked the political, industrial and agricultural dynamics of the predictably hostile Eastern regions of the country. Washington strategists may have based their calculations on instigating a Yugoslavia-style break-up accompanied by massive ethnic cleansing amidst population transfers and slaughter. Undeterred by the millions of civilian casualties, Washington considers its policy of dismantling Yugoslavia, Iraq and Libya to have been great political-military successes.

Ukraine most certainly will enter a prolonged and deep depression, including a precipitous decline in exports, employment and output. Most likely the economic collapse will lead to nationwide protests and social unrest spreading from East to West, from South to North. Social upheavals will certainly impact on the armed forces, even now, only a fraction precariously under control of the Kiev junta. The US-EU are not likely to directly intervene militarily since they would face a prolonged war on Russia's border at a time when public opinion in the US is suffering from imperial war exhaustion, and European business interests with links to Russian resource companies are resisting consequential sanctions.

The US-EU putsch resulted in a failed regime, and a society riven by violent conflicts. What in fact has ensued is a system of dual power with contenders cutting across regional boundaries. The Kiev junta lacks the coherence and stability to serve as a reliable NATO military link encircling Russia. On the contrary, US-EU sanctions, military threats and bellicose rhetoric are forcing Russia to rethink its "openness" to the West. The strategic threats to its national security are forcing Russia to rethink its ties to Western banks and corporations. Russia may resort to industrialization via public investments and import substitution. Russian oligarchs, having lost overseas holdings, may become less central to Russian economic policy.

What is clear is that the power grab in Kiev will not result in a "knife pointed at the heartland of Russia". The defeat and overthrow of the Kiev junta can lead to a radicalized self-governing Ukraine based on the burgeoning democratic movements and rising working class consciousness emerging from the struggle against IMF austerity programs and Western asset stripping of resource enterprises. Ukraine industrial workers, in throwing off the yoke of the western vassals, have no intention of subjecting themselves to Russian oligarchs: *their* struggle is for a democratic state, capable of developing an independent economic policy, free of imperial military alliances.

Epilogue: May Day 2014
Dual Popular Power in the East, Fascism Rising in the West

The predictable falling out between the neo-fascists and neoliberal partners in the Kiev junta was evidenced by large scale riots between rival street gangs and police on May Day. The US-EU strategy envisioned using the neo-fascists as "shock troops" and street fighters in overthrowing the elected regime of Yankovich and then to discard them. The EU-US favored their own neoliberal proxies to promote foreign capital, austerity policies and welcome foreign bases. In contrast the neo-fascists favor nationalist economic policies, retaining state enterprises, and are hostile to oligarchs, especially those with 'dual Israeli-Ukraine" citizenship.

The Kiev junta's lack of any semblance of an economic strategy, its violent seizure of power and repression of pro-democracy dissidents in the East, has led to a situation of 'dual power'. In many cases, troops sent to repress the pro-democracy movements have abandoned the Kiev junta and joined the self-governing movements in the East.

Apart from its outside backers—the White House, Brussels and IMF—the Kiev junta has been abandoned by its rightwing allies in Kiev for being too subservient to NATO and resisted by the pro-democracy movement in the East for being authoritarian and centralist. The Kiev junta has fallen between two chairs: it has no legitimacy among most Ukrainians and has lost control of all but a small patch of land occupied by government offices in Kiev and even those are under siege by the neo-fascist right and increasingly distant from its own disenchanted former supporters.

Let us be absolutely clear, the struggle in the Ukraine is not between the US and Russia, it is between a NATO-imposed junta composed of neoliberal oligarchs and fascists on one side and the industrial workers and their local militias and democratic councils on the other. The former defend and obey the IMF and Washington, the latter rely on the productive capacity of local industry and rules by responding to the majority.

IS UKRAINE A TURNING POINT IN HISTORY?

RODNEY SHAKESPEARE

Is the Ukraine situation a turning point in history? Is the great tide of human affairs slowing down before settling into that moment's stillness which presages a reversal—on a world scale, too—of everything that has gone before?

Is an empire—apparently omnipotent—riding for a fall?

1. Western complacency, bullying and arrogance

The USA doesn't think so. Nor do its Western allies. They are carrying on with the same mixture of complacency, bullying and arrogance as they did before. Indeed, in a very fundamental way their thinking stems from the events of the early 1990s when communism collapsed and, with a cry of triumph, it was announced that History Has Ended! No further change is possible! The West is the Perfection of God's Work!

Of course, if a little history had been studied—including that of the German philosophers who believed that the nineteenth century Prussian state was the End of History—then the cry of triumph would never have happened.

But it did happen. With insufferable hubris the West was, and is, claiming complete and absolute Victory. Moreover, it is backing the hubris with threats —"all options are on the table"—and, if military options are not thought necessary, it then flashes out four aces in a row—sanctions, sanctions, sanctions and sanctions.

Most astonishing of all, underlying the claims of Perfection and Victory, are assumptions—all of them false. For example, the West assumes that the 'free market' of finance capitalism is perfectly free, perfectly efficient and all its outcomes are just. The reality, however, is that it is not free, not efficient, and a large part of its outcomes are unjust.

Claiming perfection is not just complacent but stupid. Only complacent people could think that economic affairs have been perfected. Only stupid people are unable to see the signs, all around them, of unnecessary poverty and economic failure.

2. Global downturn

The present global economic downturn started in August, 2007 and, although the mainstream propagandists are forever claiming to see 'green shoots', 'upturns' and the like, the reality is different. In Europe, for example, Greece, Cyprus, Spain, Ireland, Italy and Portugal—with more to come—are in deep trouble.

Official unemployment is around 13%, but unemployment of young people (18-25) is double the overall unemployment figures and in some areas (e.g., the south of Spain) is over 60%. Moreover, those officially in employment are often on short-term contracts, or only in part-time work.

To which is added unrepayable debt. The Western assumption is that ever-rising debt, at compound interest, is a good thing. This expresses the reality that the present system requires ever-increasing amounts of debt if it is not to collapse.

The system creates enough money for the repayment of the principal of a loan but not for the payment of the interest. More and more debt at compound interest, therefore, must be created....

Thus in Europe, figures for government debt as a percentage of GDP are huge—e.g., Greece, 170%; Italy, 130%—and everywhere they are rising.

All this gets worse if a country's 'total debt' is considered. 'Total debt' is government debt plus the debt of financial institutions, non-financial businesses and households. In the PIIGS countries (Portugal, Ireland, Italy, Greece and Spain) total debt is almost 400% of GDP. In the UK and Japan total debt is around 500% of GDP.

The result is that the populations are being turned into debt-peons while, at the same time, there is a build-up of debt which cannot be repaid. Debt which cannot be repaid will not be repaid.

These horrific figures indicate that the economic system is flawed beyond correction.

3. Position of the 'free market' exemplar

The position of the 'free market' exemplar—the USA—is disastrous. True unemployment is around 23% and double that for young people and minorities. Forty seven million people are on 'food stamps'; the military budget is unrestrained; real wages for the middle class have been in decline for twenty five years; and jobs have been permanently exported.

The selfish elite exports jobs to countries where manufacturing is done cheaply with the products being imported at a low price. This benefits the elite and the international corporations but, because of the loss of jobs at home, it destroys national consumer demand and any hope of a genuine balance of supply and demand.

Yet the finance capitalists go further—they say that domestic manufacturing does not matter and that wealth 'trickles down' from the rich to the poor.

Moreover, in America there is a huge prison population, particularly of blacks and Latinos—the USA incarceration rate is by far the worst in the world—and rich-poor division has sharply increased. Nobel Prize winner Joseph Stiglitz has written:-

> It's no use pretending that what has obviously happened has not in fact happened. The upper 1% of Americans are now taking in nearly a quarter of the nation's income every year. In terms of wealth rather than income, the top 1% control 40%. Their lot in life has improved considerably. Twenty-five years ago, the corresponding figures were 12% and 33%.

4. Political time warp

Politically, the West is in a time warp. Despite claiming victory over communism, it thinks it is still fighting the Cold War against communism and that, in particular, nothing good can ever come out of Russia.

For the West, the Russian Bear is as dangerous as ever.

Which is all very well, but fundamental facts should (but don't) give the West cause to think. In the world, not only is economic power shifting from the West to the BRICS, which include Russia, but political power is shifting as well. Globally, recent United Nations voting on resolutions relating to the establishment of Palestinian rights are indications that the USA is not only becoming isolated but may even become a pariah state (which will soon be the fate of Israel).

5. The West's moral reputation is zilch

Morally, of course, the West's reputation is zilch. Readers might like to reflect on the following:-

- the West's upholding of the biggest lie of all—that the attack on the World Trade Centre, 9/11/2001 was done solely by a few men rather than with the help and connivance of the CIA and Mossad;

- the war in Iraq, 2003, started on a 'false flag' claim, with destruction and killing continuing to this day;

- the West's support for Saudi Wahhabism which is destroying countries throughout the Middle East;

- the West's claim of support for democracy when the reality is that it suppresses democracy e.g., in Saudi Arabia and Bahrain

- the torturing claimed to be only 'enhanced interrogation techniques';

- the continual slaughtering of women and children, let alone innocent men, by drones in the skies;

- the extraordinary revelations of Bradley Manning, Julian Assange and Edward Snowden not only as to callous slaughtering but, in particular, to the wholesale spying, in almost every conceivable way, on almost every conceivable person, almost anywhere in the world;

- the fact that while, under section 11 of the 1947 Headquarters Agreement, the United States, as the host country of the United Nations, is required to allow access to the world body for foreign diplomats, it is grossly abusing that power by refusing access to an Iranian diplomat.

All this means that, in the eyes of decent people throughout the world, the West is scum.

5. Implications of the failure to attack Syria

Not surprisingly, the worm is turning. An abused world is deciding to do things differently. In August, 2013 there was an atrocious gas attack in Syria and anybody with an iota of sense could immediately see that it was done by the Wahhabi throat-slitters, head-choppers and garroters of young girls. But the USA and the UK, relying on their almost absolute control of the media, were demanding war—indeed, Obama, Kerry, Cameron and Hague were hysterical about it.

Yet, something new, something extraordinary, then happened. Ultimately getting their information from alternative communications sources including Facebook, Twitter, TV stations such as Press TV, Russia Today and radio stations such as Progressive Radio, the UK public almost instantly began pressurizing their politicians not to attack.

In no time at all, the UK House of Commons had voted against an attack and that put the kibosh on American plans for an air assault even bigger than that on Libya.

6. New agreements are being made

The failure to attack Syria in effect coalesced thinking around the world. Economic power is shifting away from the West; political power is shifting moral power has gone; and nearly all the gold seems to have gone East.

Everywhere new agreements are being made. The Shanghai Co-operation Organization has the potential to equal NATO; the BRICS are working to construct their own independent banking system; and everywhere are the new trade and other agreements signaling a move away from Western influence, indeed, a desire to end it.

Perhaps the best recent example is the agreement between Russia and Iran to go ahead with a big oil contract which not only infuriates the USA (which is eternally committed to damaging Iran) but makes the neo-cons incandescent because financial exchange will not be in US dollars but in Russian roubles or gold.

7. The crux of the matter—Who holds the high cards over Ukraine?

Which brings us to the crux of the matter—Who holds the high cards over Ukraine? We can set aside, for a moment, the democratic implications (with nearly 97% of the Crimean population, fearing the elimination, by thugs, of their language and identity) and go straight to the subject of oil and gas.

Or rather, to the payment for oil and gas. Or rather to the type of payment for oil and gas.

When countries no longer require payment in US dollars but in their own currencies, barter or gold, the end of the American empire is nigh.

The USA has been at war, in some form or another, every year since 1945. It has about one thousand military bases around the globe (nobody, even the Pentagon, knows the exact number) and spends almost half of the world's military expenditure.

But that expenditure is totally dependent upon the USA's ability endlessly to print the dollars with which to finance it. And the ability to print dollars is ultimately dependent upon international trade being dependent upon dollars.

So what happens if the trade is no longer done in dollars? What happens when Russia—and China, and Iran, even the whole world—decides enough is enough and, besides, why buy and sell in dollars when it is just as easily done in another currency?

So is the USA really being wise not only in sanctioning Russia over Ukraine but in bringing NATO right up against Russia in what could become a major war?

Of course, the USA's intention has been, and is, to bring NATO up against Russia, but is it wise when Russia holds the key cards, particularly that of potentially ending USA financial dominance (with catastrophic economic and social consequences within the USA itself)?

8. Collapse of the Soviet Union (USSR)—and collapse of the USA

The question of wisdom, furthermore, comes into sharp focus when comparison is made between the condition of the Soviet Union shortly before its collapse and the condition of the USA as it is now.

One collapsed and the other one is going to but the harsh truth is that the USSR was better prepared for collapse then than the USA is now!

Let nobody think that the social, economic and political collapse of the USA is fantasy. For a start, the USA government itself believes in that collapse as evidenced by its recent purchase of two billion dum-dum (hollow-jacketed) bullets.

That's six dum-dum bullets for every man, woman and child in the USA! Dum-dum bullets explode on contact so as to make a hole the size of a baseball, even a football. They are illegal under international law.

So, in one sense, the USA government is most certainly prepared for domestic collapse!

Both the USSR and USA were/are empires exercising control over large areas of the world. Both went bankrupt (yes, the USA is now bankrupt and please notice that the USA is completely unable to return Germany's gold).

Both had/have huge jail populations (the USA is now in the lead). Both lost in Afghanistan and the USA has lost in Iraq (and would be most unwise to attack Iran).

Both had/have out of control military budgets. Both thought/think they are God's Gift to the human race—yet both were/are hated throughout the world.

Flashpoint in Ukraine: How the US Drive for Hegemony Risks World War III

But—readers are invited to visit Dimitri Orlov, "Closing the 'Collapse Gap'"—the USSR was better prepared for collapse than the US is.

9. A turning point in world affairs

All in all, it really is beginning to look as if the Ukraine situation marks a turning point in world affairs. An arrogant West, particularly the neo-con element, has not only gone too far but, at the same time, does not seem to realize that the ground is crumbling beneath its feet.

Time will tell, of course, but this writer, for one, looks forwards to a different world which is likely to be healthier and a great deal safer.

WASHINGTON INTENDS RUSSIA'S DEMISE

PAUL CRAIG ROBERTS

Washington has no intention of allowing the crisis in Ukraine to be resolved. Having failed to seize the country and evict Russia from its Black Sea naval base, Washington sees new opportunities in the crisis.

One is to restart the Cold War by forcing the Russian government to occupy the Russian-speaking areas of present day Ukraine where protesters are objecting to the stooge anti-Russian government installed in Kiev by the American coup. These areas of Ukraine are former constituent parts of Russia herself. They were attached to Ukraine by Soviet leaders in the 20th century when both Ukraine and Russia were part of the same country, the USSR.

Essentially, the protesters have established independent governments in the cities. The police and military units sent to suppress the protesters, called "terrorists" in the American fashion, for the most part have until now defected to the protesters.

With Obama's incompetent White House and State Department having botched Washington's takeover of Ukraine, Washington has been at work shifting the blame to Russia. According to Washington and its presstitute media, the protests are orchestrated by the Russian government and have no sincere basis. If Russia sends in military units to protect the Russian citizens in the former Russian territories, the act will be used by Washington to confirm Washington's propaganda of a Russian invasion (as in the case of Georgia), and Russia will be further demonized.

The Russian government is in a predicament. Moscow does not want financial responsibility for these territories but cannot stand aside and permit Russians to be put down by force. The Russian government has attempted to keep Ukraine intact, relying on the forthcoming elections in Ukraine to bring to office more realistic leaders than the stooges installed by Washington.

However, Washington does not want an election that might replace its stooges and return to cooperating with Russia to resolve the situation. There is a good chance that Washington will tell its stooges in Kiev to declare that the crisis brought to Ukraine by Russia prevents an election. Washington's NATO puppet states would back up this claim.

It is almost certain that despite the Russian government's hopes, the Russian government is faced with the continuation of both the crisis and the Washington puppet government in Ukraine.

On May 1 Washington's former ambassador to Russia, now NATO's "second-in-command" but the person who, being American, calls the shots, has declared Russia to no longer be a partner but an enemy. The American, Alexander Vershbow, told journalists that NATO has given up on "drawing Moscow closer" and soon will deploy a large number of combat forces in Eastern Europe. Vershbow called this aggressive policy deployment of "defensive assets to the region."

In other words, here we have again the lie that the Russian government is going to forget all about its difficulties in Ukraine and launch attacks on Poland, the Baltic States, Romania., Moldova, and on the central Asian states of Georgia, Armenia, and Azerbaijan. The dissembler Vershbow wants to modernize the militaries of these American puppet states and "seize the opportunity to create the reality on the ground by accepting membership of aspirant countries into NATO."

What Vershbow has told the Russian government is that you just keep on relying on Western good will and reasonableness while we set up sufficient military forces to prevent Russia from coming to the aid of its oppressed citizens in Ukraine. Our demonization of Russia is working. It has made you hesitant to act during the short period when you could preempt us and seize your former territories. By waiting you give us time to mass forces on your borders from the Baltic Sea to Central Asia. That will distract you and keep you from the Ukraine. The oppression we will inflict on your Russians in Ukraine will discredit you, and the NGOs we finance in the Russian Federation will appeal to nationalist sentiments and overthrow your government for failing to come to the aid of Russians and failing to protect Russia's strategic interests.

Washington is licking its chops, seeing an opportunity to gain Russia as a puppet state.

Will Putin sit there with his hopes awaiting the West's good will to work out a solution while Washington attempts to engineer his fall?

The time is approaching when Russia will either have to act to terminate the crisis or accept an ongoing crisis and distraction in its backyard. Kiev has launched military airstrikes on protesters in Slavyansk. On May 2 Russian government spokesman Dmitry Peskov said that Kiev's resort to violence had destroyed the hope for the Geneva agreement on de-escalating the crisis. Yet, the Russian government spokesman again expressed the hope of the Russian government that European governments and Washington will put a stop to the military strikes and pressure the Kiev government to accommodate the protesters in a way that keeps Ukraine togetherand restores friendly relations with Russia.

This is a false hope. It assumes that the Wolfowitz doctrine is just words, but it is not.

The Wolfowitz doctrine is the basis of US policy toward Russia (and China). The doctrine regards any power sufficiently strong to remain independent of Washington's influence to be "hostile." The doctrine states:

> Our first objective is to prevent the re-emergence of a new rival, either on the territory of the former Soviet Union or elsewhere, that poses a threat on the order of that posed formerly by the Soviet Union. This is a dominant consideration underlying the new regional defense strategy and requires that we endeavor to prevent any hostile power from dominating a region whose resources would, under consolidated control, be sufficient to generate global power.

The Wolfowitz doctrine justifies Washington's dominance of all regions. It is consistent with the neoconservative ideology of the US as the "indispensable" and "exceptional" country entitled to world hegemony.

Russia and China are in the way of US world hegemony. Unless the Wolfowitz doctrine is abandoned, nuclear war is the likely outcome.

THE UKRAINE CRISIS
DECODING ITS DEEP STRUCTURAL MEANING
JOHN McMURTRY

The "Ukraine crisis" repeats a script as old as the Cold War. The narrative features rising attacks by corporate states and media on the traditional whipping boy of Russia. As usual, "escalating the crisis" is US-led. As usual, alarm about "increasing lawless aggression" is a projection of US policy itself.

In fact, one more US-directed violent overthrow of an elected government has carved off the biggest country of Europe from next-door Russia. Yet Russia gets all the blame for "brute force" in reclaiming Crimea—although 96% of a voluntary turnout of 82% voted to rejoin its traditional mother country.

While denounced as a "violation of international law", the Crimea referendum choice expresses the "self-determination" of a society guaranteed under Article 2 of the United Nations Charter. Ukraine's coup government, in contrast, has prohibited any referendum on its rule—especially in the Eastern regions where popular uprisings with no mass deaths or beatings (as in the Kiev coup) call for self-determination against illegal rule from Kiev.

The uprising cities of East Ukraine—beginning with Donetsk, then Kharkov, Luhansk, Slavyansk (the Slav has been removed from the Westernized Sloviansk),Kramatorsk and other centers and villages—all demand a democratic referendum for their future status as equal citizens in a Ukraine federation. Integration with Russia is not favored by Russia, but the dominant popular feeling unreported in the media is peaceful and pragmatic.

Ukraine's government has been broken by the US-led coup and cannot provide what people need in jobs, healthcare, income security and pensions. Certainly "the Greek model" planned for Ukraine is not in its common people's life interests. Under the coup government of Prime Minister Arseniuy Yatsenyuk, a banker who is already prescribing mass dispossession by austerity programs, what will happen to Ukraine is foretold by has happened in Greece.

The EU's financial rule by banker mechanisms has already been almost as great a failure as the oligarch-marketization of Russia after 1990. It is a complex system of one-way powers of life deprivation and social ruin which I define in *The Cancer Stage of Capitalism: From Crisis to Cure* (1999, 2013). Elected governments lose all control to the new absolute and overriding imperative of European rule—to grow and multiply private transnational money sequences. In accord with the ruling formulae, the Greek economy has been slashed by 25 per cent, unemployment is an official 28 per cent excluding the unpaid, the public health system is dismantled to pay foreign banks, wages are cut by a quarter, the public sector is sacked and privatized, and jobless youth rises to 60 per cent even with mass emigration. These outcomes now await Ukraine.

Those in Ukraine who are not under the spell of its father cult, oligarch riches, and post-1991 dispossession know better. Outside of Kiev they have had enough, and that is why the election and presidency of the Party of Regions and its allies whose popular support lies outside Kiev have been repeatedly overturned. It is also why their decentralized federal alternative has been removed from the table.

The murderous insurrection in Kiev and violent coup of elected government reveals how far the Kiev oligarchy and plotters are prepared to go, backed by the US. Yet this time Russia has drawn a red line. With near-unanimous support of the Crimean people and the uprising of the Eastern cities and villages as I write, Russia has stopped the US-led transnational corporate-machine and NATO from further expansion for the first time in 25 years.

It is true that Ukraine—the biggest country and bread basket of Europe—has now been pried wide open for transnational Western banks, agribusiness, Big Oil and NATO to feed on. And it is true that all talk of "land grab" has been projected onto Russia even as US Greystone and Blackwater mercenaries —now called "Academi" in the Big Lie lexicon—move on the ground in Ukraine as the US and NATO propagate ever more threats of force and embargo against "Russia's aggression".

Reverse blame is always the US geostrategic game. "Russia's designs to take the whole of Ukraine" is again a US projection of its own objective, as in the old days when a "world rule plot" was attributed to the former USSR. Yet a line has been drawn at Crimea, and drawn again in Eastern Ukraine, and it is backed by a country that cannot be arm-twisted, propaganda invaded, or air-bombed with impunity. That is why the one-way threats never stop. It is the first line yet drawn by an historical power outside of China against the exponentially multiplying US-led private transnational money sequences devouring the world.

People now have a chance to reflect on who is the aggressor and who stands for democratic choice as events unfold. They can observe the patterns of Orwellian distortion day to day. Never is the other side presented. The US and NATO alone continuously denounce, lie and threaten.

Financial contracts and assets are violated by one side alone. Hate campaigns without evidence go one way. Uprisings have been mass murderous from the US-coup side and long without harm from the resisting side. Russia is behind its own borders, and the US deploys threats, covert operations and mercenaries from thousands of miles away. But this time US-NATO-led corporate globalization cannot destroy nations at will. Sometimes history can happen as it should.

The Mechanisms of Reverse Blame to Justify Destroying Societies

Reversal of blame is always the US method of pretext and justification. This is why Russia is pervasively vilified in the mass media, and Canada's big-oil regime joins in along with the UK. As always, denunciation rules without reasoned understanding. As always, the US-led financial and military forces of private money-power expansion move behind the abomination of designated enemies. Any nation or leader not serving transnational corporate control of resources and markets across borders is always the villain. This is the ruling meta program.

Thus too in Ukraine. When Europe tried to broker a peace deal between the opposition and elected government of Ukraine, the US Assistant Secretary of State Victoria Nuland continued to court the neo-Nazi coup leaders to overthrow the state, instructing "Yats" (appointed PM Yatsenyuk) to consult with the main putsch leader, Oleh Tyahnybok, "at least four times a week". When she is reminded of the EU peace talks and agreement to stop the bloodshed, her response is telling: "Fuck the EU".

The coup peaked after three days of murder by the neo-Nazi faction. When former "Orange revolutionary" and gas oligarch leader of the Fatherland Party, Yulia Tymoshenko, then got out of jail where she had been held for criminal embezzlement of state property, she expressed the logic of power shared with the US regarding Russia. She says without denial of the words: "take up arms and go and wipe out these damn katsaps" [Russian minority] ... so that not even scorched earth would be left of Russia." Yet in every Western media of record, it is Russia who remains "the aggressor", "the growing threat", "the source of the rising crisis", and "the out-of-control power that must be stopped".

There are exact thought governors at work throughout. I have analyzed these structures of delusion in learned journals as 'the ruling group-mind' (collectively regulating assumptions that are false but taken for granted) and, sustaining it, the *'argumentum ad adversarium'* (the diversion of all issues to a common adversary). The "escalating crisis in Ukraine" expresses these fallacious operations in paradigm form.

So does the false claim of "Syrian use of chemical weapons" which almost led to US bombing of Syria's civilian infrastructures a few months earlier. The mind mechanics at work form the inner logic of the lies which never stop. The grossest operations go back to the Reagan regime naming Nicaragua as "a clear and present danger to the United States" to justify US war crimes against it which in turn fed the ever- growing corporate-military complex and murderous covert operations. Always the mind-stopping mendacity and criminal aggressions are justified through the ruling group-mind and enemy-hate switch which form the deep grammar of this thought system.

At the most general level, the "Russian threat to Ukraine" diverts public attention from the really fatal problems of the world and their global causal mechanism—transnational money sequencing—which is metastasizing further in Ukraine. The air, soil and water cumulatively degrade from its transnational corporate looting and polluting.

The climates and oceans destabilize from the same cause at the same time. Species too become extinct at a spasm rate, and the world's forests, meadows and fisheries are cumulatively destroyed. The global food system produces more and more disabling junk as commodity diseases multiply.

The vocational future of the next generations is eliminated for a growing majority of people. All these trends and more are one-way, degenerate, and undeniable. All are driven by US-led private and transnational money-sequence multiplication which now moves into and through Ukraine. Without Russia's past financial and energy assistance worth tens of billions of dollars and completely destabilized by the US-led violent coup, Ukraine verges towards collapse. That is where the Greek model comes in—the stripping of Ukraine to pay for what it has lost from Russia by the US-led coup which further enables military advance to Russia's borders.

As usual, such geostrategic intervention is life destructive at every level of its consequences, but the underlying causal mechanism is unspeakable in official culture. From Africa to Europe to the Middle East to Latin America, the unspoken master trend is systematic society destruction.

Look, for example, forward and backward from the last manufactured crises geared to enable US-led destabilization to bombing—

the "weapons of mass destruction of Iraq", the "genocidal plans of the dictator Qaddafi", "Assad's chemical weapons used on his own people", or, across the ocean, Venezuela's "despotism" which prioritizes the elimination of public education, healthcare and poverty elimination. Always the victim society has more developed social programs than its neighbors. The ultimate enemy is social life bases themselves.

Observe the common pattern of social destruction. It begins with US covert forces sponsoring opposition forces in the society featuring fascist and jihadist terrorists, mounting global media campaigns against the targeted leader, murders committed by snipers pretending to be state agents, growing civil division and hate towards civil war, and absolutely one-sided reporting of the US point of view, and reverse-moral justifications for what ends as society destruction.

The US bombing stage has not yet been reached in Syria because Russia led the alternative of UN chemical-weapons destruction, even though Syria had never used the weapon. Not long after destroying Iraq and Libya on known false pretexts, the US proclaimed again and again the mass-murderous gas used in Syria was by "Assad the war criminal" although the evidence kept disconfirming the big lie mega-phoned by John Kerry.

It went all the way to a White House plan to bomb civilian infrastructures as in Iraq and Libya. In revealing contrast, Russia "the world bully" has never bombed a foreign city, not even in Germany under the Nazis. (Grozny bombing broke this higher policy of international law within Russia's borders after the NATO bombing of Yugoslavia in 1999.) Yet US reverse projection rules as a syntax of Western propaganda. Even with Assad's much-trumpeted "war crime", the truth found by multiple analysis was that "kitchen sarin" manufactured in Turkey and crude-missile lobbed by the al Nusra jihadists allied with the US and funded by Saudi Arabia and Qatar was the source of the gas massacre (as Seymour Hersh has finally made public).

Much the same generic script of engineered civil conflict and war combined with false threat and crimes of the constructed foreign enemy has been used over and over again against Iran and its "nuclear threat" with no evidence, while Israel has an illegal stockpile of them and threatens to use them to stop Iran's "nuclear threat". In all, the reverse-projection tactic has become the signature of everything the US and its allies allege of others to ruin them.

Ukraine in Motion as Another Paradigm Example of US-led Society Destruction

Serial false allegations and pretexts thus unfold again against Russia in regard to Ukraine. The US-led mayhem and violence varies widely, but the dots have not yet been joined on what is always achieved beneath the political-ideological shows—the tearing apart and dispossession of one society after another by US-led financial and armed means.

Here it is Ukraine and the set-up of Russia at once. Not only is the society decapitated, as in Ukraine or Libya or Iraq or as demanded in Syria. That is the official script. Much more deeply the society's civil bonds are rent asunder, its productive base is sabotaged, its social life supports are stripped, its environment and resources looted and its future despoiled. Always. There is no objective fulfilled except social life-system destruction.

But the connections still go unmade. As General Rick Hillier, commander of Canada's forces helping to bomb Libya said afterwards: "We did it because we could". As CIA executive director Buzzy Krongard acknowledges about the permanent US war, but still without the consequence named: "It will be won by forces you do not know about, in actions you will not see, and in ways you may not want to know about".

The supremely evil truth becomes testable by its continuous repetition. Dismantling or destroying society's very life bases is the innermost meaning of US-led "freedom" and "globalization". It includes even US society itself by ever more monstrous misallocation of public resources away from what serves life bases to what deprives them. If one reviews the post-1980 trajectory of ruin of nations, the objectively evil pattern becomes clear.

No other actually working goal has been achieved since the Reagan-Thatcher turn. It is the DNA of the global cancer system. Try to think of an exception. Since the war-criminal destruction of poverty-ridden Nicaragua's new schools and clinics by the signature method of covertly US funded and armed forces within, the society-destruction method has only grown and multiplied by terrorist as well as financial means.

When Obama says "every society must chart its own course", he follows the reverse moral syntax at work. The deliberate mass-diseasing of 500,000 children in the first manufactured crisis of Iraq as the nearby Soviet Union collapsed revealed what we could expect from the US without another superpower to contain it. In all cases, there has been one underlying principle of outcome—US-led civil disintegration of societies across the world. That is how a cancer works at the transnational level of life organization.

Engineering civil war is the favored method with effective genocide the long consequence. This is true not only in Afghanistan, Iraq, Libya, Lebanon, and Syria, but Somalia, Sudan and the Congo. Direct US invasion may lose the war from Vietnam to Afghanistan, but its defeat is, more deeply, another US-led success at destroying another society.

The Wall Street metastasis to EU banker-run Europe has worked without invasion or even proxy uprising, but society destruction is still achieved by the small print of corporate treaties and bank powers people never see. Greece, Spain and Italy are effectively ruined, and behind the dismantling of these and all victim societies is the same transnational corporate system multiplying itself through societies.

Big Banks, Oil, Military Contracting, Big Agri-Food and Pharma are themselves only vehicles of the one underlying economic disease of transnational money sequences self-multiplying across all borders without life limits or functions. They feed on ruined societies as their carrion.

Ukraine follows this macro pattern. It comes into the fold of the EU through a US-led fascist coup posing as "freedom" and "revolution", but in fact hollowing out the society's lifeblood and bases as the US-led coup and EU financial straitjacket suck it dry.

This is the unseen law of transnational money-demand multiplication to the top. In Ukraine the method features similar tools—increasingly armed and destructive oppositional forces on the ground, US bankrolling and direction of the opposition's factions in orchestrated destruction ($5 billion under aid guises, $20 million for the street reported by Secretary Nuland in a speech to business), and pervasive transnational corporate propaganda about the constructed civil war as a "struggle for Ukraine's freedom"— decoded, transnational corporate and bank freedom to loot and pollute. As always, inside allies include fascist and terrorist forces—the Svoboda and Pravy Sektor factions in Ukraine which now have key executive posts in the coup government and trace their history back to the Ukraine Insurgent Army (UPA) led by their hero.

The worst is yet to come. Never is there any US building of the victim society's economy and life support systems, and so too in Ukraine. Again we might compare Russia here to the US in Afghanistan over 14 years.

The self-multiplying corporate money sequences which reap all gains have no committed life function or obligation including to the imperial state itself. They pay ever fewer taxes to it, and bleed ever more public money and resources from it. There is only one pattern of consequence and Ukraine too is now almost occupied by its ruling mechanism to impoverish the people further to feed the rich. As always, society's common life capital bases will be further defunded, privatized for profit, and saddled by unpayable transnational bank debts.

The real economy will be flooded with more junk foods, media products and social-dumping commodities, and bred to a violence culture already hatched by the coup. Collective life capital bases will be further laid waste for multiplying private money fortunes across borders.

The Life-Blind Thought System Behind Global Society Destruction

Since using the spectacular 9-11 event as pretext for the new

PNAC plan of "full-spectrum domination", falling on the anniversary of the destruction of Chile's society in 1973, the U.S. has been on a non-stop crusade of destroying societies across the world.

The hollowing out of social bonds and bases includes within the US itself. Its impoverishment grows as non-productive riches multiply at the top, middle classes fall to ever new levels of debt, the growing majority of youth is without a future, public squalor spreads across the land, and over 2000 million dollars a day is spent on armed force threat and operations with no real enemy to justify them.

It all goes back to first principles. "There is no such thing as society," declared the fanatic Friedrich von Hayek who was mouth-pieced by his disciple, Margaret Thatcher. "We owe our very lives to capitalism". But deeper than words, the principle of no-society is built into the ruling economic paradigm. Without notice, every life coordinate is erased from account.

There are no life needs, no environment, no society, no children, no relations with others, and no history in this life model. All unpriced life goods—from water and sewer infrastructures and services to universal public education, culture and healthcare to social security support in age, unemployment, and disability—are blinkered out except as "cost burdens".

The very terrestrial biosphere on which everything depends is ruled out of this moronic frame of reference. Demand itself is never people's needs or necessity. It is private money demand minted by private banks without the legal tender to back it to indebt the great majority and to gamble on their future means of life. 'Supply' is not the life means people require.

It is ever more priced commodities for profit promoting more human and ecological ill-being as far as corporate globalization extends. Ukraine can look forward to this US-led thought system ruling over it from within the financialized European Union which is now as banker-run as America.

The ruling value mechanism can be crystallized into natural language equations: Freedom = freedom for private money demand = in proportion to the amount controlled = ever less freedom for those with less of it = no right to life for those without it. Even more generally, the underlying master equations of the globalizing system now moving to rule Ukraine into Russia can be defined as follows: Rationality = Self-Maximizing Choice = Always More Money-Value for Self is Good = Self-Multiplying Sequences of Ever More Money to the Top = All Else is Disposable Means to this Pathogenic Growth.

This is the innermost value logic of the US-led global system and it has no limit of dispossession and ruin if not stopped. It is perhaps emblematic irony that the favorite for Ukraine's post-coup President, 'Chocolate King'

Flashpoint in Ukraine: How the US Drive for Hegemony Risks World War III

Petro Poroshenko, is a billionaire sugar-commodity maker producing no food value, but more and more obesity and diabetes.

World Empire or Globalizing Disease?

Left critics coalesce around "US imperialism" as the common cause of the global meltdown on organic, social and ecological levels. Yet it is strange to call a system an "empire" whose imperial center is increasingly hollowed out on every plane; whose interventions and wars destroy productive forces at every level; and whose outcome is not more amenities for the poor, as apologists like Leo Strauss claim, but ever more societies as black holes with life support systems cumulatively devoured. "Sometimes I think they feel like they're in a lab and they're running experiments on rats and not understanding the consequences of what they are doing," Vladimir Putin wonders in partial sense of the derangement at work.

More clearly, the states which the US planned to destroy in 2001 (as reported by General Wesley Clark in his memoirs)—Iraq, Lebanon, Libya, Somalia, Sudan, Iran and Syria—are now in fact destroyed societies. All but Iran are left with civil war and majority destitution where once they had been relatively prosperous and life secure.

For example, before Western bombing of Iraq under the usual blame-the-enemy diversion to its leader (a paid CIA agent implanted in office by the US), Iraq led the Middle East in free public healthcare and higher education, and Libya provided free down payments for young couples' housing as well, prior to its bombing. U.S.-led interventions and aerial bombing have destroyed the social life-organization of both nations which now don't even have the electricity and water back on.

Syria was also a middle-income quasi-socialist nation, but was independent, friendly with Russia, and capable of fighting an expanding Israel. So Syria too was marked for destabilization. Its internal protests received US-Israel covert support, and turned quickly into civil war with US special operation forces and orchestrated funding of rival camps, including jihadists still incinerating the country. As usual the national leader is blamed for everything. All the while, Iran is periodically threatened with annihilation while Venezuela across the ocean is subjected to US-led destabilization, too, as in Ukraine, Syria, and Libya.

While gas bombs have been thrown freely in Venezuela and Ukraine with US support against democratically elected states, Venezuela's government serves the poor while Ukraine's has been oligarchic on both sides. Putin thus understands Ukraine's protestors as "tired of seeing one set of crooks replacing another". In contrast, no common life interest at all exists for the US.

When bribes of officials, street gangs and press slander are not enough, US-led destabilization by financial system levers, covert operatives and civil war follow behind reverse-projection cover stories. One can imagine if Molotov cocktails were thrown during the Wall Street uprising as they were in US-financed protests in Ukraine and Venezuela. "Violence-threatening protestors" is all they can say about peaceful demonstrations at home, however just the cause.

Concern about people's lives, in short, never arises except as a media mask. This is why the US-led coup in Ukraine murdered people and usurped democratic process and legal warrant without a pause. It is also why it demanded the *sieg-heiling* violent thug, Oleh Tyanybok of the Svoboda Party, to be a chief advisor to the coup government although he blamed a "Muscovite/Jew mafia" for Ukraine's problems and "Germans, Kikes and other scum" who want to "take away our Ukrainian state".

He is a symptom of the deep-structural derangement of US rule. In all cases—from Honduras to Paraguay, Egypt to Mali—covert funding, forces of destabilization and chaos are the modus operandi with US special operations leading the repertoire of financial destabilization, demonization of resistance, and armed civil-war training. Unlike classic imperialism, the system spreads by greed and fear, never by productive force development and universalizing rights and laws.

Invasive war in 2014 is not so acceptable to the world after the obliteration of the societies and life infrastructures of Iraq and Libya. So drones, suitcases of money, special operations, propaganda campaigns and whatever else can sabotage resistance are deployed to pry societies open for competitively self-multiplying transnational corporations to exploit foreign resources, labor and forced markets.

This is known as "the free movement of private capital and commodities". Until 1991, the former Union of Soviet Socialist Republics was still the biggest block and resource treasure of all to US-led global financialization. Thus military encirclement, pervasive international slander, ruinous armaments races and illegal embargoes followed for 50 years.

It eventually worked to cause the intended collapse of the Soviet Union by spending it bankrupt on the armaments race, and forcing repression by perpetual war threats from richer societies. But US market magic and miracles for the world's biggest country and its neighbors did not work at all. So the GDPs of the Soviet republics fell by 60%, and polls today show that 56% of Ukrainians would prefer to be governed as before. Social priorities and universal life necessities matter more to them than majority dispossession and glitz for the rich. But no Western journalist dares say it. And so the spectacularly failed global capitalist experiment has passed without a word of notice from "the free world". It remains unspeakable to name.

Yet reality catches up. The US-led empire was itself unraveling in historical time without recognition. Its most gigantic failure has come back to haunt it—running the once relatively well-off societies of the USSR into productive and cultural ruin. "Well and good", one is taught to think. "The Soviet Union repressed free speech".

But like Cuba today, a state which is continuously threatened with war, plague, assassination and hate by richer states reverts to tight control. But if one considers all the universal sciences, arts, pensions, education, and health-care provision of the Union of Socialist Republics which have been systematically destroyed, the meaning takes on a different complexion. It remains unspeakable but lies at the heart of the Ukraine-Russia crisis today. Nothing is better but only worse in collective life capital evolution.

Many prefer the language of the imperial past. In this way reality is categorized as familiar, not mutant, backward and chaotic. The repetitions are not from "tragedy" to "farce", as Karl Marx memorably observed in the case of Louis Bonaparte III of France. Today there is nothing but tragedy. It may all seem to be about oil and imperialism, what opponents focus on.

Yet possessing others' oil and territory are comparatively rational objectives compared to the actual performance of metastasizing destruction. Far more is spent on unproductive technologies of killing and terror than has been won in new oil and territory. Both land and energy sources have been largely despoiled and wasted. The oil produced in Iraq, for example, is not close to pre-1990 levels and the oil in Libya is the site of unending civil war. The pattern is destroying not producing through generational time. Corruption and insecurity are universalized, not life as human.

Ukraine's coup now binds it in the pathological direction—more civil strife towards war, more mountains of bank debt, more lack of affordable energy, more ethnic hatred, more mass homicidal weapons, and more rot of dysfunctional wealth inequality.

Can this be an advance of empire? Or is it the next sign of morbid overreach, corruption and fall? An empire has a unified center, a state in control of its subjects and private enterprises, a productive capacity that leads the societies within its imperial reach, an historical civilization of architecture, art, and culture, and most of all enduring public infrastructures and great works across its domains of command.

The US global system has ever less of any of these. Its imperial center is divided into gridlock, its productive powers have been increasingly exported or surpassed elsewhere, its architecture, arts and culture are increasingly mindless and violence-ridden, its capacities of civilization and public infrastructures are defunded and collapse at every turn.

The US now leads only in monopoly of world currency issue,

capacities to destroy life and life conditions, and mass propaganda methods. Its transnational corporations are no longer subservient to any imperial center or purpose but multiply their private money sequences on the back of monopolies of force and money-issue paid for by increasingly impoverished citizens.

The collapsing US civilization cannot comprehend its derangement. Its money-party leaders can only see more opportunity for transnational corporate profits—the moral DNA of the cancer system. This is why the destruction of Russia has been long planned by the geostrategist Zbigniew Brzezinski—first in Afghanistan where he rallied the original jihadists to fight the Soviet Union along with tens of billions in US cash and weapons which developed into 9/11 and the 9/11 wars. In Ukraine the US continues the strategy.

In Afghanistan the route to the ex-Soviet oilfields, the US funding was the beginning of the Taliban and al Qaeda forces whose US-manipulated function was and remains destroying societies by armed civil war to complement financial bleeding. This same method bled Yugoslavia dry and then the USSR, and has worked from Afghanistan through Iraq and Serbian-Kosovo wars to Syria, to Somalia, Mali and Nigeria under many names, but almost always it turns out the terror is manipulated by US money, arms and connections. Today Brzezinski has former Harvard graduate students who strategically game for the Obama administration to smash Russia into ungovernable pieces—the long game.

This is not an exaggerated sense of danger, but a long track record. Wrecking the society in crisis is the testable generalization of all US interventions. More exactly, the unseen law of the ruling system across borders including those of the US is: Ever more public money is hemorrhaged into private money sequences with ever more ruined societies the result.

Consider Ukraine with this diagnostic principle in mind. We can predict from this systemic law that only more disintegration of society and mutual life support systems will occur in Ukraine with more US-EU bank and corporate feeding on the post-coup remains. US and EU countries themselves will come apart more in the process, and the US will bleed vastly more public resources to keep metastasizing the unrecognized fatal disorder while 90% of its own people and the world grow poorer, more malnourished and life insecure.

US Script of Democracy and Freedom versus Facts of Violence and Society Destruction

To put the matter in one sentence, the collapse and overthrow of Ukraine's elected government has been financed and directed by the U.S, cored in violence by the Nazi roots of the uprising linked with the US-selected coup leaders now in power, and after the swift takeback of Crimea by Russia, fanned into hysteria by the corporate media. Revealingly, the Bandera-loving Nazis on the street leading the chaotic terror of Feb 22-24 caused the overthrow of the legitimate government exactly when the civil battle had already been won.

The elected President Yanukovych made concessions on everything—his PM was fired, the new protest laws against helmets, metal shields, and masks were revoked (even although banned everywhere else), with legitimate democratic turnover of government plainly in sight and further brokered by the EU in presidential succession. But there was no assurance of electoral victory of the US-allied Kiev forces.

They had already lost two elections to the federalist Party of Regions and its alliance governments. It was then the US-led violent overthrow happened in bloodshed, with return of the Nazi past proclaimed as "freedom" and "revolution". The violent coup was instantly validated by the US state, but the EU paused for days before diverting blame to Russia too. No media of record appeared to notice that the US had criminally led the coup, and selected and instructed the new coup-government leaders with no vote, no election, and no public discussion. All the while the democratic referendum so abused in Crimea was never imagined for Ukraine by "the free press" and "leaders of the democratic world" even when eastern Ukraine popular uprisings demanded it.

The coup was precisely rushed ahead to avoid any election. The US-backed forces had already lost two in a row. No reports mentioned this in the Free World. The track-switch of attention was instead to Russia. How could the strategy fail? If Putin draws the line at Crimea, he forwards the plan of blaming Russia. If he does not, the long game to dismantle Russia moves faster. If Putin calls a sudden referendum in Crimea to show its citizens' overwhelming support, he can be ridiculed for "the farce", "the region under military occupation", "the gun to the head". If almost all the people of Crimea want in fact to join the historic mother country in a peaceful vote, just keep repeating "Russia's annexation of Crimea", "brute force", "Russian aggression".

The violent putsch in Ukraine is thus erased from view. It disappears into reverse projection. The most basic reality test is always blocked—Does the society rise or fall in life means available and produced, social life infrastructures and services, employment levels, youth life purpose, and ecological integrity after US-induced "regime change". It always falls. Is there any exception?

Crimea joining historic Russia again after it was won from the Ottoman Empire centuries ago revealingly goes the opposite way. Bridges, roads and tunnels are promised and planned immediately in the wake of the Olympic building spree. Pensions, minimum wages and healthcare are invested in to "raise life standards".

Exposure of the world to Crimea's historical treasure begins. In contrast, the opposing US-led forces silence the EU agreement for presidential succession in Ukraine, lead a coup of the elected government with neo-Nazi snipers and violent chaos, direct IMF austerity and social dispossession for the people's collapsing life support systems, set the main languages, cultures and identifications of citizens into irreparable division and civil war footing, and proclaim virulently against Russia taking an opposite path.

Dividing society from within with no common or productive goal but only more tearing apart is the generic meaning—as in Yugoslavia before it, Libya and Syria in between, Honduras, Paraguay, where does it stop?

Direct the destabilizing in the street with billions for the purpose, play on real and invented problems, insert special forces to lead the mounting violence, bribe the people with dollars and bananas, divide classes and cultures to the death, proclaim freedom and prosperity, and run the country into the ground with no life construction undertaken nor any life base any longer secure for 90% of the people.

The special forces at work here incredibly included Israelis trained in Gaza allying with the legacy of Ukraine Nazism. But the stakes are large and undiscussed. Ukraine is the biggest land mass of Europe, a leading global grain producer, and home to newly found gas reserves of possibly trillions of cubic feet.

The US-led lockdown on all of it is clear in the new coup state. A neoliberal banker is Prime Minister, a violence script-writer and chief aide to the Fatherland Party is President, and various neo-fascists are in cabinet positions with none elected. To complete the destruction of democratic legitimacy of Ukraine took only a few hours. But public panic and appointing banker presidents has already been managed in Italy and Greece, why not here too? With no mass media noticing the growing reversal of democracy and freedom in their name, Putin-bashing is the corporate-press game.

Media Censorship and the Violation of International Law

Crimea joining Russia was the lightning rod for the defining US operation of reverse projection, always blaming the other side for what one is doing oneself as the reason for attacking it. Since the Reagan regime made this the signature operation of US propaganda which is always repeated by the media as fact, an Orwellian rule of big lies has been normalized.

Reverse projection combines with the earlier defined *ad adversarium* fallacy and ruling group-mind to overwhelm all reasoned understanding with cartoon-like masks of good (US) and evil (Them) where fact never interferes. Media-conditioned publics are in this way stampeded through one US-led war and civil war after another with official oppositions rationalizing the same belligerent stupefaction. With only the point of view of the US or its allies reported, only the US story line and point of view can be seen or heard by the great majority.

So too in "the Ukraine crisis". That Russia "invaded Crimea and annexed it against international law" has been the basic story for global denunciation of Russia. In fact over 80% of Crimeans voted, over three times the electorate participation in the US, and almost all of them for integration with Russia not "annexation by it".

The striking fact is that given the accuracy of these figures which is not denied, it is far more than could enable Quebec to legally secede from Canada even with universal language rights lacking in Ukraine. By mathematical deduction, the referendum also included the great majority of the nearly 40% identified as Ukrainians and Tatars.

How is it that all you ever heard or saw in the mass media were selected opposing voices from Ukrainian and Tatar minorities? This is the ruling censorship by unseen means—selecting out of public view all facts that are not consistent with the ruling script. More exactly, the corporate media select for public showing only what sells the transnational money-sequence system. This is why we never hear of the US placing itself above all international laws as it enforces this ruling program. Its entire record here is blinkered out a priori. So blame of others easily enters the ruling group-mind internalized by mass media audiences

This point is worth pausing on because the US is the very "rogue state", "international outlaw", "criminal violator of human rights" and, above all, perpetrator of "war crimes" and "crimes against humanity" which it is always projecting onto other states. It has refused to ratify the International Criminal Court to uphold the law against war crimes and crimes against humanity, and publicly repudiated the Court's right to investigate US criminal violations including the "supreme crime" of a war of aggression.

While it is always invoking international laws to falsely blame others of violating them (e.g., Syria's use of chemical weapons), the US has systematically undermined virtually all international laws to protect human life—treaties and conventions against landmines, against biological weapons, against international ballistic missiles, against small arms, against torture, against racism, against arbitrary seizure and imprisonment, against military weather distortions, against biodiversity loss, and against climate destabilization. Even international agreements on the rights of children and of women have been sabotaged. Yet this unrelenting profile of lawless US right to terror and destruction is nowhere published. This is how censorship by selection works without people knowing it.

What then are we to say about "Russia's brutal invasion and seizure of Crimea"? In fact the number of Russian soldiers in Crimea were fewer than agreed by contract with Ukraine long prior to the referendum.

Crimea is and was also an historic Russian port and strategic peninsula even under Ukraine's interregnum, and its place in Ukraine occurred only by a 1954 decree of the now-defunct Soviet Union. All of these facts are selected out by corporate media and states which only repeat "Russian brute force", "illegal seizure of territory", "war of invasion", and even "what Hitler did back in the 1930s" (Hillary Clinton). There is no limit to the absurd hypocrisy of accusation. Thus attention is diverted again and again onto the latest enemy as lawless and the US as law-abiding in contradiction to the facts.

In reality, no injury occurred in the peaceful and overwhelmingly popular integration of Crimea with Russia. Ukrainian troops yielded in peaceful transition and were extended offers to stay. There was no bloodshed with one exception—a soldier in Sebastopol murdered by two men at night in masks and a getaway car tied back to the Ukraine coup leaders.

They called it "the entry into the stage of military conflict" and the corporate media reported it without evidence or question. But the sniper murders of 21 people in the Kiev uprising by the US-led coup agent was already diplomatically registered by March 4.

Predictably, every detail was gagged in 'the free press' and the official 'Free World'. Even the EU's Foreign Minister Catherine Ashton to whom the facts of the mass murder were communicated by a fellow Foreign Minister, Urmas Paet of Estonia, remained silent. He reported that in fact the medical and forensic evidence proved all 21 murders were by "the same type of bullets" and from "the same handwriting" which could only be from "the new coalition" [of the coup government].

"The new coalition", concluded Foreign Minister Paet in English, "don't want to investigate what exactly happened. So that there is now stronger and stronger understanding that behind the snipers, it was not Yanukovich, but it was somebody from the new coalition."

Such mass murder is grounds for prosecution of war crimes and crimes against humanity under international law and prosecution by the International Court. But due process of law and criminal prosecution are repressed at the same time as the known diplomatic evidence is silenced in the public sphere.

Group-mind, reverse projection and blame-the-enemy operations have become so automatic that the most important historical facts and heinous crimes do not register through their prism. Thus Russia goes on being accused of the "violations of law" and "international law" with John Kerry bawling loudest against the evidence. That the violent coup itself was propelled by mass murder of protestors perpetrated by the US-led insurrection to blame on the elected government has thus never made the news.

The murderous logic was again evident in microcosm when troops of the coup state opened fire on unarmed citizens approaching their barracks to talk on the Easter eve of the Geneva agreement to repudiate armed violence. The day after the Geneva accord a worse attack exploded in Slavyansk with gunmen (named as Right Sector, the fascist armed group behind the coup whose activities the accord banned) racing up in jeeps to a checkpoint and killing at least three people including a bus-driver before disappearing. As always the US-orchestrated government in Kiev projected all attacks onto Russia with no evidence.

All the while heavily armed Ukraine forces moved into eastern Ukraine are blocked by citizens while Kiev's own central street still remains occupied by coup forces. "Putin's threats" continue to be manufactured along with "Russia's forcible annexation of Crimea" despite the inhabitants voting peacefully and overwhelmingly for re-unification with Russia in affirmation of a relationship over two centuries old. Altogether erased from reports are the facts that the Supreme Council of Crimea referred to the United Nations Charter and "the right of nations to self-determination" (Article 2, Chapter 1), the very right Ukraine invoked in seceding from the USSR in 1991, and the same right invoked for the separation of Kosovo from Serbia.

Also erased is the UN International Court ruling in July 2010 that "general international law contains no prohibition on declarations of independence". Once again we find on closer inspection that what is proclaimed as fact and law by US leaders and allied states is yet another level of a big lie system.

Conclusion

The Ukraine crisis is another variation on the great crisis of the world—the undeclared global war of transnational corporate money sequences to multiply themselves through human societies and life on earth in the diagnosable form of an invasive cancer.

Yet what is different in Ukraine is that eastern Ukrainian citizens and the world's largest nation have stood against the new metastasis across traditional borders and cultural regions. Activists with weapons and massive local support across the Donetsk region hoist their own flag and demand a referendum for constitutional independence from the fascist-led coup state.

The elected Federal Assembly of the Russian Federation, the equivalent of the US Congress, has given unanimous approval for defense of eastern Ukraine protestors against armed assault from the coup government, already underway with NATO flexing armed power all around. Yet this time the resistance cannot be just overrun or bombed. And this time the system DNA begins to be recognized—US-led destruction of societies to ensure their servile dependency and open borders for hollowing out.

The very words "Russia" and "Putin" may provoke ruling group-mind reactions pro or con, so analysis here sticks to track records, trends and policy directions—the defining past, present and future lines of system decision on both sides.

What is clear now are set-point differences and shifts towards recognition of the society-destroying forces. The most visible shift has been set into motion by the overthrow of Ukraine's elected government, big-lie pretexts and serial murders in another US-made civil chaos.

But Russia has moved decisively to stop it in the historical process still unfolding. The never-named enemy behind the coup and behind the collapse of evolved social and natural life systems across the planet has been blocked on the ground. Neither Putin nor Russia are a model, but like Venezuela and much of Latin America, they now stand against the invasive disorder overrunning life bases and needs in every region.

The deepest issue is the US money-cancer system. In murderously destabilizing and overthrowing Ukraine's elected government and advancing towards Russia's borders in the latest metastasis, the pathogenic forces are now confronted by the world's largest country, the longest-tested army and once socialist superpower.

All the lies in the world cannot overwhelm this resistance. Everywhere the US-led collapse of world life security is being decoded outside corporate states and media. The Ukraine crisis, perhaps linked to Russia-China movement from the US oil-dollar, could be a new turning point against the Great Sickness of our world.

CONTRIBUTORS

Robert Abele is Professor of Philosophy at Diablo Valley College, CA. His books include *Democracy Gone* and *Anatomy of a Deception*, discussing the Iraq invasion, occupation, and preparation for the next deception.

Michel Chossudovsky is Professor Emeritus of economics, University of Ottawa and Founder/Director of the Centre for Research on Globalization (CRG). His most recent book is *Towards a World War III Scenario: The Dangers of Nuclear War*.

Edward S. Herman is Professor Emeritus of finance at the Wharton School, University of Pennsylvania. He's written extensively on economics, political economy, and the media. Among his books are *Corporate Control, Corporate Power*; *The Real Terror Network*; *The Political Economy of Human Rights* (with Noam Chomsky); and *Manufacturing Consent* (with Noam Chomsky).

Nolan Higdon is adjunct faculty in history at several colleges in the San Francisco Bay Area and a faculty research affiliate with Project Censored.

Michael Hudson is Distinguished Research Professor of Economics at UMKC, and former Professor of Economics and Director of Economic Research at the Latvia Graduate School of Law. His most recent articles on the post-Soviet economies are "Stockholm Syndrome in the Baltics: Latvia's neoliberal war against labor and industry," in Jeffrey Sommers and Charles Woolfson, eds., *The Contradictions of Austerity: The Socio-Economic Costs of the Neoliberal Baltic Model* (Routledge 2014), pp. 44-63, and "How Neoliberal Tax and Financial Policy Impoverishes Russia – Needlessly," *Mir Peremen* (The World of Transformations), 2012.

Mickey Huff is professor of social science and history at Diablo Valley College in northern California where he is department co-chair; director of Project Censored; and co-host of the Project Censored Show on Pacifica Radio, a weekly public affairs program.

Andrew Kolin is Professor of Political Science at Hilbert College. His research focuses on state power and how authorities use force and violence. His books include *State Power and Democracy* and *State Structure and Genocide*, which elaborates his thesis that America is now a police state.

John Kozy is a retired philosophy professor, now writing on social, political and economic issues. He taught for many years and has been writing for many more.

Stephen Lendman is a writer and broadcaster, hosting The Progressive Radio News Hour on The Progressive Radio Network. Lendman was awarded the Mexican Press Club's International Investigatory Journalism Award in 2011 in an awards ceremony televised throughout Latin America. His books, *How Wall Street Fleeces America* and *Banker Occupation* have since been published in China. He holds a BA from Harvard and an MBA from Wharton

John McMurtry is an internationally recognized moral and political philosopher. He is an elected Fellow of the Royal Society of Canada and University Professor Emeritus at the University of Guelph, Ontario. He is the author of the multi-volume Philosophy and World Problems, written for the UNESCO Encyclopedia of Life Support Systems, and most recently *The Cancer Stage of Capitalism: From Crisis to Cure*.

Mahdi Darius Nazemroaya is an interdisciplinary sociologist, award-winning author, and noted geopolitical analyst. He is a researcher at the Centre for Research on Globalization in Montreal, Canada, an expert contributor at the Strategic Cultural Foundation in Moscow, Russia, and a member of the Scientific Committee of Geopolitica, a peer-reviewed journal of geopolitics in Italy. He is author of *The Globalization of NATO*. In 2011, he was awarded the prestigious First National Prize of the Mexican Press Club for his work in international investigative journalism.

Michael Parenti (Ph.D., Yale University) is an internationally known, award-winning author, scholar, and lecturer who addresses a wide variety of political and cultural subjects. Among his recent books are *The Face of Imperialism* (2011), Waiting for Yesterday (an ethnic memoir), *God and His Demons* (2010), *Contrary Notions: The Michael Parenti Reader* (2007), and *The Culture Struggle* (2006).

David Peterson is an independent journalist and researcher. He and Edward Herman co-authored *The Politics of Genocide*.

James Petras is Professor Emeritus at Binghamton University, New York, a noted figure on the left, author of numerous books, winner of the American Sociological Association's Lifetime Achievement Award, and longtime chronicler of Latin American popular struggles and the power of Israel in the US. HIs most recent book is *The Politics of Empire: The US, Israel and the Middle East*.

Peter Phillips Ph.D., is professor of sociology at Sonoma State University in northern California; president of the Media Freedom Foundation/Project Censored; and co-host of the Project Censored Show on Pacifica Radio, a weekly public affairs program.

Jack Rasmus teaches politics and economics at St. Mary's College in Moraga, California and is a lecturer in labor economics and US economic history at the University of California, Berkeley. He is the author of several recent books on Political Economy in the U.S., including *Obama's Economy: Recovery for the Few* and forthcoming in late 2014, *America's Ten Crises*. He is the host of the weekly New York hourly radio show, 'Alternative Visions' on the Progressive Radio Network.

Paul Craig Roberts was former Assistant Treasury Secretary under Ronald Reagan, a *Wall Street Journal* Associate Editor/columnist, and holder of numerous academic appointments, including the William E. Simon Chair, Center for Strategic and International Studies, Georgetown. His latest books are T*he Failure of Laissez-Faire Capitalism* and *How America Was Lost*.

Rick Rozoff is an activist, anti-war supporter, and Stop NATO web site editor. He extensively documents and opposes global militarist trends in expanding imperial theaters of war.

Rodney Shakespeare is a Professor of Binary Economics at Trisakti University, Britain. He teaches postgraduate Islamic Economics and Finance.

Jeffrey Sommers is Associate Professor and Senior Fellow of the Institute of World Affairs at the University of Wisconsin, Milwaukee. He is also Visiting Faculty at the Stockholm School of Economics in Riga. He is co-editor with Charles Woolfson of *The Contradictions of Austerity: the Socioeconomic Costs of the Baltic States* (Routledge Press, 2014).

Matthew Witt is Professor of Public Administration at the University of La Verne in California where he teaches courses in public administration theory, integrative ethical leadership, urban environments and managing sustainable communities. He has published in leading academic journals examining how race and racism shape and are shaped by public institutions and practices. He has also published on state crimes against democracy (SCADs), serving as lead editor for the first published SCAD symposium, appearing in American Behavioral Scientist in May, 2010.

INDEX

9/11 231, 249

A

Afghanistan 20, 21, 33, 48, 54-56, 61, 71-73, 116, 134, 175, 191, 197, 213, 239, 249, 250, 255
aggression 20, 25, 35, 54, 60, 74-76, 88, 168, 172-177, 184-186, 197, 203-206, 212, 244-247, 256-258
Akhmetov, Rinat 128
anti-missile defense 174
Anti-Semitism 12-14, 70, 73, 91, 136, 149, 173, 210
austerity 10, 29, 31-49, 129, 133, 138, 146-148, 152-155, 208, 224, 232, 245, 257

B

bailouts 113, 121, 128, 133, 219, 220
Balkans 176, 227-231
Bandera, Stepan 91, 156, 187, 256
banks 27, 28, 33, 39-41, 47, 88, 120-123, 127-130, 144-146, 232, 245, 250-251; *see also* Wall Street
Beijing 107
Belarus 10, 69, 85, 104-107, 128, 132-137, 141-142
Black Sea 16-20, 22-25, 31, 36-39, 107-109, 110-116, 184, 229-231, 241
Bosnia 85, 101, 206
Breedlove, Gen. Richard 188, 189, 193, 198
Brennan, John O. 189, 190, 230
Bretton Woods 138, 143
bribes 21, 133, 156, 253, 257
BRICs 160, 236-238
Britain/United Kingdom 76, 94, 106, 107, 116, 163, 211
Brzezinski, Zbigniew 10, 29-32, 107, 132, 142, 150, 154, 255
Bush, George H.W. 29, 33, 70, 140

Bush, George W. 21, 29, 31, 45, 60, 72, 73, 113, 140, 141, 143, 160, 224

C

Cameron, David 136, 193, 237
Carter, Jimmy 21, 30, 44
Chavez, Hugo 51, 82-84, 88, 172, 194
chemical weapons 84, 247, 248, 258
Cheney, Dick 29, 65
Chevron 156, 160
China 22-25, 29, 32, 65-67, 70, 83-87, 100, 107, 112, 121-125, 143, 160, 239, 243-245, 261-263
Churchill, Winston 163, 167, 170
CIA 56, 61, 69, 85, 93, 155, 158-162, 230, 237, 249, 252
civil society 66, 156-162, 183
civil war 11, 22, 71, 134, 151, 231, 248-250, 252-258
Clinton, Bill 21, 23, 29, 33, 65, 140, 224
Clinton, Hillary 83, 88, 115, 259
Clinton Foundation 129
Cold War 26-29, 31-33, 41-43, 57-61, 67, 68, 87, 108, 114, 154, 165, 168-172, 175, 176, 194-199, 236, 241, 244
Collective Security Treaty Organization (CSTO) 108
Commonwealth of Independent States (CIS) 105, 143-1445
Communist Party 27, 99, 134
corruption 29, 30, 67, 106, 133, 143-145, 150, 161, 191, 254
Crimea 15-17, 19-24, 30, 44, 46, 48, 50, 51, 52, 60, 62, 96, 101-104, 109-112, 116-119, 130, 135, 139, 141, 149-151, 163, 171, 174-177, 181, 184-187, 195-199, 209-212, 221, 228, 230, 244, 245, 256-260
crony capitalists 124, 128
Cuba 57, 60, 85, 254
cyberwarfare 69

265

D

debt 10, 26, 31, 32-37, 48-53, 82, 83, 85, 130, 133, 144-148, 152, 157, 225, 235, 251, 254
destabilization 30, 47, 69, 77, 86, 188, 192, 214, 247, 252-258
Diego Garcia 136
Donetsk 102, 113, 129, 139, 147-151, 183, 189, 190, 244, 260
Duma 27, 33, 101,
Duty to Protect / R2P; see Humanitarian intervention

E

elections 29, 32, 38, 52, 68-69, 125, 156, 179, 190, 209, 222, 227, 229, 242, 256
Estonia 70, 87, 114, 194, 206-211, 231, 259
EU/Ukraine Association Agreement 104, 105, 144
EuroMaidan 90 ff.; see also Maidan coup
European Union (EU) 12, 16, 48, 67, 68, 81, 92-96. 104-106, 119, 123, 133-137, 152, 156, 178,219, 223, 251
Exxon 33, 124, 160

F

fascism 12, 14, 70, 113, 129, 172, 173, 209, 228-233, 257
FBI 164, 165, 192, 230
federalization 53, 100, 102, 113
finance capitalism 41, 234; see also Wall Street
Finland 114, 117
Finlandization 149
Foreign Policy Initiative (FPI) 65
fracking 126, 160
France 23, 47, 76, 81, 94, 96, 106, 124, 136, 142, 178, 181, 190-198, 254
free markets 26, 27, 41, 67, 234, 235
Freedom House 32, 65, 158, 225
Friedman, Milton 154

G

gas 28, 31, 32-37, 42-49, 56, 105-110, 120-129, 139, 143, 155, 160, 161, 162, 178, 208, 237,238, 246, 248, 252, 257
genocide 13, 197, 204, 206, 249
Georgia 15, 24, 69, 88, 115, 116, 117, 137-140, 176, 183, 206, 224, 229, 241, 242
Germany 12, 16, 21-28, 31, 47, 48, 76, 96, 106, 110, 121-126, 132-136, 140-146, 160, 167, 175,178, 194, 211, 227, 248
Gorbachev, Mikhail 24, 26-29, 42, 70, 134, 140, 141, 175, 195, 206
Greece 102, 133, 134, 137, 168, 194, 235, 244, 245, 247, 250, 257
Greek Catholic Church 102

H

Hague, William 83, 193, 237
Hamas 229
hegemony 25, 49, 55, 71, 87, 151, 168, 212, 243
Herszenhorn, David M. 172, 173, 189, 194-198
Humanitarian intervention 56, 57, 58, 77, 203, 204
Hussein, Saddam 52

I

IMF 10, 26, 32, 33, 38-43, 49-57, 66, 67, 82, 112-119, 120-130, 148, 160, 208, 224, 225-233, 257
International Court of Justice (ICJ) 203-210
International Financial Institutions (IFIs) 153-158
International law 20, 23, 34, 35, 42, 52, 53, 74-77, 177, 184, 185, 197-214, 239, 244, 248, 257-260
Iran 22, 43-48, 56-62, 67, 84, 106, 107, 159-162, 183, 193, 225-229, 238, 239, 248-252
Iraq 20, 21, 29-33, 52-63, 73, 116, 134, 142, 143, 175, 176, 185, 197, 212, 225, 231, 237, 239, 248-255
Israel 72, 80, 193, 229, 236, 248, 252

J

Jews 12-16, 51, 92, 102, 103, 136, 156, 190, 198, 209

Index

K

Kagan, Robert 65, 86, 142, 155
Kazakhstan 69, 107, 112, 142
Kennan, George 165-170
Kerry, John 17, 47, 60, 63, 159, 174, 178, 184-198, 214, 237, 248, 259
Kharkov Agreement 35
Khrushchev, Nikita 15, 20, 24, 101, 139
Klitschko, Vitali 66, 178, 224
Korean War 168
Kosovo 19, 34, 44, 177, 184, 193, 197, 210, 214, 255, 260
Kuban, Stepan 129
Kyrgyzstan 69, 107, 176

L

Latvia 27, 38, 42, 43, 70, 87, 114, 150, 151, 194, 206, 207, 211
Lavrov, Sergei 25, 34, 39, 44, 45, 68, 169
Lenin, Vladimir 20, 24, 139, 166
Libya 20-29, 33, 54-57, 61, 73, 80-89, 175, 193, 211, 212, 229, 231, 238, 248, 249, 252-257

M

Maidan coup 29-31, 38, 66, 179, 181-183, 187, 190, 192, 216, 217; see also EuroMaidan
Marshall Plan 169
Marx, Karl 42, 254
McCain, John 20, 115, 125, 173, 197, 208
Medvedev, Dmitri 33-36, 48, 85, 112, 189
mercenaries 22, 51, 82, 245, 246
Merkel, Angela 136, 151, 193, 221
Mossadegh, Mohammad 51
multinational corporations 47, 60, 116,127, 128, 130; see also transnational corporations

N

Napoleon 131, 132
National Endowment for Democracy (NED) 32, 56, 65, 156-161
national security 32, 65, 91, 159, 168, 173, 176, 186, 223, 232
Nationalism 16, 17, 21, 22, 30, 39, 49, 52, 58, 88, 90-96, 100- 106, 113, 116,141, 156, 160, 161, 187, 229, 232, 242
neoconservatives 20, 22, 39, 125, 142, 159, 162, 199,
neoliberalism 26, 40, 41, 42, 82, 146, 147, 157-162
neo-Nazis 11, 34, 51, 73, 156, 215, 230
NGOs 16, 50, 83, 128, 140, 207, 224-228, 242
Norway 114, 194
nuclear war 18, 243
nuclear weapons 24, 58, 61, 84, 106, 114
Nuland, Victoria 16, 29, 50, 65, 66, 86, 96, 97, 142, 151-158, 179-188, 195, 196, 208, 224, 246, 250

O

Obama, Barack 9, 17, 21, 29, 46, 49, 52-66, 70, 76, 80-88, 115, 116, 125, 135, 146, 159, 160, 162, 174, 179, 182, 184, 189, 190, 193, 195, 196, 211, 212, 221, 222, 224, 237, 249, 255
Odessa massacre 11, 150, 215-218
oil 33, 42, 48, 52, 82, 110, 124, 126, 139, 143, 160, 229, 238, 245, 246, 250, 254
oligarchs 17, 28, 29, 30, 37, 40-48, 105, 113, 124, 143-148, 208, 227, 232, 233
Orange Revolutions [just look up Orange] 64, 91, 92, 106, 115-128, 155, 178, 227, 246

P

Pakistan 58
Partnership for Peace 115, 116
Party of Regions 92, 99-105, 128, 245, 256
Paul, Rand 20, 21, 44, 86, 168
Pentagon 190, 238
petro-dollar 160, 162
Pinchuk, Victor 128, 129
pipelines 31, 110, 112, 126
Poland 10, 15, 24, 28, 47, 53, 70, 86, 87, 96, 106, 113, 114, 129-139, 143, 144, 174, 178, 190, 194,206, 207, 211, 227, 231, 242
police state 73, 225, 226, 263
privatization 26, 27, 32, 38, 41, 49, 121, 153, 224, 225, 228

Project for a New American Century
(PNAC) 65, 86, 142, 251
propaganda 21-25, 46, 58, 81, 104, 149,
156, 163, 164, 171, 173, 174, 186-
199, 203, 225, 241-257
Putin, Vladimir 9, 17, 20-24, 32-36,
40-49, 51-68, 71-81, 109, 113,
124, 144, 151, 155-160, 163, 169,
173-178, 181, 183, 184, 190, 191,
211, 220-222, 238, 248, 252, 256,
257, 260, 261
putsch 46, 47, 96-102, 178, 195, 107,
214, 228-233, 246, 256
Pyatt, Geoffrey 66, 78, 96, 97, 156, 157,
179, 180, 188, 195, 208, 224

Q

Qaddafi, Mu'ammar 51, 80-88, 193, 229,
248

R

Rada 90, 97-102
Rawls, John 201, 205, 209, 214
regime change 50,-56, 65-69, 73, 95, 97,
106, 107, 195, 208, 214, 222, 229,
256
reset 33, 147, 161
Right Sector (Pravy Sektor) 13, 14, 21, 22,
91-94, 113, 129, 139, 173, 181-190,
208, 210-217,260
Roman Catholics 102
Roman Empire 10, 70, 136
Russo-Turkish War 133

S

sanctions 17, 20, 47, 48, 49, 53, 57, 124,
125, 175, 198, 203, 221, 229-234
secession 34, 101, 130, 147, 184, 187,
209-214
Second World War 24, 104, 106, 134; see
also World War II
self-determination 19, 22, 171, 184, 200-
213, 244, 260
Serbia 15, 19, 21, 34, 69, 85, 177, 210,
260
Shanghai Cooperation Agreement 107
snipers 29, 84, 93, 96, 180, 183, 248,
257, 259
Snowden, Edward 59, 159, 237

Soros, George 26, 43, 65
South Ossetia 15, 24, 91, 115
sovereign debt 133; see also debt
sovereignty 10, 20, 24, 71-77, 170, 171,
185, 201, 203-213, 221, 222
Soviet Union 15, 16, 22, 26, 28, 33, 41,
42, 44, 65, 87, 104-109, 128, 131-
139, 154, 166, 174, 174, 206, 239,
243, 249, 253-259; see also USSR
Stiglitz, Joseph 157, 161, 236
street gangs 129, 232, 253
structural adjustment 10, 67, 143, 148
subsidies 35, 40, 49, 120-129, 146-150,
208, 224, 230, 231
Svoboda 30, 51, 90-99, 129, 139, 156,
181, 190, 208, 210, 250, 253
swarming 64, 69
Syria 20, 21, 29, 54, 56, 60, 61, 73, 78,
83, 84-88, 106, 107, 159, 193, 211,
213, 229, 237, 238, 248, 249, 252,
255, 257

T

Tartars 92, 103
Tartuta, Sergey 129
Tiahnybok, Oley 178, 179
Transnationalcorporations 54-61,
245-260; see also multinational
corporations
Treaty of Versailles 138, 143
Truman Doctrine 165
Turchynov, Oleksandr 98, 99, 129, 197
Turkey 81, 114, 168, 194, 223, 229, 248
Tymoshenko, Yulia Timoshenko 23, 36,
39, 92, 106, 115, 146, 147, 155,
178, 195, 246

U

UK 22, 25, 44, 45, 61, 120, 124, 143, 163,
235-238, 246
Ukrainian Orthodox Church 102
Unemployment 10, 31, 32, 38, 49, 67,
123, 145, 146, 231, 235, 245, 251
United Nations 31, 57, 74, 84, 85, 101,
113, 156, 177, 185, 186, 193-198,
200-206, 236, 237, 244, 260
US State Department 140, 142
USAID 27, 56, 158
USSR 57, 61, 134, 139-148, 152-167, 206,
228, 239-245, 254-260

Index

V

Von Hayek, Friedrich 154, 251

W

Wall Street 27, 33, 41-48, 59, 71, 129, 249, 253; *see also* banks
Warsaw 106, 167, 174
Warsaw Pact 29, 33, 64, 70, 139, 140-146, 174
Washington Consensus (WC) 152-160
White Book 11
World War I 21, 23, 40, 104, 143
World War II 38, 57, 110, 138-140, 143, 144, 187; *see also* Second World War

Y

Yanukovich, Victor 28-30, 40, 105, 120, 128, 129, 181, 219-224, 259
Yatsenyuk, Arseniy 29, 35, 92, 102, 115, 121-129, 132, 142, 147, 155, 156, 178-180, 222, 224, 244, 246
Yeltsin, Boris 38, 40, 141, 143, 230
Yemen 84
Yugoslavia 32, 33, 54, 56, 61, 100, 102, 150, 174-177, 183, 193, 204, 209, 213, 231, 248, 255, 257
Yushchenko, Victor 91, 92, 101, 106, 115, 116, 155